Pope and Berkeley

Pope and Berkeley

The Language of Poetry and Philosophy

Tom Jones

First published 2005 by
PALGRAVE MACMILLAN
Houndmills, Basingstoke, Hampshire RG21 6XS and
175 Fifth Avenue, New York, N.Y. 10010
Companies and representatives throughout the world

PALGRAVE MACMILLAN is the global academic imprint of the Palgrave Macmillan division of St. Martin's Press, LLC and of Palgrave Macmillan Ltd. Macmillan® is a registered trademark in the United States, United Kingdom and other countries. Palgrave is a registered trademark in the European Union and other countries.

ISBN-13: 978–1–4039–4172–5 hardback
ISBN-10: 1–4039–4172–6 hardback

This book is printed on paper suitable for recycling and made from fully managed and sustained forest sources. Logging, pulping and manufacturing processes are expected to conform to the environmental regulations of the country of origin.

A catalogue record for this book is available from the British Library.

Library of Congress Cataloging-in-Publication Data
Jones, Tom, 1975–
    Pope and Berkeley : the language of poetry and philosophy / Tom Jones.
        p. cm.
    Includes bibliographical references and index.
    ISBN 1–4039–4172–6 (cloth)
    1. Pope, Alexander, 1688–1744—Technique.   2. Language and languages—Philosophy—History—18th century.   3. Art and literature—Great Britain—History—18th century.   4. Berkeley, George, 1685–1753—Influence.   5. Pope, Alexander, 1688–1744—Philosophy.   6. Pope, Alexander, 1688–1744—Language.   7. Philosophy, Modern—18th century.   8. Poetics—History—18th century.   9. Philosophy in literature.   10. Economics in literature.   I. Title.

PR3637.T4.J66 2005
821'.5—dc22
                                                                        2005040216

10   9   8   7   6   5   4   3   2   1
14   13   12   11   10   09   08   07   06   05

Contents

Acknowledgements

I would like to thank Oxford University Press for permission to reproduce some material from my article 'Plato's *Cratylus*, Dionysius of Halicarnassus, and the Correctness of Names in Pope's *Homer*', *Review of English Studies* in Chapter 1. I am very grateful to Bill Zachs for the great generosity he showed me with his time and in allowing me to inspect a presentation copy of Hume's *Treatise*; and to William Stoneman of the Houghton Library, Harvard University, for helping me to locate that book. My thanks go to Andrew Murphy and Nick Roe for helping me to plan this project and to Emily Rosser and Paula Kennedy for being such helpful and considerate editors. The anonymous readers at Palgrave Macmillan helped a great deal in giving this book its final shape. For reading parts or all of my work in draft I would like to thank Natalie Adamson, Constantine Caffentzis, Alex Davis, Joseph Jones and Susan Manly. Remaining errors are, of course, my own.

This seems like the right time to thank all those who have taught me over the years and who continue to teach me: Gavin Alexander, Peter Brennan, Colin Burrow, John Casey, Howard Erskine-Hill, Simon Jarvis, Fred Parker and Jeremy Prynne. I owe particular thanks to Howard, Simon and Fred. Thanks are also due to Penny Wilson and Brean Hammond. A number of friends and colleagues have offered support and encouragement to me during the writing of this book: Andrea Brady, Emily Butterworth, Anya Clayworth, Alex Davis, Robert Douglas-Fairhurst, Alex Hale, Jeremy Hardingham, Freya Johnston, Chris Jones, Kai Kresse, Sam Ladkin, Susan Manly, Kate McGladdery, Lizzie Muller, Tony Paraskeva, Philip Parry, Malcolm Phillips, Gill Plain, Corrina Russell, Keston Sutherland, Bharat Tandon. I owe them all my gratitude. Lastly, I would like to thank Natalie, my brothers Ben, Joseph and Dan and my mum, Margaret, for helping me to get on with this, and even taking an interest.

A Note on Texts

Throughout this book I will refer to the following editions of the works of Alexander Pope and George Berkeley, unless otherwise specified:

The Works of George Berkeley Bishop of Cloyne, ed. A.A. Luce and T.E. Jessop, 9 vols (London: Thomas Nelson, 1948–57).

The Correspondence of Alexander Pope, ed. George Sherburn, 5 vols (Oxford: Clarendon Press, 1956).

The Twickenham Edition of the Poems of Alexander Pope, ed. John Butt, 11 vols (London: Methuen, 1939–69).

Introduction: Pope and Berkeley

In *An Essay on Criticism* Alexander Pope says that if one wants to write truly correct and impressive verse it is 'not enough no Harshness gives Offence, / The *Sound* must seem an *Eccho* to the *Sense*' (ll. 364–5). He goes on to illustrate this direction with a series of lines whose sound echoes their sense, whose sonic, syntactical and metrical effects seem to imitate the actions being described in the semantic content of the lines. This book asks how it might be possible for the sound to echo the sense.[1] It asks what Pope might have thought language was, and how language works, if the sound can be made to echo the sense of a passage of verse. In a note on these lines from *An Essay on Criticism*, the Twickenham Edition of Pope's poems gives full details of analogous statements made by Pope in his letters, and by earlier poets, including Marco Girolamo Vida, Dryden and the Earl of Roscommon. The last's 'Essay on Translated Verse' provides the most direct analogue for Pope's statement. Roscommon says that in good verse the 'The *sound* is still a *Comment* to the *Sense*.'[2] Pope, one might say, is naturalising what Roscommon presents as an artificial activity: only people can offer a comment, whereas an echo is a naturally occurring phenomenon. But Pope says the sound should 'seem' an echo. He does not say that it is an echo, a natural imitation of the sense, but only that it should seem to be so. This kind of natural imitation incorporates artifice, or seeming, without acknowledgement. Pope's version of the statement might seem to present imitative versification as a more natural phenomenon than Roscommon's, but both versions of the statement lean more towards artifice the longer they are considered.

The longer one dwells on Roscommon's '*Comment*', the less likely it seems that he is invoking the image of a Restoration wit offering an extempory gloss on an event, and the closer his sense seems to move

1

towards the tradition of literary and biblical commentary: he seems to be talking about planned rather than spontaneous comment. A comment as 'the action of commenting; animadversion, criticism, remark' is given as the fourth sense by the *Oxford English Dictionary*, which provides no example before Tennyson. The preceding definitions (1, 'an exposition; a commentary', 2, 'A remark or note in explanation, or criticism of a literary passage') are perhaps closer to Roscommon's sense. The sound is not a sharp and witty gloss on what is going on in the sense of the verse, but a learned shoulder note that spells out its ramifications. The preposition 'to', rather than 'on', pushes the line towards this more bookish, less immediate sense.

Pope's lines on the echo of sense in sound also tend to sound more artificial the longer they are considered. I have already said that they assert only the appearance of naturalism, that the sound need only seem an echo to the sense. One might also ask what Pope's echo is. The *OED*'s third listed sense for echo is 'an artifice in verse, by which one line is made to consist of a repetition (such as might be given by a literal echo) of the preceding line.... Hence, the name of the species of verse in which this was done.' The dictionary cites Addison as an example here. An echo is both a natural phenomenon and a type of writing. Pope may be playing a naturalistic sense of the word off against a highly artificial sense of the word, suggesting that his imitative versification is at once natural, a reflection of the natural order of things, and also the product of skilled human artistry and artifice.

Pope might also be engaging in an allusion, thinking of Ovid's story of Echo and Narcissus. Ovid's story begins at a time when '*Eccho* was ... a Body not a Voyce'. Juno punishes Echo for helping Jove to get away with his adulteries by depriving her of any speech but an echo of what has just been said. Echo falls in love with Narcissus and follows him into the woods in an attempt to seduce him, but he rejects her:

> Her wretched body pines with sleeplesse care:
> Her skin contracts: her blood converts to ayre.
> Nothing was left her now but voyce and bones:
> The voyce remaynes; the other turne to stones.
> Conceal'd in Woods, in Mountaynes never found,
> Shee's heard of all: and all is but a Sound.[3]

An echo, in the Ovidian mythology, is a natural phenomenon resulting from the transformational power of human and divine love and jealousy. One might say that Pope is thinking nostalgically of a time when echo was a body not a voice, and that he is attempting in his imitative technique to give language body again, to make the sound that echoes the sense into something substantial, to make the sound truly embody the sense once more, reversing the metamorphosis of substantial into insubstantial words. Or one might say that Pope is aware of the impossibility of reaching back into such a naturalistic period before human artifice and human relations have altered the phenomena of the divinely created natural world, and that he is merely making a submerged literary allusion pointing out that the existence of such periods is always mythical, that such origins are always the concoctions of art. Either way, the echo is not as simple a natural phenomenon as it might appear; it is laced with artifice. As in those other stories in Ovid in which people are turned into trees, the human puts its roots down into the natural world.

Thinking about language often follows a similar trajectory to Pope and Roscommon's lines, a trajectory from the natural to the artificial. The more people consider the words they use, the more artificial those words seem to be, the less purchase they seem to have on the world, the more they seem to form an entirely disjunct set of relations that has no necessary connection to the world, the more they seem merely to represent an inadequate and probably deceptive human mental construct. And quite often thinking about language in this way draws one towards a mythical moment of origin when people first decided to institute language. I will argue in this book that these considerations about the nature and function of language are important for understanding the arguments and techniques of Pope's poems. I will emphasise Pope's connection to George Berkeley, whose philosophical writing provides one of the best contexts for understanding Pope's poetic language, and also for understanding Pope's philosophical disposition in his *Moral Essays* and *Essay on Man*. I go on from general linguistic questions to discuss the ethics of Pope's philosophical poetry in the light of Berkeley's work.

In the first chapter, I explore what Pope and Berkeley read on the nature and origin of language, and ask some questions about what it is for language to be natural or artificial. I hope to recuperate concepts of both nature and artifice in language, suggesting that naturalist theories of language need not be naïve, and that an emphasis on the artificiality of language need not necessarily lead on to vertiginous scepticism concerning its capacity to work. I will try to develop a moderate position in which custom bridges the 'immense divide that separates the pure state of nature from the need for language', about which Rousseau wrote.[4] In Chapter 2, I will go on to explore the association between language and the visual world and the visual arts in both Pope and Berkeley, and then in Chapter 3 the association between money and language, suggesting that visual and economic signs acquire their meaning through customary human experience of the world. In Chapter 4, I will look at *An Essay on Man* and Berkeley's theological dialogue *Alciphron* as exercises in Christian utilitarian ethics, as works that present the world as the language of God. I conclude with an epilogue, looking at the relationship between Pope, Berkeley and Hume. Throughout this book I want to suggest that Pope's technique and argumentative strategies require readers to ask fundamental questions about language, and that Berkeley's writings on language provide the best available answers to those questions, both historically, in as much as Pope knew Berkeley's work, and theoretically, in as much as Berkeley's linguistic theory is far better able to accommodate the poetic use of language than theories concerned primarily with reference and propositional meaning. In doing this I hope to contribute to the understanding of eighteenth-century linguistic and poetic theory and practice, and to the understanding of poetic language in general. This book, then, attempts three things: to describe the possible relationships between the work of Pope and Berkeley; to revise the linguistic context in which early eighteenth-century poetry is studied; and to revaluate Pope's place in eighteenth-century philosophical writing with reference to the group of philosophers sometimes known as the 'British Empiricists' – Locke, Berkeley and Hume.

I want now to review the existing biographical scholarship on the relationship between Pope and Berkeley, to give a context in which to read the more speculative accounts of the intellectual relationship of their work in the following chapters. Gregory Hollingshead is the only person to have worked extensively on the relationship between Pope and Berkeley: the following account draws on and adds to his work. He suggests that 'Berkeley probably met Pope through Steele at Steele's house in Bloomsbury in late February or early March 1713.'[5] Both writers contributed papers to Steele's *Guardian* and were mixing in the catholic intellectual and political environment of London in 1713.[6] They certainly met on 6 March 1713, as Berkeley writes to John Percival that Pope had that day presented him with a copy of *Windsor-Forest*.[7] How much they knew of each other's work at this point is uncertain, but one might conjecture that Berkeley presented Pope with his own work in return. Berkeley's *New Theory of Vision* and *Principles of Human Knowledge*, two of his major early works, were at first printed only in Dublin, not being given a London printing until 1732 and 1734. Yet Addison held in his library editions of the *New Theory of Vision* and *Three Dialogues between Hylas and Philonous*, and Swift owned the *New Theory*, *Three Dialogues*,

Alciphron and the *Discourse to Magistrates*.[8] There can be little doubt that Pope, a frequent borrower of books, would have seen some of these works early in his career. Indeed, one of Pope's *Guardian* essays that I will discuss in Chapter 3 seems to echo Berkeley's *New Theory of Vision*, suggesting Pope read this work almost immediately after he met Berkeley.[9] Pope certainly thought of Berkeley in association with these early works, and not just those it can be proved he read. When he comes to publish the letters that he received from Berkeley, Pope identifies him in a footnote as 'Afterwards Bishop of Cloyne in Ireland, Author of the Dialogues of Hylas and Philonous, the Minute Philosopher, &c.', indicating that Pope thought of Berkeley as the immaterialist philosopher of his early life, as well as the Bishop and polemical divine of his later years.[10]

Pope and Berkeley must have established a sound friendship very rapidly, as on 1 May 1714 Berkeley wrote to Pope from Leghorn in Italy where he was staying '(by favour of my good friend the Dean of St. *Patrick's* [Swift]) in quality of Chaplain to the Earl of *Peterborough*'.[11] Berkeley shows in this letter the level of his interest in Pope as a poet and friend:

> I have accidentally met with your Rape of the Lock here, having never seen it before. Stile, Painting, judgment, Spirit, I had already admired in others of your Writings; but in this I am charm'd with the magic of your *Invention*, with all those images, allusions, and inexplicable beauties, which you raise so surprizingly and at the same time so naturally, out of a trifle. And yet I cannot say that I was more pleas'd with the reading of it, than I am with the pretext it gives me to renew in your thoughts the remembrance of one who values no happiness beyond the friendship of men of wit, learning, and good nature.[12]

Berkeley spends the remainder of the letter attempting to persuade Pope into a continental trip (that Pope would always be too ill to make) in order 'to store his mind with strong Images of Nature'.

Berkeley continued to follow Pope's work when he returned from the continent. Pope printed in all of his own editions of his letters (excepting the first authorised edition of 1737) an excerpt from a letter from Berkeley that enters into the controversy surrounding the rival translations of the *Iliad* that were appearing in 1715, the one by Pope, the other by Addison's friend Thomas Tickell. Berkeley writes that he and the friends together with whom he is comparing the translations were 'unanimously of opinion that yours was equally just to the sense with Mr. ———'s, and without comparison more easy, more poetical, and more sublime'

(*Correspondence*, I, 304, Berkeley to Pope, 7 July 1715). Berkeley is prepared to weigh in behind Pope in this charged controversy, in which to approve of one or other translation could be read as an indication of political as well as literary taste.[13] On his second trip to the continent, as tutor to St George Ashe, Berkeley again writes to Pope with the hope of providing him with a poetical image, this time of the island of Inarime, saying that 'the imagination of a Poet is a thing so nice and delicate, that it is no easy matter to find out Images capable of giving Pleasure to one of the few, who (in any Age) have come up to that Character' (*Correspondence* I, 445–7, 22 October 1717). Berkeley thinks of Pope as a poet, always mentioning Pope's talents when writing to him, and esteeming them highly.

Pope and Berkeley maintained contact throughout the 1720s. Berkeley stayed with Pope for a week in the summer of 1721, during which time they dined with Francis Atterbury. Pope invites Berkeley in such a way as to write him into Pope's satirical and moral opposition to the vices and follies of the town, one of the emergent themes of his writing in this period:

> as I take You to be almost the only Friend I have, that is above the little vanities of the Town, I expect you may be able to renounce it for one week, and to make trial how you like My Tusculum because I can assure you it is no less yours, & hope you'l use it as your own Country Villa, the ensuing season. (*Correspondence*, II, 63)

Berkeley was again in London during 1726–27 when Swift was visiting Pope and working on the publication of *Gulliver's Travels*. Berkeley was engaged in some serious lobbying and fundraising for his project of founding a college in Bermuda. He asked Pope to translate Horace's sixteenth epode, several lines of which he used to apply to his Bermudan scheme.[14] Berkeley went on to spend two years in Newport, Rhode Island, waiting for the funds that were promised him by the Walpole government, and which never arrived. On his return to London in 1731 Berkeley must have been in close contact with Pope, as Pope reads and comments on *Alciphron*, the work Berkeley had written in Rhode Island, and which was published in London in 1732. Pope, in a joint letter with Bolingbroke to Swift, prefers *Alciphron* to Patrick Delany's *Revelation Examined with Candour*: 'Dr D——'s Book is what I can't commend so much as Dean Berkeley's' (*Correspondence*, III, 276, March 1731/2). This interest in *Alciphron*, Berkeley's most immediately popular work to that point, and its influence on Pope's philosophical masterpiece *An Essay on Man*, I discuss at length in Chapter 5. Joseph Spence records that Pope had asked

Berkeley's advice on the inclusion of an invocation of Christ in that poem, modelled on Lucretius' invocation of Epicurus in *De Rerum Natura*, and that Berkeley had advised Pope to exclude the passage.[15] This remark remains the only piece of direct evidence that Pope sought Berkeley's opinions when composing, yet it is a remark the full implications of which have not been followed through in a reading of Pope's poetry: Pope, at least at this point in his career, regards Berkeley as a suitable advisor on literary, philosophical and religious questions. It is clear from the posthumously published works of another of Pope's friends, Henry St John, Viscount Bolingbroke, that Pope and he had been discussing Berkeley's *Alciphron*, or at least some of its major themes, at around this time: Bolingbroke's *Letters or Essays Addressed to Alexander Pope, Esq* and *Fragments or Minutes of Essays* are said by Bolingbroke to be accounts of the conversations he had with Pope whilst Pope was working on the *Essay on Man*, and these essays and fragments frequently and explicitly take issue with Berkeley.

Berkeley must have regarded Pope's translations and original poetry highly in 1733, the year in which the publication of *An Essay on Man* began, as Pope's *Homer* and *Dunciad* both appear in a gift of books Berkeley made to Yale University in 1733, along with a very wide range of books that indicate the extent of his intellectual interests.[16] Pope maintains a high opinion of Berkeley throughout the 1730s. In the second dialogue of the *Epilogue to the Satires* (1738), Pope famously attributes 'To *Berkeley*, ev'ry Virtue under Heav'n' (*TE*, IV, 317, 1. 73), continuing Pope's presentation of Berkeley as the man of public life who resists public follies and vices. Pope had also praised the Anglican bishops Rundle, Secker and Benson in the lines leading up to his encomium of Berkeley. A letter from Thomas Secker, then Bishop of Bristol, later Bishop of Oxford, to Berkeley, 1 February 1734/5 suggests that Berkeley needed to be kept up to date with the English literary scene once he took up his bishopric in Cloyne. Secker's letter tells Berkeley of the Bishop of London's project to reprint 'by subscription the most considerable tracts against popery that were written in and about King James the 2ds time'. He goes on:

> Your friend Mr Pope is publishing small poems every now and then full of much wit & not a little keenness. Our common friend Dr Butler hath almost completed a set of speculations upon the Credibility of Religion from its Analogy to the Constitution and course of Nature which I believe in due time you will read with pleasure.[17]

Secker may be referring to the epistles to Cobham or Arbuthnot, Satire II.ii from the *Imitations of Horace, Sober Advice from Horace*, or the final epistle of *An Essay on Man*, all of which were published in the year leading up to his letter. The variety of genre in this selection of poems means that Secker could be talking about Pope's satirical or his philosophical 'keenness'. The transition from Pope to Butler's *Analogy of Religion*, however, suggests Secker was thinking of Pope's vindication of providence by analogical argument in the *Essay on Man*, a poem whose earlier epistles some had taken to be by Secker himself.[18] Berkeley then, if he needs to be informed by Secker, seems to have followed Pope's publications less closely after taking up his bishopric in 1734. The library sold by Sotheby's from 6 June 1796 that formerly belonged to Berkeley, his son and grandson, is thought to contain many of the books in the library at Cloyne, as many of the works referred to in Berkeley's last major piece, *Siris*, are present in the sale catalogue.[19] This catalogue contains only three items by Pope, and of these only one is at all likely to have belonged to Berkeley, 'Pope's Miscellaneous Poems, 2 vol. 1722'.[20] Berkeley had, however, just before moving to Cloyne sent works by Pope to Yale. Whether Berkeley followed Pope's work closely or not, Pope continued to read Berkeley. He read *Siris*, a treatise on the medical benefits of drinking pine resin diluted in water, a month before dying: 'I have had the bishop's book as a present, and have read it with a good deal of pleasure' (*Correspondence*, IV, 514, Pope to Bethel, April 1744). Presumably the present came direct from Berkeley himself.

The evidence that connects Pope and Berkeley biographically and intellectually seems to me sufficient to support Hollingshead's claim that 'Of all the wits, including even Addison, Swift, and Arbuthnot, it is perhaps Pope who most clearly comprehends the nature and significance of the Berkeleian argument.'[21] Hollingshead's main concerns are the influence of Berkeley's critique of Newton on Pope's, and the influence of *Alciphron* on the four-book *Dunciad*: he suggests that Pope uses some of the arguments of *Alciphron* when revising *The Dunciad* in order to save himself from charges of deism that had been levelled against him after the publication of the *Essay on Man*.[22] I will therefore not deal with these subjects at length, adding only some support to the idea that Berkeley is important to the 1740s Dunciads, and commenting on William Warburton's editorial mediation between Berkeley and Pope. I will be arguing more generally that Berkeley's philosophy, particularly his writing on language, provides a very important set of positions for reading Pope's work. There is no record of Berkeley having a greater involvement with any living poet than Pope, and Berkeley must run a close second to Bolingbroke as the living philosopher with whom Pope had greatest involvement, whilst remembering that the compositional history of Bolingbroke's philosophical works is uncertain, and that they were in the main unpublished until 1754. Berkeley had some reputation as a philosopher as early as the 1710s, a reputation that was greatly enhanced by *Alciphron*. Bolingbroke's reputation as a philosopher has never been as high as his reputation as a statesman and historiographer. In the following chapters I shall be arguing that an interpretation of Pope's work benefits from a sensitivity to this biographical connection, and also that Berkeley's philosophical projects and positions help readers of Pope to understand the themes and procedures of Pope's work.

1
Reading about Language

What did Pope think about language? He says that in good poetry the sound should seem an echo to the sense, and this statement might imply that he held an Adamic view of the relationship between words and their meaning: language is divine and gives the right names to the right things – as Adam did in the garden – and poetry is the best expression of the divinity of language. If Pope held this view he would be a nostalgic poet, adhering to views of language popular in the seventeenth century and earlier, views that Milton might have held, and that see divine appropriateness in onomatopoeia and etymological relationships between words.[1] Yet, as I have already noted in the Introduction, Pope's echo is a matter of artifice, or seeming, and not simply a natural or divine phenomenon. Other statements in Pope's *Essay on Criticism* place him closer to other schools of thought on language. He says that 'Expression is the *Dress* of *Thought*, and still / Appears more *decent* as more *suitable*' (ll. 318–19), perhaps implying that words are external signs that more or less correctly reflect thoughts that exist independently in the mind of a speaker. Stephen Land for one takes these lines by Pope as evidence that 'Pope's concept of language is very close to that of Locke', who, as I will demonstrate shortly, holds something like the view of language just sketched.[2] The lines, however, belie a model of language as an arbitrary system of contractually established connections between certain articulate sounds and mental states known as ideas. Dress does not represent the body that it clothes, it conceals and transforms that body, makes it practical in daily social life, prevents its original, natural state from being offensive, presents and enacts the social status of the body. Pope has also been claimed to represent a general turn from referential to syntactic thought in the later seventeenth and early eighteenth centuries, a turn that hinges on the Port Royal grammarians' insistence that the relationship between ideas, and so between the words that represent them, is not arbitrary because it accurately reflects the structure of the world: 'Grammar becomes, preeminently, the syntax of connectives, and this characterization of language brings us close to one of the distinctive qualities of literary language in the period.... Pope associates value, morally and literarily, with composition, with the well-connected series of verse paragraphs and the syntactic sophistications of cleverly composed couplets.'[3] Pope, then, might be claimed by Adamic theorists of language (sometimes also called Cratylic theorists for reasons that should become clear below), by supporters of Locke, or supporters of Port Royal. The relationship of his poetry to theories of language is contested. The statements he makes about language are not simple; they do not attach him to any one dominant school of thought about language. I aim in this chapter to explore the complex relationship between Pope's overt statements about language, his technical achievements in the use of language, and the work of writers on language with whom he was familiar, in an attempt to get closer to knowing how Pope meant that the sound should echo the sense.

1.1 Locke

Any account of the relationship between philosophical writing on the nature of language and literary writing in the eighteenth century ought to take account of the apparent dominance of John Locke. This chapter will account for Locke by trying to undermine his position in literary and intellectual history, and by presenting other ways of thinking about language that were available to Pope and Berkeley.[4] Locke receives a good deal of attention in critical writing on the influence of philosophy on literary production in the eighteenth century.[5] Roy Porter suggests that Locke achieved a philosophical monopoly, and describes Bolingbroke and Pope as his publicists:

> 'Locke is universal,' declared William Warburton. By 1760, the *Essay* [*Concerning Human Understanding*] had raced through nine English editions, as well as four in his collected works, and Latin versions came out in London and on the Continent. . . . a host of writers publicized his views. Bolingbroke, for instance, proclaimed the potential, yet also the limits, of human knowledge – notions versified in Pope's *Essay on Man*.[6]

Literary critics frequently cite Locke's work when trying to reconstruct what early eighteenth-century poets might have thought about language.[7]

Whilst Locke was, of course, an extremely influential writer, the degree of his influence on Pope is uncertain. Pope says he found him 'insipid',[8] and Pope's friend Berkeley writes against Lockeian semantics and epistemology in his *Treatise Concerning the Principles of Human Knowledge* (1710), forming arguments that I will look at later in this chapter, and which resurface in a theological context in *Alciphron* (1732). Beginning with a criticism of Locke that acknowledges some of the main strands in the interpretation of his work, I will work my way towards a more positive position by the close of the chapter, suggesting that Pope and Berkeley's reading opened up to them a number of ways of thinking about language that offer partial solutions to the traditional objections to Locke's account, and which also do a great deal more to make possible an understanding of poetic language in the early eighteenth century than Locke himself. I will refer to Plato's *Cratylus*, Lucretius, Montaigne, Thomas Stanley's *History of Philosophy*, Bayle's *Dictionary*, the Port Royal writers and Hobbes. I will explore the position of custom in writing about language, and emphasise ways in which the natural aspects of language use become confused with or indistinguishable from its conventional and artificial aspects. What I say about custom, habit, the natural and the artificial in language should be relevant to all subsequent chapters of this book.

1.1.1   Names for ideas

The third book of *An Essay Concerning Human Understanding*, 'Of Words' is the most obvious place to start in any discussion of eighteenth-century linguistic theory and its relation to poetry. This book, that Locke claims was not a part of his original scheme for the composition of the *Essay*, sets out the relationship between words, ideas and things. Words are articulate sounds that men use *'as Signs of internal Conceptions'*.[9] I would like to emphasise two very important details of Locke's definition: words refer only to ideas, and the relationship each word has to the idea to which it refers is perfectly arbitrary. Locke runs these points together.

> Thus we may conceive how *Words*, which were by Nature so well adapted to that purpose [indicating internal conceptions], come to be made use of by Men, as *the Signs* of their *Ideas*; not by any natural connexion, that there is between particular articulate Sounds and certain *Ideas*, for then there would be but one Language amongst all Men; but by a voluntary Imposition, whereby such a Word is made arbitrarily the Mark of such an *Idea*. The use then of Words, is to be sensible Marks of *Ideas*; and the *Ideas* they stand for, are their proper and immediate Signification. (III.ii.1, p. 405)

The latter of these two points requires further definition. Words are only signs of the ideas in the mind of the person that uses them, and they cannot be 'Signs either of Qualities in Things, or of Conceptions in the Mind of another' (III.ii.2, p. 406). Locke is required to qualify his point in this way because he has limited the scope of human knowledge to people's ideas of things or qualities in the world: knowledge of things or qualities in the world is only possible through the mediation of ideas, and as these ideas exist only in the minds of particular individuals, the words that refer to those ideas can only refer to ideas in the minds of particular individuals, not, as it were, to the idea in general, or a common idea of a thing or quality in the world.

The problems with such an internalised, mentalised account of the reference of words seem apparent to Locke:

> though Words, as they are used by Men, can properly and immediately signify nothing but the *Ideas*, that are in the Mind of the Speaker; yet they in their Thoughts give them a secret reference to two other things. (III.ii.4, p. 406)

These two other things are the ideas that other people have in their minds and the things or qualities of things to which those ideas themselves refer. Locke argues that these secret references cause problems in signification. People take it for granted that the word they are using refers to exactly the same idea in other people's minds as in their own, and they also presume that the word they use refers to a thing or quality rather than the effect a thing or quality produces in them. These two problems Locke expands upon throughout the book. He does not seem to realise that as well as creating some problems in the chain of signification, he relies upon these two secret references to make his account of signification possible. If words refer only to the ideas a person has in his or her mind, there is no criterion for ascertaining whether or not another person using the same word signifies by it the same idea, or at least the equivalent idea in his or her mind. Likewise, there is no criterion for knowing whether the idea to which a word refers itself refers to the appropriate thing or quality in the world to which the person in question takes it to refer. Internalising the process of signification to this extent deprives users of language of any criteria they might have hoped for to let them know whether or not they are using language correctly, or using language at all, if the purpose of language is to externalise internal conceptions.

This criticism of Locke's account, its dependence on a 'double conformity' between thing and idea, and between idea and word, a conformity for which there are no criteria, is by no means new, and has been identified as a principal topic in the history of linguistics.[10] Locke tackles some of the problems adjacent to this lack of criteria for verifying the double conformity necessitated by his account of signification, but never identifies it as the central problem it is. He acknowledges that words do not work well either in ordinary or in philosophical use 'when any Word does not excite in the Hearer, the same *Idea* which it stands for in the Mind of the Speaker' (III.ix.4, p. 477). This problem does not arise from words, says Locke, as no word is more or less fit to signify any one idea rather than another, but from ideas themselves and their relative complexity, instability and so on. He talks of ideas that have no standard in nature against which they may be compared, of ideas that are made up of a large number of other ideas, without addressing the fact that his two speakers have no means by which to be assured that they are referring to the same ideas when they use the same words, however simple or complex the ideas happen to be.

In the discussion of the particular problems that arise with the names of mixed modes, Locke introduces common use as a possible criterion for determining to what thing an idea refers (perhaps strangely he is not suggesting that common use is a criterion for determining what ideas words refer to). The ideas that must be combined to constitute the idea 'murder' necessarily lack any standard in nature:

> 'Tis true, *common Use*, that is the Rule of Propriety, may be supposed here to afford some aid, to settle the signification of Language; and it cannot be denied, but that in some measure it does. Common use *regulates the meaning of Words* pretty well for common Conversation; but no body having an Authority to establish the precise signification of Words, nor determine to what *Ideas* any one shall annex them, common Use is not sufficient to adjust them to philosophical Discourses; there being scarce any Name, of any very complex *Idea* (to say nothing of others,) which, in common Use, has not a great latitude, and which keeping within the bounds of Propriety, may not be made the sign of far different *Ideas*. Besides, the rule and measure of Propriety it self being no where established, it is often matter of dispute, whether this or that way of using a Word, be propriety of Speech, or no. (III.ix.8, p. 479)

Locke here necessarily slides between his stated position that it is the nature of ideas that causes problems for signification, and the more common position that the nature of words causes problems for signification: there is no way of telling the idea and the word apart when it comes to ideas that may only be defined by the rule of propriety, by particular ways of behaving, and principally speaking, in certain places and at certain times. The confusions are manifold. It is presumed that there are several distinct ideas of murder, glory, gratitude (Locke's examples in this section) and that in a more philosophical language these distinct ideas would be distinguished verbally. Yet these more distinct ideas are already distinguished in words such as 'fratricide' and 'vainglory', for example. Locke is not prepared to admit that 'murder' does not indicate a determinate set of ideas, but a range of ideas, and he wants to blame language, not ideas, for any difficulties that arise from this fact. Locke has difficulty in separating words from the ideas they are said to signify when dealing with his more complex categories of ideas.

The appeal to common use and propriety is also confused. Common use is said to define the meaning of words well enough for common conversation – tautologically, as common use *is* common conversation. Locke then says that common use is not definitive enough for philosophical use (employing the conjunction 'but' whose ambiguity he begins to set out III.vii.5, p. 473) because no body has the authority precisely to define the meaning of words – a contradiction, as the use of no one singular authorised person constitutes *common* use. Likewise, talk of establishing the rule of propriety in a particular time and place seems contradictory as propriety, in an important sense, is only ever propriety for the particular time and place in question. Locke's use of the word 'propriety' is an excellent example of the problems for signification that his more complex categories of ideas create: it is unclear which sense of 'propriety' he relies on most heavily. But in addition to this it is an example of Locke's failure to grasp the utility of a criterion of common use for verifying the reference of a word to an idea, as he misunderstands altogether what common use is, being unable to divorce his notion of linguistic usage from a notion of individual right and authority over one's own actions, in this case the action of referring by one combination of sounds to an idea in one's own mind. He has precisely the same problem, no doubt related to his notion of political liberty, when discussing the arbitrariness of the connection between the sound of words and the ideas to which they refer:

> *Words* by long and familiar use, as has been said, come to excite in Men certain *Ideas*, so constantly and readily, that they are apt to suppose a natural connexion between them. But that they *signify* only Men's peculiar *Ideas*, and that *by a perfectly arbitrary Imposition*, is evident, in that they often fail to excite in others (even that use the same

Language) the same *Ideas*, we take them to be the Signs of: And every
Man has so inviolable a Liberty, to make Words stand for what *Ideas*
he pleases, that no one hath the Power to make others have the same
Ideas in their Minds, that he has, when they use the same Words, that
he does. And therefore the great *Augustus* himself, in the Possession
of that Power which ruled the World, acknowledged, he could not
make a new Latin Word: which was as much as to say, that he could
not arbitrarily appoint, what *Idea* any Sound should be a Sign of, in
the Mouths and common Language of his Subjects. (III.ii.8, p. 408)

The right to refer to one's own ideas is intensely private, and conceived
of analogously to the right over the products of individual labour as
Locke describes it in his second *Treatise on Government*: no political
interference can alienate this right of propriety.[11] But this privacy and
individual authority prevents the model of language from working
altogether, as it removes any possibility of being sure that another person
uses the same sounds to refer to the same idea, and makes all language
impossibly private language. Locke's account of signification creates
problems that he refuses to solve by invoking any effective criterion of
common use.

The imperfections of words, abuses of language and remedies for the
abuses of language which Locke goes on to discuss are concerned primarily with the ideas to which words refer. Again he introduces a weak
idea of common use:

For Words, especially of Languages already framed, being no Man's
private possession, but the common measure of Commerce and Communication, 'tis not for any one, at pleasure, to change the Stamp
they are current in; nor alter the *Ideas* they are affixed to; or at least
when there is a necessity to do so, he is bound to give notice of it. . . .
Propriety of Speech, is that which gives our Thoughts entrance into
other Men's Minds with the greatest ease and advantage: and therefore
deserves some part of our Care and Study, especially in the names of
moral Words. (III.xi.11, p. 514)

Here, however, the individual liberty of nomination seems to be sacrificed
to a common good: this is language after the moment of original
contract, the decision to sacrifice complete individual liberty for some
kind of social security. But common use is still not the criterion of
language, it is merely one of its lesser functions. None of Locke's remedies
acknowledge that it is only the fact that words are exchanged in common

use in an apparently successful manner that indicates the appropriate use of language, that is, by his own definition, successfully referring to an idea or sequence of ideas in an individual's mind.

1.1.2   Metaphor and figure

I would like to move on from this linguistic critique to a deconstructive critique of Locke. The deconstructive critique begins by noting Locke's mistrust of language and carries this mistrust of language back into a reading of his epistemology ('back' only in terms of the structure and argument of the *Essay*) in order to quiz his prioritisation of ideas over words, of the literal over the figural, of the philosophical over the rhetorical. The critique suggests that whilst attempting philosophically to describe the understanding, Locke only ever describes certain linguistic tropes or rhetorical figures, with the implication that all philosophical activity is thus limited: Paul De Man, the most eminent practitioner in this school, suggests that 'philosophy either has to give up its own constitutive claim to rigor in order to come to terms with the figurality of language or... it has to free itself from figuration altogether'.[12] This statement implies a radical reconsideration of the nature and purpose of philosophy, and more specifically philosophical writing, a reconsideration played out in the last forty years of theoretical debate in the humanities or human sciences.

Locke is of course aware of the existence and use of figurative language:

> It may also lead us a little towards the Original of all our Notions and Knowledge, if we remark, how great a dependence our *Words* have on common sensible *Ideas*; and how those, which are made use of to stand for Actions and Notions quite removed from sense, *have their rise from thence, and from obvious sensible* Ideas *are transferred to more abstruse significations*, and made to stand for *Ideas* that come not under the cognizance of our senses; *v.g.* to *Imagine, Apprehend, Comprehend, Adhere, Conceive, Instill, Disgust, Disturbance, Tranquillity*, etc. are all Words taken from the Operations of sensible Things, and applied to certain Modes of Thinking. (III.i.5, p. 403)

Locke clearly conceives of a primitive language that contains words for sensible things in the world, the senses of which, by means of a mental power of comparison and judgement, are transferred to more abstract things, here mental operations themselves. The move in this list from infinitive verbs to nouns is a jolt that indicates Locke's atomised sense of language and his occasional but shocking syntactic insensitivity, a lack of interest in connectives. By choosing just these examples, Locke opens himself up to the critique: when he uses such abstract terms to describe mental processes, all he is doing is saying that they are comparable in some respect to sensible objects. To admit the figurative nature of philosophical language is to admit that it lacks purchase on the items or faculties it is supposed to describe. Immediately a reader begins to scrutinise Locke's text in this manner examples of figurative language leap out and upset the *Essay*'s veneer of discursive rationality. Locke describes the processes of acquiring ideas and abstracting:

> The Senses at first let in particular *Ideas*, and furnish the yet empty Cabinet: And the Mind by degrees growing familiar with some of them, they are lodged in the Memory, and Names got to them. Afterwards the Mind proceeding farther, abstracts them, and by Degrees learns the use of general Names. In this manner the Mind comes to be furnish'd with *Ideas* and Language, the Materials about which to exercise its discursive Faculty: And the use of Reason becomes daily more visible, as these Materials, that give it Employment, increase. (I.ii.15, p. 55)

The domestic and proprietary metaphors here are barely beneath the surface of the text, with the mind somewhere between a guest house, a display case and a manufactory. As in Locke's discussions of propriety and the individual right of nomination, mental and linguistic processes are inflected by a specific realm of political vocabulary, the neutral philosophical position reveals itself as political rhetoric. Even the plainest phrases, names being 'got to' ideas, for example, have either an acquisitive edge or no possible explanatory power: unless a name is 'got to' an idea by the expenditure of labour as a form of acquisition, no process is being described at all. Likewise, if ideas are 'let in' to the mind as a guest is 'let in' to a house, then the mind is a landlord admitting ideas as tenants of its property; if the phrase is stripped of this and other possible figurative meanings, it is altogether empty. There is, in this sense, only figurative meaning.

Locke in these instances would like his language to be thought to refer to clear and distinct ideas or determinate sets of ideas, but the ideas he refers to refer to other ideas rather than to things in the world or their qualities. And it is not just Locke's language that behaves in this way, because the understanding as he describes it itself behaves in a manner modelled on the sensible world; it only operates by reference to some other operation. As has been pointed out, Locke does not require any form of resemblance between sensible and reflective ideas for them to be included under the same denomination, and in this respect they resemble ideas that need bear no resemblance to the things to which they refer (II.viii.7, p. 134), and words that need bear no resemblance to the ideas to which they refer.[13] Locke's philosophical language appears in this critique to be terribly vacant, only ever figurative. Philosophical language is figurative, the operations of the mind are figurative, being like sensible operations, and knowledge itself is figurative as what is known is only ever known by being like other things. The deconstructive critique, by conflating Locke's figurative description of the understanding with the understanding itself, shows that any attempt to describe the mind or the limits of human knowledge becomes a description of language. That the empirical world has a rhetorical structure is one of the main contentions of deconstructive criticism and philosophy.[14]

1.1.3 Reference and meaning

Locke's account of language is already fairly mired in critical difficulties. I would like to add one more before looking at other writings available to Pope and Berkeley that provide solutions to some of these difficulties. This third difficulty is raised by philosophers in the Anglo-American tradition, and states in broad terms that Locke thinks he describes meaning when he only ever describes reference. That is, by saying that one is using language when one utters certain articulate sounds that are the sign of an idea in the mind, Locke says that those sounds refer to that idea. But he provides no criterion for knowing that the person uttering those sounds means that idea, means to invoke its presence in his or her mind or to evoke its presence in another person's mind. This difficulty is closely associated with the lack of a criterion for knowing whether or not other people use the same sets of sounds to refer to the same ideas as oneself. The difficulty may be divided into two parts. Locke describes no mechanism by means of which reference takes place: how do sounds point to ideas in the mind? Nor does he provide any explanation, if the pointing is successful, of how the pointing might be taken to mean something, that is, point to an idea for a particular purpose.[15]

Locke's expansion of his notion that words should externalise the inward conceptions of the mind reveals something about the kind of language he is describing in the *Essay*. He states that words are '*for the recording our own Thoughts* for the help of our own Memories' as well as 'for the communicating of our Thoughts to others' (III.ix.1–2, p. 476). The word 'thoughts' here is clearly doing something other than that common word 'idea'. There is little indication of what Locke considers a thought, but the implication seems always to be that a thought is a proposition:

> Besides Words, which are names of *Ideas* in the Mind, there are a great many others that are made use of, to signify the *connexion* that the Mind gives to *Ideas*, or *Propositions, one with another.* The Mind, in communicating its thought to others, does not only need signs of the *Ideas* it has then before it, but others also, to shew or intimate some particular action of its own, at that time, relating to those *Ideas.* This it does several ways; as, *Is,* and *Is not,* are the general marks of the Mind, affirming or denying. But besides affirmation, or negation, without which, there is in Words no Truth or Falshood, the Mind does, in declaring its Sentiments to others, connect, not only the parts of Propositions, but whole Sentences one to another, with their several Relations and Dependencies, to make a coherent Discourse. (III.vii.1, p. 471)

Locke only really conceives of affirming, negating or relating different parts of speech in order to construct sequences of propositions. He is interested in a propositional language, one that records a set of relations between ideas and between things or qualities in the world. I cannot think of one instance in the *Essay* when Locke shows an interest in any other function of language. Locke's interest in propositional language is reflected in his focus on words rather than phrases, expressions, sentences and so on. He writes continually of what the word 'gold' means, when he really asks to what it refers. He reports a discussion amongst a group of learned men about whether 'any Liquor passed through the Filaments of the Nerves', that was resolved by Locke's suggestion that they decide 'what the Word *Liquor* signified' (III.ix.16, pp. 484–5). Locke is interested in refining the significance of these words by defining and determining the idea to which they refer. This task of refinement and determination would be far harder with a phrase or sentence, even a proposition, than with a single word. Apparently most of the physicians agreed (like doctors after much dispute has passed) that a 'fluid and subtile Matter' passed through the nerves. But presumably, then, they did not agree about what it was to 'pass through', or how this passage occurred, which seem to be the more interesting and demanding scientific *and* linguistic questions. And if the phrase or sentence were not propositional (Jonathan Bennett uses the example 'pass the salt'), it is hard to see how Locke's set of refinements would work at all. If somebody says 'pass the salt' when there is no salt on the table, how will the refinement of an idea of salt remove whatever imperfection of language might be said to have revealed itself in the utterance?

I have been treating two ideas simultaneously that now I would like to distinguish. First, Locke thinks he is talking about the meaning of words when he is in fact only talking about their reference. Secondly, Locke thinks he is talking about the meaning of a language when he is in fact talking about the meaning of a proposition, or set of propositions. Locke writes as if defining these two uses of language is to define language altogether. I will refer briefly to three twentieth-century linguistic philosophers as a contrast to Locke. Saul Kripke makes a clear distinction between the reference of a word and its meaning. He suggests that

> in the case of species terms as in that of proper names, . . . one should bear in mind the contrast between the *a priori* but perhaps contingent properties carried with a term, given by the way its reference was fixed, and the analytic (and hence necessary) properties a term may carry, given by its meaning.[16]

This is to say that a name, gold, for example, has some contingent properties that depend on scientific understanding of what makes gold what it is, properties that will change as people understand more about gold and metals in general (when people first learnt about atomic numbers, for example, the atomic number for gold was added as such a contingent property). The necessary, analytic properties of the name are those associated with its meaning. When people talk of the love of gold, it does not matter how many of the contingent referential properties they associate with the word, as long as they know it refers to gold, and that gold is thought of as an object of desire that causes covetousness, greed and strife. The necessary, analytical properties of the word combine its basic reference with the position that basic reference occupies in the culture of the people speaking the language.[17]

Naming is a part of language rather than its total function. Wittgenstein has argued that naming is one of the games that makes up a language.[18] It is not the aim of a language just to create a full and accurate nomenclature, but to put that nomenclature to work. J.L. Austin was preoccupied with how this nomenclature was put to work, and also considers the act of naming: one of his favourite examples of using language is the naming of a ship.[19] Austin's point is that the occasion of naming the ship does not take place as a super-linguistic event in order that the name may then be used in propositions about the world (where the ship is, how long it is and so on – although being able to form such propositions is one of the desirable outcomes of naming the ship), but that the act of naming is the use of language that should attract the hearer's attention: it is an action, a ceremony, a performance, a use of language in itself, rather than the preface to the propositional uses of language that might follow from it. Berkeley too is aware that pointing to ideas in the mind, referring, is not the only purpose of language.

> [T]he communicating of ideas marked by words is not the chief and only end of language, as is commonly supposed. There are other ends, as the raising of some passion, the exciting to, or deterring from an action, the putting the mind in some particular disposition; to which the former is in many cases barely subservient, and sometimes entirely omitted, when these can be obtained without it, as I think doth not infrequently happen in the familiar use of language.[20]

Berkeley writes about a language that is more than propositional, that does more than refer to ideas and place them in certain relations one with another in order to make propositions and sets of connected propositions about the state of the world. As a result Berkeley's language is much more able to accommodate poetry than Locke's language. If Locke's language admits poetry at all it would only admit a poetry that referred to ideas in the mind of the poet, and in which any set of words would have to be taken as referring to the mental state of the poet. Paradoxically, perhaps, with regard to poems like Wordsworth's 'Thoughts of My own Mind', this might not seem unreasonable, but with regard to discursive writing, such as Pope's *Moral Essays*, the model becomes severely limiting. A reader would have to believe that Pope was making propositions about the relationships between ideas in his mind that he wishes also to raise in the reader's mind in order that the reader may decide whether or not that set of propositions reflects a mental reality that adequately reflects the real reality of the world. But this is precisely what the poems refuse to do. They argue, attempt to change people's minds, say that if the reader thought about the world in the way the poet is thinking about the world, then maybe things would not be so bad.

Pope is as curious about gold as Locke.

> What Nature wants, commodious Gold bestows,
> 'Tis thus we eat the bread another sows:
> But how unequal it bestows, observe,
> 'Tis thus we riot, while who sow it, starve.
> What Nature wants (a phrase I much distrust)

Extends to Luxury, extends to Lust:
And if we count among the Needs of life
Another's Toil, why not another's Wife?
Useful, I grant, it serves what life requires,
But dreadful too, the dark Assassin hires:
Trade it may help, Society extend;
But lures the Pyrate, and corrupts the Friend:
It raises Armies in a Nation's aid,
But bribes a Senate, and the Land's betray'd.

(*Epistle to Bathurst*, ll. 21–34)

Knowing what Pope is talking about here is not a matter of knowing what his idea of gold is, what its contingent referential properties are, because this is an argument about what, broadly speaking, its meaning is. 'Gold' here does not mean the metal, but the position that metal has in the culture Pope inhabits and informs. The three sentences that make up this quotation are mostly propositional in form, but not in purpose: these are not the kind of propositions one might hear and then either accept or reject depending on their agreement or disagreement with the real world (if a reader does this, he or she might not be reading poetry). Perhaps no ethical, moral or political propositions can be treated in this manner, although Locke seems to think they can, as he suggests propriety is to be paid particular regard in the determination of the significance of moral words, and this presumably goes for moral propositions too. There could be a broader question here about kinds of thought that are determinable and deductible from sets of propositions, and those to which an incompleteness or irresolubility is inherent.[21] But this is not the real point either, because the propositions Pope sets out only achieve part of their effect by being propositions in the strictest expository sense. They also accumulate, imply, suggest, and this is even before they have really been considered as poetry. The question 'if we count among the Needs of life / Another's Toil, why not another's Wife?' (ll. 27–8) compacts two ideas, that it is acceptable to take another person's labour and that it is acceptable to take another person's wife, in order to hint at a disparity that the poem in part argues against: there is a difference between the two ideas, but Pope yokes them together so that if one accepts the legitimacy of alienating labour and buying it off another person, one must not do so without thought, one must do it warily and with care not foolishly to extend the idea beyond its useful bounds. The rhetorical question is really a compacted argument. It is an argument that illustrates one of Pope's most constant techniques, the argumentative antitheses which, through parallels and inversions of word order and syntax, through rhymes that confirm or upset the arguments they clinch and through repetitions and modulations of sound, give vigour even to Pope's most baldly expository paragraphs. Pope's linguistic act is not really referential in the way Locke's theory might seem to demand. It is rhetorical, it attempts to persuade, to argue for the propositions it instantiates, even to perform them.

But I do not want to stop here, as is normally the case in the deconstructive argument, and imply that Locke was actually right about language and all these objections add up to is the fact that people cannot use language or do philosophy without the kinds of errors Locke himself identifies and fails to solve. I would like to suggest that there are numerous ways of thinking about language that remove some of Locke's difficulties and that can account far better for the kinds of effects that Pope achieves in this passage and others like it. I will concentrate on writings that discuss common use and custom in relation to language, aspects of language that I suggest Locke fails to understand and use as fully as he might have done in his own work. I will base my discussion on texts available to Pope and Berkeley, texts they are known to have read or are exceedingly likely to have read. These texts were for the most part widely known in the late seventeenth and early eighteenth centuries, and so offer resources not solely relevant to the two figures with whom I am most concerned. I will begin by looking at Plato's *Cratylus* and some of the ways in which it challenges the Lockean account.

1.2 *Cratylus*

Most of the points discussed in the previous section relate to Locke's statement that words refer only to ideas. Locke also emphasises that the relationship each word has to the idea to which it refers is perfectly arbitrary. Although this point might seem to have little bearing on the objections to Locke I have just set out, looking at the ways in which the point has been contended clarifies some of the difficulties in which Locke finds himself. Pope affirms that 'all the World must conspire in affixing steadily the same Signs to their Sounds, which affixing was at first as arbitrary as possible; there being no more Connexion between the Letters, and the Sounds they are expressive of, than there is between those Sounds and the Ideas of the Mind they immediately stand for', strongly supporting the arbitrary relationship. But in the same piece he also wonders whether the invention of letters should not be attributed to 'the Assistance of a Power more than Human'.[22] The possible divinity of human letters may force a reconsideration of how the arbitrariness of ideal and linguistic representation is understood. The arbitrary relationship between a word and the idea it signifies also seems particularly worth discussion in relation to poetry, in encountering which a reader is frequently inclined to ask whether there is not something other or more than an arbitrary relationship between the words being used and the ideas to which they refer (if, indeed, words in poems refer to ideas at all in Locke's sense).

Pope says famously that it is 'not enough no Harshness gives Offence, / The *Sound* must seem an *Eccho* to the *Sense*'[23] (*An Essay on Criticism*, ll. 364–5). It is impossible, if Locke is right about what words do, that this should happen. It may be that readers of poetry feel that there is some echo between the sound (or orthographic form) of a word and the nature of the thing to which it refers, but, according to Locke, they would be experiencing a psychological illusion, or simply making a mistake about the nature and purpose of language, because they take what is simply their familiarity with the word to be a measure of its natural appropriateness to the idea or thing to which they use it to refer. My discussion of the *Cratylus* will look at some ways in which the perception of this echo might not be an illusion or a mistake, and will also extend into a questioning of what it is to be arbitrary, artificial or natural, points that will be relevant to later chapters of this book.[24]

Plato's *Cratylus* concerns itself almost exclusively with the relationship between the form of words and the ideas to which they refer, and whether or not this relationship is natural or a matter of arbitrary imposition and custom or convention.[25] Berkeley thought enough of the dialogue to use a quotation from it as an epigraph to the second volume of *Alciphron*: Socrates says 'there is nothing worse than self-deception', expresses doubt about the explanation of language that he has just given, and moves on to think of language as a tool that is used to instruct people.[26] That Pope knew this dialogue is clear from a note in his translation of the *Iliad*.

> We find in *Plato's Cratylus* a Discourse of great Subtilty, grounded chiefly on this Observation of *Homer*, that the Gods and Men call the same thing by different Names. The Philosopher supposes that in the original Language every thing was express'd by a word, whose Sound was naturally apt to mark the Nature of the thing signified. This great Work he ascribes to the Gods, since it required more Knowledge both

in the Nature of Sounds and Things, than Man had attained to. This Resemblance, he says, was almost lost in modern Languages by the unskilful Alterations Men had made, and the great Licence they had taken in the compounding of Words. However, he observes there were yet among the *Greeks* some Remains of this original Language, of which he gives a few Instances, adding, that many more were to be found in some of the barbarous Languages, that had deviated less from the Original, which was still preserv'd entire among the Gods. This appears a Notion so uncommon, that I could not forbear to mention it. (XIV.328n)

Pope's note is tonally complex, not indicating clearly whether he thinks Plato's dialogue is simply unusual, or actually ridiculous. The dialogue has three participants. Cratylus holds that names 'are natural and not conventional . . . that there is a truth or correctness in them, which is the same for Hellenes as for barbarians' (383b). He is led by Socrates to state that if a stranger in a foreign country addressed him, Cratylus, as 'Hermogenes, son of Smicrion', then 'he would be putting himself in motion to no purpose, and that his words would be an unmeaning sound like the noise of hammering at a brazen pot' (429e–430a). Cratylus adheres so strongly to the view that words reflect the nature of the idea to which they refer that he believes 'if we add, or subtract, or misplace a letter, the name which is written is not only written wrongly, but not written at all, and in any of these cases becomes other than a name' (423a). This is an extreme position, almost the mirror image of Locke's, whereby the nature of a word must reflect the nature of the idea to which it refers in order to be a word at all, just as Locke's words had to be used to refer to ideas if they were to be words.

Hermogenes, on the other hand, asserts that the name for a thing is just what any person agrees to call it, as Locke sometimes argues. Socrates immediately asks Hermogenes whether there is any difference if the name is given by an individual or by a city (385a–b), suggesting that some criterion of common use might be relevant to the function of words. Hermogenes, however, thinks there is no difference. Names can be conferred by a convention with oneself as much as by convention with others. Socrates tries to show that the function of names is to form propositions which are true or false, and that just as any other instrument has a function which is not relative to the individual using that instrument, so the truth or falsehood of propositions is not relative to particular individuals. And if all the parts of a proposition must be true in order for the whole to be true, then there must be a certain correctness in names which is independent of individual or private practices of naming: 'the argument would lead us to infer that names ought to be given according to a natural process, and with a proper instrument, and not at our pleasure; in this and no other way shall we name with success' (385b–388d). Socrates is interested in propositional language here, but, as I shall go on to show, he believes that propositional language has a function beyond describing relationships between ideas that reflect relationships between things or qualities of things in the world: propositional language is an instrument of teaching and dialectical progression.[27]

Whilst arguing against Cratylus and Hermogenes, Socrates shows that words can be used badly: mistakes can occur and they are not meaningless, they are understood to be mistakes. Words are still being used even if they do not produce true propositions or accurately reflect the nature of that to which they refer. Socrates' arguments open up the possibility of a form of correctness in words which does not depend on their propositional content or their natural relation to the external world (or ideas of the external world, to be true to the double conformity).[28] The two parts of Socrates' suggestion that language has a purpose beyond naming, that words have a function like any other tool and that this function is to divide up reality and to teach one another, form the basis of this possibility.

Socrates moves away from the referential arguments of Hermogenes and Cratylus to a certain extent by introducing an analogy between language and tools. Naming objects is not necessarily the criterion for language being used. Socrates suggests that the criterion for language being used is that a certain function is performed. In this respect, Socrates' position has more in common with Austin's performative view of language, in which reference serves other purposes, than those which take reference to be the sole purpose of language. I have already said that the possibility of error is important to Socrates' position.

> In cutting, for example, we do not cut as we please, and with any chance instrument, but we cut with the proper instrument only, and according to the natural process of cutting, and the natural process is right and will succeed, but any other will fail and be of no use at all. (387a)

It is not clear here that Socrates conceives of degrees of success in the use of words, but the possibility is important. Cutting cloth with a flint might have very little success, but it might well have some. The attempt could not be described as a complete misconception of the action of cutting. Only if someone attempted to cut cloth with an entirely blunt

instrument, or perhaps by talking to it, has that person entirely miscon-
ceived the action of cutting. So it is also with the specific functions which
the participants agree that language should perform, the division of reality
and teaching one another. A person's words might provide evidence that
they have divided up reality in the wrong way, or that they have been
taught incorrectly, or failed to learn properly. For Socrates, this would be a
situation over which the dialectician has jurisdiction. The provision of
words is the work of the legislator (388d–e), whose work is to be judged by
the dialectician (390c), as the work of the shipwright is judged by the pilot.

Socrates gets both Cratylus the naturalist and Hermogenes the
conventionalist to drop the extreme version of their views. He does so
in part by adopting at different times parts of the naturalist and parts of
the conventionalist position, but with the important difference that an
instrumental has been substituted for a referential basis for describing
the use of language: Socrates is more interested in what words do than
what they stand in for.[29] He tells Hermogenes that there is a natural
process for assigning names to things. He tells Cratylus that the indication
of a meaning 'may proceed from unlike as well as from like', from words
whose parts fail to depict their referent as well as those whose parts
succeed. 'But if this is true, then you have made a convention with
yourself, and the correctness of a name turns out to be convention,
since letters which are unlike are indicative equally with those which
are like, if they are sanctioned by custom and convention' (435a–b).
The natural process by which names are assigned cannot always be
carried out with like success: 'have courage to admit that one name may
be correctly and another incorrectly given' (432e). It is only in the perfect
state of the language that all names are correctly given, that is, function
as much by means of the like as the unlike (435c–d). The principles of
operation for the imperfect state of language are more or less those of
natural languages. There are natural likenesses between certain sounds
and certain qualities of external objects (hence onomatopoeia), but words
need not employ just these natural likenesses, as reference may also be
made by means of unlike sounds, which come to have their meaning
through convention.[30] It could be said that any likeness depends on
convention to some extent. Socrates himself points out that if an image
of Cratylus were infused with motion, character and everything that
makes Cratylus what he is, there would not be Cratylus and an image of
Cratylus, but two Cratyluses (432b–c). Representation necessarily involves
what is unlike, as if any two things were exactly like they would be the
same. Socrates is, perhaps, adopting a form of the conventionalist position,
a form that subsumes naturalism as a type of convention.

The instrumental view of language should be remembered. The function of language is to divide up reality and to allow people to teach one another. Abandoning the notion that the legislator and dialectician govern the formation and use of language as an indication only of how an ideal language might work, the division of reality and the responsibility of teaching are now left ungoverned. It might be said that these functions of language are matters of convention also, that the manner in which reality is divided up, and the way in which people are taught (that is, shown that they are in error and persuaded to change their views) are merely conventional. Yet the kind of convention involved in these functions of language is quite different from those of which Hermogenes conceived. Those conventions might be altered quite readily by means of brief exchanges between users of the same language (if Hermogenes' language were capable of forming such exchanges, which is doubtful): they are the kind of conventions that govern the use of one word, not the use of an entire language. The kind of convention which might be said to govern the division of reality could not be so easily altered. Such a division of reality may not really be a matter of choice, of deciding to look at the world in a certain way. It might constitute occupying a certain sort of reality.[31] The way in which different people divide up reality may not be available to attributions of correctness or incorrectness, truth or falsehood. They are only to be recognised as different in significant if inexplicable ways. Considering the function that language is said to perform in the dialogue brings one to the point at which nature and convention are confused, and the lines along which reality is divided up are open to all kinds of contention.

It seems implausible that Plato intended his dialogue to be read in this manner, or that Pope would have read it so. One text, however, which might have affected the way in which Pope read *Cratylus* does blur the distinction between naturalist and conventionalist positions so extremely that it might suggest the two are compatible, or at least lead one to seek a resolution between them. Thomas Stanley, in an unfamiliar passage which I shall quote in full, says:

> The Summ of that which he [Plato] saith *in Cratylo*, is this; he enquireth whether *Names* are by the power and reason of *Nature*, or by *Imposition*. He concludeth that the rectitude of names is by a certain imposition, not temerarious or casual, but seemingly to follow the nature of things themselves; for rectitude of names is nothing but an imposition consonant to the nature of the thing: Hence every imposition of names is not sufficient for rectitude, neither the nature nor first sound

of the voice, but that which is composed of both; so as every name is conveniently and properly applyed to the thing. For any name applyed to any thing will not signifie rightly, as if we should impose the name of Horse upon Man. To speak is a kind of Action: Not he that speaketh any way speaketh rightly, but he who speaketh so as the nature of the thing requireth. And for as much as expression of Names is a part of speaking, as Noun is a part of Speech, to name rightly, or not rightly, cannot be done by any imposition of names, but by a natural affinity of the name with the thing it self. So that he is a right imposer of names who can express the Nature of the things in their names; for a Name is an Instrument of the thing, not every inconsiderate name, but that which agreeth with its Nature. By this benefit we communicate things to one another whence it followeth, that it is nothing else but an instrument accommodated to the teaching and discerning of a thing, as a Weavers shuttle to his Webb. It belongeth therefore to a Dialectick to use Names aright; for as a Weaver useth a Shuttle rightly, knowing the proper use therof after it hath been made by the Carpenter; so the Dialectick rightly useth that name which another hath made. And as to make a Helm, is the Office of a Ship-wright, but to use it rightly of a Pilot; so he who frameth names, shall impose them rightly, if he do it as if a Dialectick were present, who understandeth the nature of those things which are signified by the names. Thus much for Dialectick.[32]

Naming is an act of imposition, but a form of natural, or at least 'seemingly' natural, imposition. Even though it is natural, the imposition requires effort, the particular kind of effort aimed at knowledge of things exercised by the dialectician. An instrumental or even performative view of language is emphasised towards the end of the passage. The abrupt transition from the discussion of imposition and nature in signification to the idea that 'To speak is a kind of Action' has the force of a solution. The solution lies in the fact that words are instruments used in the action of teaching and discerning things. The effort involved in the imposition, and perhaps also in the use, of names is an effort of discerning reality inseparable from the use of language. It is possible to be right or wrong in the imposition and use of names, as has been said before, only in as much as the dialectician has jurisdiction over the relationship between words and what they name. Stanley weakens the Socratic position. It is not that the dialectician alone may judge of the correctness of names provided by the legislator. Anyone may impose, and therefore use, names just as long as 'he do it as if a Dialectick were present'. Stanley does not discuss Socrates' investigation of etymology and sound symbolism, but it seems likely from Pope's note on the *Cratylus* that he remembered this section quite clearly. Considerations of etymology and sound symbolism are what Socrates seems to think the efforts of the dialectician should consist of. It does not seem unreasonable to suggest that Pope could have seen the effort exercised by a poet in the creation of imitative verse as parallel to that of the dialectician.

The etymological section of Plato's dialogue remains to be discussed. It is hard to know whether to take seriously the etymologies which Socrates offers, or to take them ironically, as parodies of the kinds of etymology offered by earlier Greek thinkers from whom Socrates is attempting to distinguish himself.[33] The problem with the first course is that the etymologies seem absurd in the light of more recent linguistic thought. The problem with the second course is that so much of the dialogue is spent in discussing these etymologies. It is possible, however, to regard the etymologies as serious and dubious at the same time. This possibility is particularly attractive if, as I have argued, Socrates is attempting to occupy a position that mixes parts of the naturalist and conventionalist arguments concerning the correctness of names. The etymological section of the dialogue is an investigation of the point at which nature and convention become confused, when it is no longer easy to say whether signification is achieved by the like or the unlike elements of words, or even how they become like or unlike. Socrates himself describes the kind of wisdom which his etymologies reveal as 'rather ridiculous, and yet plausible' (402a).

A consideration of Socrates' avowed state of mind and the way in which he is looking at and using language in this section goes some way to explain why his wisdom should be plausible and ridiculous. It is hard not to see Socrates' explanation of his state of mind as ironic.

Hermogenes: You seem to me, Socrates, to be quite like a prophet newly inspired, and to be uttering oracles.

Socrates: Yes, Hermogenes, and I believe that I caught the inspiration from the great Euthyphro of the Prospaltian deme, who gave me a long lecture which commenced at dawn. He talked and I listened, and his wisdom and enchanting ravishment have not only filled my ears but taken possession of my soul, and today I shall let his superhuman power work and finish the investigation of names – that will be the way – but tomorrow, if you are so disposed, we will conjure him away, and make a purgation of him, if we can only find some priest or Sophist who is skilled in purifications of this sort. (396d–397a)

Socrates is inspired and ravished. Even if he is ironic, the state of mind to which he is referring is a poetic state. In the poetic state, the meanings which can be derived from words almost mystically are rather ridiculous and yet plausible. Without saying anything more about poetry and poets in Plato's dialogues, I would like to suggest that the etymological section of *Cratylus* admits a poetic understanding and use of language into discussion of the correctness of names, as such an understanding and use of language is particularly apt to probe the confusion of nature and convention in signification.

Before arriving at the conclusion that the elements of words (syllables or letters) have fundamental significance, Socrates offers a number of etymologies which work by metonymy. He etymologises 'd'affinité' not 'de filiation'.[34] It is only the theory of elemental phonetic signification, the association of particular phonemes with particular qualities of objects or actions, which prevents the etymological process from being entirely circular, and elemental phonetic signification can be achieved by the unlike as well as the like as long as the users of the language in question make conventions with themselves to that end. The convention which gives a phoneme a natural significance can hardly be called a convention. It is more like a way of dividing up reality, or even of constituting the reality which the user of language occupies: it is hard to say if such natural conventions are right or wrong, and to what degree they are voluntary. Just how natural or how conventional the reality which users of language occupy is, is called into question by a consideration of the way in which words acquire their seemingly purposeful relationship with that to which they refer.

I will attempt an illustration of the relevance of my argument about the dialogue to Pope's technique. The index Pope added to the *Iliad*, 'VERSIFICATION. *Expressing in the Sound the Thing describ'd*', seems to have been constructed on several different criteria. Of the twenty-seven headings, the first five are representations of states of mind through direct speech. The remainder employ a mixture of effects drawn from syntax, onomatopoeia or sound symbolism and manipulations of the poetic line as a unit of meaning. The fifteenth heading, 'Bounding of a Stone from a Rock, 13.198', combines these techniques.

> As from some Mountain's craggy Forehead torn,
> A Rock's round Fragment flies, with Fury born,
> (Which from the stubborn Stone a Torrent rends)
> Precipitate the pond'rous Mass descends:
> From Steep to Steep the rolling Ruin bounds;

At ev'ry Shock the crackling Wood resounds;
Still gath'ring Force, it smoaks; and, urg'd amain,
Whirls, leaps, and thunders down, impetuous to the plain:
There stops – So *Hector.* Their whole Force he prov'd,
Resistless when he rag'd, and when he stop'd, unmov'd.

(XIII.191–200)

The repeated *r*s of ll. 191–92 may be taken to depict the roughness of
the rock and its passage. The adjective 'crackling' in l. 196 imitates the
sound of the breaking wood. The accumulation of verbs in the first
half of l. 198, particularly with the adjective 'impetuous' functioning as
a transferred adverb applying to all three verbs and 'down' as a preposition applicable to all three suggests increasing momentum through
syntactical organisation. The long pauses after the second and fourth
syllables of l. 199 reflect the movement of the object described in the
movement of the poetic line. After admiring Homer's simile and preferring it to Virgil's and Tasso's imitations, Pope's note on this passage
states that

> There is yet another Beauty in the Numbers of this Part. As the Verses
> themselves make us see, the Sound of them makes us hear what they
> represent, in the noble Roughness, Rapidity, and sonorous Cadence
> that distinguishes them.
>
> Ρηξασ ασπετω ομβρω αναιδεοσ εχματα πετρησ, &c
>
> The Translation, however short it falls of these Beauties, may
> serve to shew the Reader, that there was at least an Endeavour to
> imitate them.

The lines seem to imitate the qualities of things and actions in an external
physical world by means of the sonic properties, sequential organisation
and distribution in space and time of words.

There is at least one passage referred to in the index whose imitative
qualities are not immediately evident. 'The quivering of Feathers in the
Sun' is said to be represented by the final line of this passage:

> Next, his high Head the Helmet grac'd; behind
> The sweepy Crest hung floating in the Wind:
> Like the red Star, that from his flaming Hair
> Shakes down Diseases, Pestilence and War;

So stream'd the golden Honours from his Head,
Trembled the sparkling Plumes, and the loose Glories shed.

(Iliad, XIX.410–15)

The unusual metrical form of this line (two pairs of unstressed syllables, the second and third, and the seventh and eighth, making it a relatively fast alexandrine), and its heavy consonance are perhaps intended to contribute to the imitative effect, but it is unclear how precisely they do so. Simon Alderson has added to the understanding of this effect by drawing attention to the etymological section of a popular grammar of English with which Pope might have been familiar. 'Both the words "trembled" and "sparkling" possess, according to Wallis's analysis [in his *Grammatica Linguae Anglicanae*], a strong phonetic representation of "frequent small movements" because of the modifying effect of the syllabic or syllable-initial l on the previous (stressed) syllable.'[35] The line is considered imitative by Pope on the basis of a piece of sound symbolism which has lost its currency. Alderson argues that overt theoretical statements in line with Locke and the Port Royal grammarians do not prevent popular English grammars from retaining sections on motivated signification (in which the phonetic construction of a word reflects the nature of its referent), despite the contradiction this seems to entail. It is necessary to consider the idea that sound symbolism exhibits an essential connection between the structure of words and their referents in order to grasp Pope's intention, even if such a doctrine has been presumed to be as unorthodox in the early eighteenth century as it is now. But I think it is also worth bearing in mind Socrates' view that these kinds of connections seem plausible and yet ridiculous, that they make readers think of the point where nature and artifice meet in language. When Pope imagines Virgil looking through Homer and discovering that nature and Homer are the same (*Essay on Criticism*, ll. 130–5), perhaps as well as saying that Homer's poems give the most perfect account of human manners and behaviour, the best descriptions of the operations of the natural world, Pope also suggests that Homer's language divides up reality in the most vivid and performative manner.

1.3   Port Royal and Montaigne

I have been trying to suggest that when reading Pope's verse it is helpful to think of language as customary in the sense that it emerges at the point where nature and artifice meet, that language is, as it were, *the* custom. I make this suggestion because I think it gets readers of Pope, and those interested in poetic language more generally, out of two difficulties. The first is Locke's lack of criteria for knowing if words refer to ideas, ideas to things, and if both of those references are the same for one person as for another. I have tried to point out the confusions in Locke's account of the extent of individual human liberty in choosing how to use language. The second difficulty is that of the distinction between views of language that suggest there is a natural relationship between a word and that to which it refers, and views that suggest the relationship is entirely a matter of arbitrary imposition. I have tried to show in my reading of *Cratylus* that if custom is considered as a matter of the way in which people divide up reality, rather than a matter of a handshake, a signature or superficial social convention, then the naturalist and the conventionalist arguments are to some extent compatible. The grand convention of language is that which blurs the distinction between the natural and the artificial. I think that Pope, in the ethical and political arguments of his verse, and in the technical shaping of his verse, explores the fact that comprehensible human existence, that is, existence in language, is customary in this broad sense.

1.3.1 Natural signs

I will introduce some works from the Port Royal tradition, mentioned by Alderson above, with which Pope and Berkeley were probably or definitely familiar: the Port Royal *Logic* and Pierre Nicole's *Moral Essays*. Pope mentions the essay on human weakness in the *Essais de Morale* in a letter to John Caryll.[36] Berkeley used the *Moral Essays* when constructing *The Ladies Library* [sic], an anthology of instructive literature for women that Steele commissioned from him.[37] As Pope had read Pascal, both the *Provincial Letters* and the *Pensées*, I presume he would have looked at the Port Royal *Logic*.[38] Bolingbroke, in the works claimed to be transcriptions of the philosophical conversations he had with Pope whilst Pope was working on *An Essay on Man*, addresses his reader during discussion of the *Logic*: 'Turn, if you please, to the fourth chapter of the first part, and to the fourteenth of the second, which treat of the ideas of things and the ideas of signs, and of the propositions wherein the names of things are given to their signs.' The casual imperative suggests Pope had a copy of the book to hand in the early 1730s. Bolingbroke calls it 'a book which is put into the hands of young men, as I remember that it was into mine, in order to improve their reason, by teaching them a right determination of their ideas, and a right conduct of their understanding', although Bolingbroke, as I shall show later, thought it failed to do this.[39]

Both Pope and Berkeley could have read about Antoine Arnauld, the main author of the *Logic*, in Bayle's *Dictionary*, where they could also have read about Cornelius Jansenius, the founder of the Jansenist sect of which Port Royal was a part, and Pierre Nicole.[40] I will briefly discuss Montaigne, against whom the Port Royal writers often argue, as a contrast to some of their views. The Port Royal writers, whilst attempting in a particularly sophisticated way to suggest that language is a set of signs arbitrarily imposed on ideas in the mind for the purpose of forming propositions about the world, find themselves compromised by custom: they recognise so many complexities in such mental operations as the arbitrary association of a word with an idea that they make those complexities more prominent than their proposed solutions. Montaigne's more phenomenological approach to language provides some contrast, and constitutes a different response to the weakness that both he and the Port Royal writers present as central to human experience.[41]

The editor of the most recent English edition of the Port Royal *Logic* points out its indebtedness to Descartes in

> the view that thought is prior to language, that words are merely external, conventional signs of independent, private mental states. On this view, strictly speaking, linguistic utterances signify the thoughts occurring in the speaker's mind. Although the association between words and ideas is conventional and thus arbitrary, language can signify thought insofar as both are articulated systems: there is a correlation between the structure of a complex linguistic expression and the natural structure of the ideas it expresses.[42]

One of the classic histories of linguistic thought in this period says that the Port Royal *Logic* and *General Grammar* helped to 'redirect the search for the rational basis of language from the order of things to the order of the mind' and cites Pope as literary evidence of a move from referential to syntactic thought.[43] Arnauld and Nicole are keen to emphasise that the association between an idea and the sign that represents it is arbitrary. The way in which they present their case, however, makes its weaknesses apparent:

> those who say that the Signification of Words is *Arbitrary*, do speak in a very obscure and equivocal Manner. For tho' it is true that it is a thing merely arbitrary to join such an Idea to such a Sound sooner than to another, yet the Ideas, especially such as are clear and distinct, are very far from being Arbitrary, or dependent upon our Fancy.[44]

In attempting to refute the argument that reasoning concerns relationships between words only, and has nothing to do with the world, Arnauld and Nicole make the association between a word and an idea stronger. Although the application of a particular sound to a particular idea is arbitrary, the ideas themselves are not at all arbitrary, and reflect the true nature of the world as it is manifest to the mind. Words, then, if they reflect ideas, might have arbitrary relationships to ideas when considered singly, but just as the internal relations of ideas are not arbitrary, so neither are the internal relations of language, with the further qualification that the internal relations of language must reflect precisely the internal relations of ideal or mental structures.[45] As soon as the decision, if indeed it is a decision in any recognisable sense, to use certain sounds to represent an idea is made, the relationship between those sounds, that idea, all other sounds and all other ideas is no longer at all arbitrary. Arnauld and Nicole present a sophisticated but weak version of the argument for arbitrary imposition.

The argument for arbitrary imposition is further compromised by Arnauld and Nicole's desire to prove that not all ideas are derived from the senses. They say that ideas are the product of the mind, which may refer to the senses to provide an image of an idea. They say that the association of the idea of an incorporeal thing with a sound or image is merely the effect of custom, using the example of the idea of thought:

> For this Image of the Sound of Thought which we imagine, is not the Image of Thought itself, but only of a Sound; and it cannot serve to make us conceive it any further than that the Soul having used herself when she conceives that Sound to conceive Thought also, does at the same time form to herself an Idea of Thought altogether Spiritual, and which has no relation with that of the Sound, but is only united to it by Custom: Which is apparent in deaf People, who tho' they can have no Images of Sounds, have yet Ideas of their Thoughts, at least when they reflect upon what they think. (I.i, p. 42)

The *Logic* presents the odd idea that ideas and the sounds used to represent them occur simultaneously and yet entirely separately in the mind, that their customary association is, as it were, coincidental. Yet Arnauld and Nicole recognise the closeness of the connection between ideas and the sounds used to represent them: 'the one is hardly ever conceived without the other; so that the Idea of the Thing excites the Idea of the Sound, and the Idea of the Sound that of the Thing' (II.i, p. 117).

Arnauld and Nicole's willingness to identify these special and liminal cases makes their argument more complicated and opens it to doubt: words seem to have many points of contact with ideas that are not best described as arbitrary, that are not simply acts of willing human institution. They state, for example, in an attempt to distinguish between natural signs (such as reflections or pictures) and conventional signs (such as words) that there are some signs of which the same things can be truly said as are truly said of the ideas they represent, such as the reflection in a mirror (I.iv, p. 53). The argument is developed at II.xiv. Arnauld and Nicole suggest that one can say of a picture of Caesar, a sign, many of the things one could say about Caesar himself, a thing (II.xiv, p. 189). They argue, however, that one cannot always affirm of the signs what can be said of the things themselves. This distinction seems particularly relevant to Pope's imitative versification: he certainly attempts to make it possible to say truly of the signs that he employs the same things as one might say truly of the things to which his signs refer. When Pope says the sound must echo the sense, he says that in poetry, real poetry, one should always be able to assert that of the signs that is true of the things to which they refer: the sound of the poetry describing the rock should have the same qualities as the sound of the rock. Pope is attempting to make his conventional signs behave like natural signs and the effect he achieves questions the point at which the natural and the conventional are distinguished.

Arnauld and Nicole object to the idea that metaphors, by associating a sign of a thing too closely with the thing itself, blur the distinction between natural and conventional signs. They fear that these metaphorical associations foreclose the category of preposterous statements, as every thought that seemed preposterous may be explained as a reasonable thought in a metaphorical dress. One of the examples they choose to illustrate this idea is unfortunate, particularly to a British audience, as they say how absurd it is that a King should be said to be a tree, when the historical association of the Stuart monarchy with the oak makes it seem a perfectly reasonable metaphorical description in English. Arnauld and Nicole allow room for this kind of historical and cultural contingency by saying that when such figurative language is used, care should be taken to prime the audience: figures or metaphors cannot be introduced by private imposition. So if cultural and historical contingency can be allowed to prevent even this absurd figure from being absurd, by means of a shared cultural heritage that amounts to an agreement, or the priming of one's audience, then surely there is no example of figurative language that remains impossible, given the right historical and cultural conditions? Customs of meaning, customary associations make it possible to form distant figures that are not preposterous; those customs close the gap between arbitrary and natural signs by making the apparently arbitrary seem natural. The complexity of Arnauld and Nicole's argument, their desire to distinguish between classes of signs and to point out that a confusion of these classes of signs is an abuse of language (taking the metaphorical for the literal), leads a reader to ask whether the customary associations of words, with the ideas for which they might stand, with other words, or other kinds of signs, are not more important in the formation of meaningful statements than Arnauld and Nicole seem willing to allow in their account of propositional statements. Their position is compromised by custom.

1.3.2 Expressive behaviour

The *Logic* gives a much more tempered version of the Christian sceptical view of language presented by Nicole in his essay 'On the weakness of Man', the essay Pope mentions in his letter to Caryll:

> I easily grant, that men are able to make a great progress in the science of words and signs, that is, in the knowledge of that arbitrary connexion they have made of certain sounds, with certain Idea's. I can well admire the capacity of their memory, which are able to contain, without confusion, so many different images of things: provided it be granted me, that this kind of knowledge is a great proof, not only of our great ignorance, but also of our being almost incapable of knowing any thing; For, of it self it is of no price, or benefit.[46]

Here knowledge of words is degraded as revealing nothing of spirit or God. As exercises in Christian scepticism it may be appropriate to contrast Nicole's *Essays* with Montaigne's, and to note that Montaigne has an entirely different relationship to language than the Port Royal writers.[47] In the *Logic*, Montaigne is attacked for his self-interest, 'entertaining his Readers with nothing but an account of his Humours, Inclinations, Fancies, Distempers, Virtues, and Vices' (III.xx, p. 346). Montaigne, however, shares many things with the Port Royal writers: he distrusts rhetoric and he has doubts about the extent of human knowledge. Yet Montaigne is, as the Port Royal writers themselves clearly recognise, a completely different kind of writer. His discussion of the various topics that present themselves to him are not just prompts for him to belittle human knowledge, point out the contrarieties and vagaries in human behaviour and defer any understanding of the world to God.

Montaigne's writing is performative rather than expository: rather than attempting to prove by deduction that people can understand little of the world, he presents examples of the difficulty of understanding the world. His writing is not a description of the states of mind that one has when one knows, doubts, thinks and so on, but a performance of those states of mind. Montaigne is one of the great philosophers of custom, one of the sceptical thinkers who manages to make things more rather than less certain through his presentation of the variety of human practices and behaviour. His sense that custom governs everything is not always negative, as it does not remove the possibility of writing one's own customs, as it were, forming the shape and altering the horizons of one's own existence by means of the grand custom that is language.

Montaigne uses words and writing to do something inconceivable in the propositional languages most of the writers so far considered in this chapter have described, in as much as he fashions a self:

> I dare not only speak of my self, but speak only of my self. When I write of any thing else, I miss my way, and wander from my Subject; . . . I, who am *Monarch* of the matter whereof I treat, and who am accountable to none, do not nevertheless always believe my self; I often hazard sallies of my own Wit, for which I very much suspect my self, and certain Quibbles, at which I shake my Ears . . . [48]

This is a use of language inconceivable to the Port Royal writers that nonetheless is relevant to them. Montaigne's writing is an act of acquiring meaning, of being meaningful. He presents the world as a world of signs in which everything is meaningful: the expressions of human faces, the noises animals make, phenomena of climate and geography and the revolutions of human history. He presents all forms of behaviour as expressive behaviour, all prompted by basic desires and feelings of pleasure and pain: 'There is not a motion that does not speak, and in an intelligible Language without discipline, and a publick Language that every one understands' (*Essays*, II, 193, 'An Apology for Raimond de Sebonde'). This expressive behaviour is a language, a natural and public language. Montaigne recognises a human need for expression: 'For my part, I hold, and *Socrates* is positive in it, That whoever has in his Mind a spritely and clear Imagination, he will express it well enough in one kind or another, and, though he were Dumb, by Signs' (*Essays*, I, 261, 'Of the Education of Children'). People tend towards this kind of expressive behaviour and Montaigne himself is no exception. [49]

A view that presents the world as in some sense significant is deeply traditional, and Montaigne shares it with the Port Royal writers (as well as Hobbes and Berkeley, to whom I shall come shortly). Arnauld and Nicole's classification of signs into types deals with the various kinds of natural signs that are not, as it were, created dedicatedly to be signs in the way that a painting is, even though painting is classified as a type of natural signification. Arnauld and Nicole suggest that many objects have the potential to be signs if looked upon as signs: 'when we look upon a certain Object only as it represents another, the Idea we then have of it is an Idea of a Sign, and this first Object is called a Sign' (I.iv, p. 50). Again, the sophistication of the Port Royal position leads to objections to that position. It is said that 'There are Signs annexed to the Things, as the Air of the Countenance, which is a Sign of the Movements of the Soul, is annexed to those movements which it signifies' (I.iv, p. 51). So the natural signs of this kind are attached to the things they signify, in a non-arbitrary manner. Certain kinds of facial expression always signify certain emotions. But one might find exceptions, differences in behaviour across different communities, and question the naturalness of this kind of sign, just as Montaigne in his essay on custom exposes differences in behaviour across different communities: if the facial expression for disgust is different in different places, can it be a natural sign? Precisely this argument is used to dispel the idea that words are naturally tied to their referents, as if this were the case there would be but one natural language.

One response to this argument is to say that the facial expression for disgust in one place is a natural sign for disgust: it is the natural sign in that place. These signs are not made unnatural because they are different from one another. Berkeley points out that nature is not always the same in all times and places:

> The plant being the same in all places doth not produce the same fruit – sun, soil, and cultivation making a difference ... things may be natural to men, although they do not actually show themselves in all men, nor in equal perfection; there being as great difference of culture, and every other advantage, with respect to human nature, as is to be found with respect to the vegetable nature of plants.[50]

Human culture is historical and geographical and natural signs may differ according to time and place: the conventions governing visual representation in painting, for example, change drastically from place to place and time to time. One might apply this inversion of the

argument to words. Words need not be unnatural, conventional or
artificial signs because they seem to bear little or no relationship to
the thing or idea they represent or to which they refer. The different
words that represent or refer to a horse in different languages are the
natural signs for a horse in that language at that time. They are the
only possible words in that language at that time. This is as much as
to give a strengthened sense to the term 'natural languages', as the
emergence of human languages is not an arbitrary matter. It may be
a contingent matter, but it is of the kind of contingency that is made
necessity by the historical, physical and geographical existence of
people in the world.

It is difficult to see the distinction Arnauld and Nicole intend between
this kind of natural sign annexed to the thing it represents, and a kind
of signification they say is impossible: 'tho' a Thing in some one State
cannot be the Sign of itself in that same State, since every Sign requires
a Distinction between the Thing representing and the Thing represented;
nevertheless it is very possible for a Thing in a certain State to represent
itself in another State' (I.iv, p. 52) (Bolingbroke feels that the *Logic* is
sophistical at this point and challenges 'the ablest professor in bedlam
to crowd more nonsense into fewer words', *Works*, IV, 169). Surely the
signs that are joined to the thing they signify are of this sort, the facial
expression for disgust not just pointing to disgust but being disgust,
being at least a part of the feeling of disgust? The same must be true of
signs like fire, signs that Arnauld and Nicole classify as certain signs. The
fire signifies heat (to use a common example), and could be described as
a sign of itself in the same state. One might attempt to think about
language, particularly poetic language, as a sign that signifies itself in
the same state, that instantiates its own meaning, that does not point to
something else in order to gain its meaning, that does not, in fact, really
signify anything at all, but simply means. To follow this line of thought
is to move from thinking about the world as signifying to thinking
about the world as significant, and it is this line of thought in Pope and
Berkeley's reading to which I would now like to turn.

1.4   Hobbes, Zeno, Epicurus, Bayle

1.4.1   The significant world

Both Pope and Berkeley had read Hobbes, Pope owning a copy of
Leviathan, Berkeley referring, in traditional manner, to Hobbes' 'wild
imaginations'.[51] Hobbes, whatever the complexities of his reception,

provides a prompt for thinking about the world as a signifying system in his definition of signs:

> A *Signe*, is the Event Antecedent, of the Consequent; and contrarily, the Consequent of the Antecedent, when the like Consequences have been observed, before: And the oftner they have been observed, the lesse uncertain is the Signe. And therefore he that has most experience in any kind of businesse, has most Signes, whereby to guesse at the Future time[.][52]

He goes on to note that words are used by people to recollect privately their own thoughts, and also 'to signifie . . . one to another, what they conceive, or think of each matter; and also what they desire, feare, or have any other passion for. And for this use they are called Signes' (*Leviathan*, I.iv, p. 25).[53] Hobbes' view of signification is functional. Signs do not form propositions about the world, but purposive statements in the world, statements that allow people to guess with more or less accuracy according to their experience what the world or people in the world will do next.

Hobbes demonstrates the function of signs that do not refer to clear and distinct ideas, a very important subject for Berkeley, in the use of the word 'God': 'the Name of *God* is used, not to make us conceive him; (for he is *Incomprehensible*; and his greatnesse and power are unconceivable;) but that we may honour him'[54] (I.iii, p. 23). Human language is presented as an extension of those properties of things in the world that instruct people in what to do or not to do with them: fire should be used to heat, or avoided; the angry person should be placated, the hungry person fed. In parallel with the purposive aspect of many human uses of language, Hobbes can see in the world a linguistic structure.

Berkeley, in attempting to explain the system of rational organisation that reveals itself to the person who investigates God's creation, argues against there being a causal relationship between one phenomenon and another. He prefers a linguistic explanation:

> the connexion of ideas does not imply the relation of cause and effect, but only of a mark or sign with the thing signified. The fire which I see is not the cause of the pain I suffer upon my approaching it, but the mark that forewarns me of it. In like manner, the noise that I hear is not the effect of this or that motion or collision of the ambient bodies, but the sign thereof.[55]

Hobbes and Berkeley are describing the operation of natural signs, a class of signs that Arnauld and Nicole recognise, but they both extend the function of natural signs into the function of human languages, that is, to indicate something about what can or cannot be done in the world, rather than presenting human language as a signifying system that forms propositions about the world. This view eliminates the idea that there is anything beyond other signs in the signifying system to which signs refer. In Berkeley's system, as the fire exists only in the perception of the fire, and the pain it signifies only exists in the perception of the pain, the idea of the fire does not signify anything beyond another idea. A deconstructive application of this position to human language might suggest that words, as signs, do not refer to anything beyond the realm of signification, that is, they do not refer to ideas: the move from signifier to signified is never made, and ideas, essences and things are lost in the continual deferral of signification. Berkeley, on the other hand, suggests that human linguistic signs take their place in the system of signs that is the world, and perform perfectly adequate functions in that world of informing other people of desires, thoughts, feelings, persuading them of one thing or another, urging them to act in one way or another. Berkeley, in a passage I have already quoted, is emphatic that these are the most common uses of language:

> Besides, the communicating of ideas marked by words is not the chief and only end of language, as is commonly supposed. There are other ends, as the raising of some passion, the exciting to, or deterring from an action, the putting the mind in some particular disposition; to which the former is in many cases barely subservient, and sometimes entirely omitted, when these can be obtained without it, as I think doth not infrequently happen in the familiar use of language.[56]

Seeing the world as made up of signs makes it possible to develop a theory of meaning that does not place prime importance on the reference of a word to an idea, that is, a theory of meaning that is outside the tradition of Lockean linguistics that has dominated discussion of eighteenth-century poetic practice and poetics.

What would it be to read a poet according to this kind of theory of meaning? Instead of asking to what Pope refers when he writes about a rock descending a hill, and how his words conjure up images of the action they describe, one would be more inclined to ask the purpose of this kind of writing, to ask what it is to forge this kind of epic image, what the purpose of inspiring readers with ideas of heroism and valour is, what Pope wanted to achieve, what he wanted to persuade his readers of and so on. Instead of asking to what Pope refers when he talks about gold, a reader would ask why he is talking about gold, what he wants the reader to believe the value or purpose of gold is, and, ultimately, whether gold is something to be sought or shunned. Undoubtedly, Pope makes play of the fact that words can refer to ideas or things, but he often asks what a particularly chimerical thing, like gold, is, in order to show that the scientific answer such as Locke might produce (it is a yellow, solid body...) is not as important in the development and discussion of human behaviour as the ethical answer (it is a substance people pursue because they believe riches will bring them happiness, but they are wrong because...). Pope is clearly more interested in the latter kind of question than the former: he wants to use language to explore human purpose rather than scientific essence.

I will look a little more at Stanley's *History of Philosophy* to show that Pope had access to such views of language, presented in considerable technical detail. Stanley's article on Epicurus suggests that the origin of language is in human desire for things in the world, and that it is a form of expressive behaviour. Man perceived that his tongue was a powerful organ, and invented speech,

> by which Men ordinarily discourse with one another, expressing the passions of the Mind, and other things, no otherwise than as by nodding the Head, or pointing with the Finger.
>
> Here, because it is usually demanded, How Men came at first to impose Names on things? We must know, that *Names were not imposed merely by Invention of Man*, nor by some Law; *but the very Natures, or natural Dispositions of Men, which were in several Nations, being, upon the presentment of things to them, affected with particular motions of the mind, and compelled by images proper to the things, sent forth the Air out of their mouths, after a peculiar fashion, and broke and articulated it, according to the impulsion of the several affectations or phantasies, and sometimes according to the difference of places*, as the Heaven and the Earth is various in different Countries. The words which were thus pronounced, and particularly with a will of denoting things to others, became the names of things....
>
> For this Reason, I conclude, That the first Man imposed Names on things, not out of certain Science, or by the Command or Dictate of any one Man; for how should he come by that Science, or have power to compel many Men to use the words which he dictated? But rather, that they imposed them, being moved by a certain natural Impulsion,

like those who cough, sneeze, bellow, bark, sigh. And therefore we may say, that Names are not by Institution, but by Nature, seeing they are the Effects and Works, as it were, of Nature; for, to see and hear things (which are certain Effects and Works of Nature,) are of the same kind, as the giving of Names to Things. (p. 592)

Language is natural to people as barking is to dogs, and has its origins in the same set of needs and desires as other animals feel. Stanley again offers a complex account of the imposition of names that recuperates the natural aspect of language.

Pope's main source of Epicurean knowledge also recuperates the natural aspect of language development, and also its social character.[57] Lucretius, in a passage from which Stanley's account is derived, insists that language is always a social enterprise, as one speaker could not impose his will on another in the matter of naming, nor would he or she be understood if he or she decided to impose a name at will:

> if others us'd not *words* as soon,
> How was their *use*, and how the *profit* known?
> Or how could He instruct the Others mind,
> And make them understand what he design'd?
> For *his*, being *single*, neither force, nor wit
> Could conquer *many* men, nor *they* submit
> To learn his *words*, and practise what was fit.[58]

The Epicurean view of language as an expressive, appetitive natural reaction to the environment that could only occur in communities is fully available to Pope, and is another view that presents meaning as a property of the world rather than a property of propositions about the world.

Stanley's account of the sceptical critique of natural signs is also complex. Stanley puts forward the dogmatic view of signs, which shares some of its classifications with the Port Royal *Logic*. He explains that two different classes of things require signs to demonstrate their existence:

> *the unmanifest for a time, by the Hypomnestick (admonitive) the unmani-*
> *fest by nature, by the Endictick (indicative.) Of Signes therefore, some are*
> *according to them, Hypomnestick, others Endictick. A Hypomnestick sign,*
> *they call that which being observed to be with a significate, evident, assoon*
> *as ever the sign evidently incurreth to our sense, tho' the significate appear*
> *not, yet it causeth us to remember that which was concomitant to it, tho'*
> *at present not evident, as smoak and fire.*

An Endictick sign, (say they) is that, which is not observed together with an evident significate, but of its own nature and constitution signifieth that whereof it is a sign; thus the motions of the body are signs of the Soul. (p. 498)[59]

The dogmatics distinguish between two kinds of natural sign, those whose presence indicates the absence of some other observable thing, and those whose presence indicates the presence of some unobservable thing, for which, in fact, the presence of the sign is the only criterion. I am suggesting that Pope's poetry be considered as the second kind of natural sign, not as a poetry that indicates the absent existence of some other entity – a set of thoughts Pope has or a set of things he describes – but as a complex natural sign, *'which is not observed together with an evident significate, but of its own nature and constitution signifieth that whereof it is a sign'.* It is poetry that instantiates its own meaning, and its own meaning is one act amidst the totality of meaningful human acts.

1.4.2 Abstraction and signification: Berkeley, Warburton and *Dunciad* IV

A connection with Berkeley's early philosophical project should be evident here. Berkeley does away with one part of the double conformity of Locke's linguistic theory by conflating ideas and things, and saying that reality exists in the perception of God, spirits and humans. He does away with the duplicate realities of ideas and of things that are at the centre of Locke's philosophy. Berkeley's reality is an indicative rather than an admonitive sign: it does not point to another absent reality, but is itself the only reality. The idea of a meaningful reality, a significant world, which does not point beyond itself to the realm of transcendent meaning is an important idea for understanding the works of both Pope and Berkeley.

Berkeley's famous rejection of Locke's account of abstract ideas employs the notion that people never think about a triangle in the abstract: people always think about some triangle in particular (*Principles*, Introduction, 13, p. 95).[60] He says that when a geometer demonstrates the method of dividing a line, and draws 'a black line of an inch in length, this which in it self is a particular line is nevertheless with regard to its signification general, since as it is there used, it represents all particular lines whatsoever' (*Principles*, Introduction, 12, p. 94). Berkeley's method is to regard the line as a sign not of an abstract idea of the line, not as a sign that refers to an abstract duplicate reality of ideas, but as a sign that can refer to other signs like itself in its own world. He treats the line as part of a language that need not refer to anything beyond that language in order to achieve its function of demonstrating the method of bisecting a line. He does away with the need for a separate realm of ideas to which signs refer. Berkeley is interested in the languages in which human activities, such as geometry, take place, not in another realm that somehow transcends and verifies those languages. He is interested in language as it enables human activities such as demonstration and persuasion, not simply as a means of forming propositions about the world (although this activity is clearly very important in demonstrating and persuading). For this reason his writing on language is better able to accommodate and describe poetry as a discreet form of human activity with its own aims of pleasing and instructing, not as an abuse of the true, scientific, propositional and descriptive functions of language.

Berkeley does not believe in the infinite divisibility of the visual plane, nor in infinite geometrical entities.[61] In order to prevent error, he wants reason to occupy itself with real things rather than abstractions derived from observed reality. It is very easy, for example, to imagine a unit of measurement of extension that can be divided infinitely: one simply imagines continually halving the unit. Berkeley discourages people from imagining that the same kind of division can be practised upon a body or figure having extension. The black line of an inch in length can only be divided into the smallest particles, it can be divided as far as the limits of human science and observation extend and no further – until the limits of human science and observation are extended. It may even cease to be possible to divide up reality any further than a certain point: perhaps physicists will one day decide that they have identified the smallest possible sub-atomic particle, and then that will be the minimum extension. Berkeley discourages his readers from contemplating a world that exists in parallel to the real, observable world because the world of abstractions leads people into errors about the real world, a world that is made up of fabric and not units. Berkeley's thinking on these points is influenced by Zeno, not the stoic, but Zeno of Elea, and his paradoxes. Zeno's paradoxes are paradoxes only if one admits the infinite divisibility of extension: only if one continually divides the distance Achilles is behind the tortoise does Achilles fail to catch the tortoise up.[62]

Both Pope and Berkeley used Pierre Bayle's *An Historical and Critical Dictionary*.[63] Bayle's entries on both Zenos, the stoic and the forger of paradoxes, investigate the question of the infinite divisibility of matter in a deeply sceptical manner, questioning the mathematicians' grasp of concrete reality. Bayle makes similar points in his entry on

Hobbes, whose attempt to apply geometrical rigour to moral reasoning Bayle derides:

> See how it is when Mathematicians attempt to apply their Speculations, about Lines and Points, to Matter: They do what they please with their Lines and Superficies, which are only meer Idea's of our Mind; they suffer us to divest them of their Dimensions, whereby we Demonstrate the finest things imaginable concerning the nature of the Circle, and the infinite Divisibility of Matter. But all this is found defective when apply'd to that Matter which exists out of our Minds, that is a hard impenetrable Body.[64]

Berkeley's world already has a linguistic structure, so it does not need to refer to a realm of abstract ideas in order to acquire meaning. His physical and visual theory attempt to remove constant reference to this other world of ideas because the presumption that such reference is necessary to meaning is a source of error and misunderstanding in philosophical discourse.

In the later versions of *The Dunciad* Pope investigates the moral consequences of abstracting a 'real' world from the observable world. It has recently been argued that Pope's *Dunciad* is a complex poetic failure because of the abstraction necessarily involved in language: 'According to the empiricist linguistic tradition that begins with John Locke, abstraction is unavoidable when we seek to refer to objects . . . : abstraction of language causes a complicated failure of poetic reference; this in turn causes the poem's failure to achieve material effects on real people.' The poem cannot act as a corrective satire because the words in the poem always fail adequately to refer to things in the world:

> If any general feature of language is to blame, it is that words do not 'hook on' to the world. And the poem's fascination only increases when we adopt a charitable stance towards Pope's intentions, understanding his massive attempts to suture words and the world. The poem's dualism results from Pope's ambitious and increasingly strident desire to engage in reference.

Pope's intellectual project in the poem is compared to Locke's linguistic system:

> The analogy between Pope's early Dunciads and Locke's system looks surprisingly apt when we realize that both writers distinguish between

abstraction and figurativeness (a special variety of abstraction), and that both are committed to naming the latter as the true cause of rupture between reference and meaning. . . . By 1742 Pope embraced abstraction in order to get around language's figurative habit of not referring to things.[65]

I would like to argue against this suggestion that *The Dunciad* is a failure because its moral programme is disabled by the failure of the referential function of language, and look at the fourth book of the poem with Berkeley in mind, as Gregory Hollingshead suggests.[66] The poem does not fail because it cannot refer in as precise a way as it needs to: it succeeds in satirising people who regard ideas and words as systems of reference to a separate external reality, rather than recognising the linguistic structure, the meaning, of the world as it is in human perception. It is not an 'allegory of the privatization of meaning', a retreat from reference to private meaning, but a satire on those who entertain the idea that meaning could ever be private, that it is the exclusive property of propositions reflecting an internal perception of an ultimately unknowable external reality.[67]

The argument of the *New Dunciad* (published in 1742 and added to the poem as its fourth book in 1743) concerns the state of contemporary learning and education. The goddess Dullness warns her minions, the tutors, university lecturers and students, '*not to proceed beyond* Trifles, *to any useful or extensive views of Nature, or of the Author of Nature. Against the last of these apprehensions, she is secured by a hearty Address from the* Minute Philosophers *and* Freethinkers' (*TE*, V, 338). Using the terminology of Berkeley's *Alciphron, or The Minute Philosopher* (1732), Pope ironically suggests people should never look beyond superficially observable phenomena to discover any providential scheme in nature.[68] Pope's despair is not with the failure of words to 'hook on' to the world, but with the failure of people to see meaning in the world without the interposition of their own vain imaginings. The observable world for these pedants is inert, and must await the language of scientific description in order to give it meaning: they see meaning as the gift of words, not as the gift of a providentially organised world. Having separated 'real things' from their existence in human perception and language, the minute philosophers find all meaning in themselves, in their attribution of systematic, mechanical existence to the world.

The poem and its notes mock the vocabulary of the physical sciences in the same way that Berkeley attacks the notions of matter, substance, force, gravity, fluxions and other occult qualities. The opening of the book asks Dullness to keep the poet from dark obscurity for just long enough to write his poem: 'Suspend a while your Force inertly strong, / Then take at once the Poet and the Song' (IV.7–8). A note attributed to P.W. (that is Pope and Warburton) explains 'Force inertly strong': 'the *Vis inertiae of Matter*, which, tho' it really be no Power, is yet the Foundation of all the Qualities and Attributes of that sluggish Substance'. The note satirises the idea that there is a world that exists behind the world of human perception, a world of occult qualities that subsist beneath the signs of the phenomenal world as people observe them. Berkeley in his *De Motu* of 1721 writes against philosophers who believe in the existence of these occult qualities without being able to say anything about them other than by giving a list of their symptoms or effects:

> [gravity] is, therefore, an occult quality. But what an occult quality is, or how any quality can act or do anything, we can scarcely conceive – indeed we cannot conceive. And so men would do better to let the occult quality go, and attend only to the sensible effects. Abstract terms (however useful they may be in argument) should be discarded in meditation, and the mind should be fixed on the particular and the concrete, that is, on the things themselves. Force likewise is attributed to these bodies; and that word is used as if it meant a known quality, and one distinct from motion, figure, and every other sensible thing and also from every affection of the living thing. But examine the matter more carefully and you will agree that such force is nothing but an occult quality. Animal effort and corporeal motion are commonly regarded as symptoms and measures of this occult quality.[69]

And of course when Berkeley mentions the 'things themselves' he means the things as they exist in perception, not in an unobservable and purely physical reality. The poem attacks the practice of naming an abstraction from observable phenomena, and deriving 'knowledge' from the manipulation of unverifiable terms attached to that abstraction. 'Mad *Mathesis*' is satirised for 'the strange Conclusions some Mathematicians have deduced from their principles concerning the *real Quantity of Matter*, the *Reality of Space*, &c' (IV.30n). The problems of giving meaning to an inert, unobservable reality are pointed out in a note on Aristarchus's speech to the goddess:

> Here the learned Aristarchus ending the first member of his harangue in behalf of *Words*; and entering on the other half, which regards the

teaching of *Things*; very artfully connects the two parts in an encomium on METAPHYSICS, a kind of *Middle nature* between words and
things: communicating, in its obscurity with *Substance*, and in its
emptiness with *Names*. SCRIBL. W.[70] (IV.248n)

In this way of understanding the world there is no possible connection
between things and words: metaphysics is required to bridge the gap
between the obscurity of an unobservable set of abstracted qualities,
and the emptiness of an arbitrary set of names.

Through the speech of the 'gloomy Clerk' (IV.465–92) Pope continues
to satirise mechanists and free-thinkers.[71]

> Let others creep by timid steps, and slow,
> On plain Experience lay foundations low,
> By common sense to common knowledge bred,
> And last, to Nature's Cause thro' Nature led.
> All-seeing in thy mists, we want no guide,
> Mother of Arrogance, and Source of Pride!
> We nobly take the high Priori Road,
> And reason downward, till we doubt of God:
> Make Nature still incroach upon his plan;
> And shove him off as far as e'er we can:
> Thrust some Mechanic Cause into his place;
> Or bind in Matter, or diffuse in Space.
> Or, at one bound o'er-leaping all his laws,
> Make God Man's Image, Man the final Cause,
> Find Virtue local, all Relation scorn,
> See all in *Self*, and but for self be born:
> Of nought so certain as our *Reason* still,
> Of nought so doubtful as of *Soul* and *Will*.

(IV.465–82)

The clerk wants to abstract nature from providential organisation, thrusting
'some Mechanic Cause' into the place of God, binding God in matter,
diffusing God in space: God is lost in the abstractions the natural scientist
forms from observable phenomena. Pope may well have been thinking
of Berkeley's arguments against the free-thinkers at this point, and indeed
throughout the poem. Pope's attacks on matter draw on Berkeley's
Principles and *Three Dialogues*, and his attacks on the use of the word
force draw on *Alciphron*, which I discuss in more detail in Chapter 4. Pope

uses one of Berkeley's less subtle tactics during the speech of the gloomy clerk, quoting Shaftesbury in a footnote, but transposing Shaftesbury's prose into blank verse, as Berkeley had done in *Alciphron*. Pope draws on Berkeley for his critique of the abstraction of general ideas from observable phenomena, and for his moral indictment of thinkers who behave as if the world was given meaning by the human ability to form propositions about these abstract ideas. Pope, as Berkeley, is more interested in seeing the world as the product of providential design. He writes against the occult quality of names, their reference beyond a general context of human significance, just as he writes against other occult qualities. Pope is dismayed by the confusion of categories of understanding, by the fact that '*Physic* of *Metaphysic* begs defence, / And *Metaphysic* calls for aid on *Sense!*' (IV.645–6). In this confusion any sense of the providential organisation of the world, of its availability to human interpretation through custom and experience, is lost in abstraction.

Warburton wrote a note to the lines just quoted, explicating them by remarking that 'Certain writers, as Malebranche, Norris, and others, have thought it of importance, in order to secure the existence of the *soul*, to bring in question the reality of *body* . . . Thus between these different reasonings, they have left us neither Soul nor Body.' Some early readers of Warburton's edition of Pope's works might have thought, having read this note, that Warburton was a supporter of Berkeley's identification of things and ideas. The third volume of Warburton's 1766 edition of Pope contains an essay on satire 'inscribed' to Warburton by John Brown. This essay picks up on the tone of *Dunciad* IV, and imagines the collapse of all human learning. It links Berkeley and Warburton in the opposition to false and superficial knowledge:

> Hence mighty Ridicule's all-conqu'ring hand
> Shall work *Herculean* wonders thro' the Land:
> Bound in the magic of her cobweb chain,
> YOU, mighty WARBURTON, shall rage in vain,
> In vain the trackless maze of Truth you scan,
> And lend th'informing Clue to erring Man:
> No more shall Reason boast her pow'r divine,
> Her Base eternal shook by Folly's mine!
> Truth's sacred Fort th'exploded laugh shall win;
> And Coxcombs vanquish BERKLEY by a grin.[72]

One might think the two bishops shared opinions and rallied around Pope. Warburton cannot, however, have been in total sympathy with Berkeley: when he rewrites his note to *Dunciad* IV.465–6 for the same 1766 edition of Pope, he adds Berkeley's name to those of Malebranche and Norris.[73] He goes much further than this in annotating the passage in the second dialogue of the *Epilogue to the Satires* in which Pope names and praises Berkeley:

> Dr. Berkeley was, I believe, a good man, a good Christian, a good Citizen, and all, in an eminent degree. He was besides very learned; and of a fine and lively imagination; which he unhappily abused by advancing, and, as far as I can learn, throughout his whole life persisting in, the most outrageous whimsy that ever entered in the head of any ancient or modern madman; namely, the impossibility of the real or actual existence of matter, which he supported on principles that take away the boundaries of truth and falshood; expose reason to all the outrage of unbounded Scepticism; and even, in his own opinion, make mathematical demonstration, doubtful. (IV, 319–20)

Warburton here, by misreading Berkeley's immaterialist arguments, attempts to write Berkeley out of Pope, just as Bolingbroke does with regard to *An Essay on Man* (see Chapter 4). Warburton is pleased to say in the preface to the 1766 edition of Pope that it contains

> a correcter and completer Edition of the *Dunciad* than hath been hitherto published; of which, at present, I have only this further to add, That it was at my request he laid the plan of a fourth Book. I often told him, It was pity so fine a poem should remain disgraced by the meanness of its subject, the most *insignificant* of all Dunces, bad Rhymers and malevolent Cavillers: That he ought to raise and enoble it by pointing his Satire against the most *pernicious* of all, Minute philosophers and Freethinkers. (I.v)

Warburton is happy to adopt Berkeley's vocabulary to characterise the object of Pope's satire in *Dunciad* IV, whilst at the same time masking Pope's proximity to Berkeley's arguments against abstraction and demeaning Berkeley's thought.

I hope to have shown here something of the variety and complexity of linguistic and philosophical thought available to Pope and Berkeley, and to have shown how it might be relevant to thinking about Pope's poetry and poetry in general. Moving away from a Lockean account of language with its unsupportable insistence on the reference of words to ideas and ideas to things, the role of custom in the creation of meaning has been emphasised. Custom blurs distinctions between what one might say is natural and what one might say is artificial about language and the meanings of words. I have tried to point out various ways in which one might view language as natural in a complex sense, natural in as much as people are natural and everywhere use language, at each point showing how linguistic and philosophical arguments might be applied to reading Pope's poetry, and how they might alter the way in which poetry is read. In the next chapter I will consider parallels between Pope and Berkeley's writing on the visual environment.

2
The Language of Vision and the Sister Arts

In this chapter I shall begin to indicate the role Berkeley's philosophy can play in a reading of Pope's work by placing Pope's poems on the sister arts of poetry and painting in the context of Berkeley's work on vision. I will begin with Pope's presentation of the sister arts in the 'Epistle to Mr Jervas'. The linguistic background to the sister arts comparison is often presented as dependent on a pseudo-Lockean view that describes words as signs for ideas, with ideas being pictures in the mind of things in the world. From this position, eighteenth- and twentieth-century critics and theorists of painting and poetry talk about painting as a universal language, and say that poetry, in the hands of an exceptional practitioner such as Pope, attains the universality of pictorial signs by including imitative sonic and syntactic effects in its descriptions of the world. These imitative and iconic effects in Pope, however, do not often have reference to things in the world. Most of the iconic descriptions in Pope are descriptions of artificial images, images created by humans through poetry or painting, or both. The iconic passages of *An Essay on Criticism* and the description of Achilles' shield in *Iliad* XVIII are not pictures of things in the world but pictures of pictures of things that may never have been in the world. The extreme artificiality of Pope's iconic poetry pushes the picture theory of language to something of a crux. Readers of iconic poetry do not seem to see pictures of things at all, just pictures of pictures, or pictures of words.[1]

I am going to use Berkeley to try to defuse this crux. Berkeley says that the visual world is the language of nature (later he adjusts this to the language of the author of nature). If the things of which we have pictures in our minds are not things but signs of things, it is not surprising that pictorial poetry does not refer to things but to more signs. Because Berkeley describes the visual world as a language and eliminates the dual reality of things and ideas, a reader of poetry need not expect to be referred beyond language when reading pictorial poetry; indeed, he or she should fully expect to be referred back continually to language, because that is what the visual world is. Berkeley, by reversing the idea that language is verified by reference to visual images, by saying that visual images are verified by being part of a language, provides an alternative context in which to read iconic and pictorial poetry. This alternative context is to be found in his utilitarian view of visual language. The visual world is, as it were, a series of clues from God that lead the attentive person towards ways of behaving that are good for him or her, and the attentive person may learn to understand these clues by accumulating experience of the world. The importance of accumulated experience, or custom, in Berkeley's work, I suggest, has a corollary in Pope's poems on the visual arts. The historical reverence and conservatism of Pope's work on the visual arts is there because the visual world is meaningful only in the light of the accumulated experience of humanity. Pope's iconic classicism, then, may be understood in the context of a Berkeleian theory of the visual world as a language that is understood by means of accumulated experience and custom. I will close by offering a reading of the *Epistle to Burlington* as a poem that fuses the natural, architectural, pictorial and literary environment through its classicising, conservative presentation of a world that acquires its meaning through adherence to customary modes of life.

2.1   The 'Epistle to Mr Jervas'

Pope's 'Epistle to Mr Jervas' is an explicit discussion of the relationship between the sister arts of poetry and painting. Its addressee and the circumstances of its publication tie it into a complex of poetical and painterly relations. Jervas is a friend of Pope's with whom Pope studied painting in London in 1713. He was a student of Sir Godfrey Kneller, and painter to George I and II.[2] The poem is framed as a presentation to Jervas along with John Dryden's translation of Charles Alphonse du Fresnoy's poem *De Arte Graphica*, in the second edition of which Pope's poem was first published. Du Fresnoy was a painter as well as a poet. So the mere situation of the poem evokes the poetico-pictorial relationships between du Fresnoy's poetry and his painting; between poetry and painting in general in du Fresnoy's treatise; between du Fresnoy's poem on painting and Dryden's translation of it; between Pope and

Dryden as pictorial poets; between Pope and Jervas as painters; between Pope as poet and Jervas as painter; and again between poetry and painting in general in Pope's poem. The relationship between the sister arts is a complex of relationships between practices and practitioners.

Having encouraged Jervas to read du Fresnoy, Pope describes his relationship to Jervas:

> Smit with the love of Sister-arts we came,
> And met congenial, mingling flame with flame;
> Like friendly colours found them both unite,
> And each from each contract new strength and light.

> (ll. 13–16)

The second couplet here begins a process of describing the relationship between the poet and the painter in terms of art derived from the practice of painting, here the harmony of two colours, a process that continues throughout the poem. It is striking that the relationship between the two arts is described in terms of the one art. Pope presents an idealised view of the working relationship he has with Jervas in which 'images reflect from art to art' (l. 20), and the fancy works 'flatt'ring scenes' (l. 23). Again, the fancy 'builds imaginary *Rome* a-new' (l. 32), it has the power to turn a work of the imagination into a series of real images, the power to overcome the pun on 'imaginary' – ancient Rome was not imaginary but real, yet all that is left of it is an image – by creating a new image of ancient Roman glory.

Along with 'fancy', Pope uses other words associated with philosophical descriptions of the workings of the mind, particularly the word 'idea'. The image of imaginary Rome is one of the 'ideas of fair *Italy*' (l. 26) that spur Pope and Jervas on. Pope suggests that 'endless streams of fair ideas flow' from the painter's breast, and are imaged forth in his work (ll. 42–4). It seems that the poem presents not only poetry in terms of pictures and painterly images but also thought, the endless stream of ideas. It seems that an account of ideas as sensory pictures of things in the world supports Pope's description of the artistic imagination as primarily pictorial. Even though the poem seems to celebrate the continued and combined life of the sister arts, with Pope saying that his poetry will 'conspire' (l. 69) with Jervas' painting and that the work of both artists will endure (ll. 71–6), painting is the main focus of the poem, and images rather than words seem to be the most important artefacts and the most dependable means of human communication.

Jervas is compared to Zeuxis, Pope to Lansdowne: the painter's art is enduring and classical, famous for its verisimilitude; the poet's art is of the present. It is not of course surprising that a poem about the sister arts should appeal to the sense of sight, should talk about ideas and thoughts primarily in visual terms, as images. The reader of the poem imagines pictorial effects whilst reading, imagines Raphael's monument and Virgil's urn (ll. 27–8), imagines the attractive features of the various ladies who are depicted in portraits. It is the purpose of this chapter to explore how the reader imagines pictorial effects whilst reading, to ask how pictorial poetry is pictorial. I will begin this exploration by looking at the kind of linguistic thought that talks about words as signs of ideas that are pictures of things in the mind.

2.2   The pseudo-Lockean picture theory

It is a very common contention in writing on pictorial poetry and pictorial effects in poetry of the early eighteenth century that John Locke's linguistic theory sponsors these effects and this kind of poetry by saying that words are signs of ideas that are pictures of things in the mind. It may be that this reading is a misreading of Locke (hence I call it a pseudo-Lockean theory), as he says that ideas derived from sensation are 'no more the likeness of something existing without us, than the Names, that stand for them, are the likeness of our *Ideas*, which yet upon hearing they are apt to excite in us'.[3] Nonetheless, some scholars suggest that Locke thought of ideas as pictures or mental images of things. Carol Gibson-Wood, in her recent study of Jonathan Richardson, says that Locke's writing provides a particularly good context for Richardson's work on the art of attributing paintings to painters 'since Locke sometimes actually refers to ideas as if they are mental images'.[4] Gibson-Wood cites a passage that applies the explicitly visual terms 'clarity' and 'obscurity' to ideas. Locke frequently compares the understanding to sight in this manner: 'The Understanding, like the Eye, whilst it makes us see, and perceive all other Things, takes no notice of it self' (*Essay*, I.i.1, p. 43). It seems to me most likely that Locke did not think that ideas derived from sensation are images of the things sensed, as he would have foreseen the difficulty in talking about an image of heat, which is no less an idea derived from sensation than that derived from sight. What happens when Locke employs specular language to talk about ideas is simply a relaxation of his language to permit the language of vision to stand in for the language of all the other senses.

The belief, then, that ideas have a pictorial quality to which words refer is based on an understandable misreading of Locke. It has influenced quite strongly the way in which people have written about visual and pictorial effects in eighteenth-century poetry. Morris Brownell says that a picture theory of language is important to the success of pictorial effects in Pope's poetry, and he associates these effects with Locke's description of the state of reverie.[5] Ralph Cohen has argued that visual theories of the imagination and pictorial language are equally important in understanding the style and reception of James Thomson's *The Seasons*.[6] It is not just on a misreading of Locke that this picture theory is based. Stephen Land puts pictorial theories of ideas in the context of the development of new empirical scientific practices and the Royal Society: 'Words are thought to work like pictures: they "represent" things either by convention or by virtue of actual resemblance.'[7] Cowley's poetry can be taken as an example of this linguistic pictorialism. In his ode 'To the Royal Society', he says the 'Words . . . are but Pictures of the Thought.'[8] One may find such expressions of a pictorial view of language earlier in the seventeenth century. Ben Jonson says that the 'conceits of the mind are Pictures of things, and the tongue is the Interpreter of those Pictures'.[9] There is some variety in these expressions of the basic thesis that language works by referring to visual images of things. Some of these expressions suggest that words are pictures of things, others that ideas are pictures of things. In Jonson's case there is further scope, as words do not simply refer to pictures, but are the interpreters of pictures: words seem to lack the referential certainty of pictorial thoughts, but they can be used to make sense of those thoughts.

Pursuing this line of thought one might say the reason that the 'Epistle to Mr Jervas' relies on terms derived from the visual arts when describing the relationship between poetry and painting is that the medium of poetry, language, works by means of pictorial images of things. The ideas to which words refer are pictures of things in the mind. Therefore, words only work at all because they refer to pictures – language is dependent upon pictures or images of things to communicate ideas and to describe the external world. The suggestion that linguistic reference has a pictorial aspect is made to lend certainty to language. If ideas are pictures of things in the mind then the conformity between idea and thing is not subject to the same vagaries as the conformity between words and ideas. Ideas are a natural likeness of the things they represent in the mind, and so cannot be confused or misused in the way that words can. The criterion for knowing that an idea refers to a thing is that it looks like that thing, and a user of language can be assured of this criterion by the evidence of the senses: one does not look at a horse and have the idea of a sheep.

This certainty of reference guaranteed by ideas being pictures or images of things elevates painting in relation to language as a means of communication, and implies that if language were to become more like painting it too could be more certain of its power to communicate. If words could be more like pictures, natural signs that refer to a thing by means of resemblance rather than convention, then language would be a better medium of communication. Jonathan Richardson, Pope's friend and collaborator, makes the first suggestion; Simon Alderson, the most recent and exacting critic of the relationship between verbal and pictorial modes of reference in the eighteenth century, makes the second.

Pope and Richardson were close friends and collaborators. Richardson painted several likenesses of Pope and helped Pope with his edition of Shakespeare.[10] Richardson's son, also Jonathan, helped Pope collate the published editions of his poems and their manuscripts.[11] It seems extremely likely that Pope collaborated with the Richardsons on their *Explanatory Remarks and Notes on Milton's Paradise Lost*, as he sends Richardson an edition of Milton and offers to 'look over' Richardson's notes in 1731.[12] Pope would presumably have been familiar with all of Richardson's published art-theoretical writings, as he appears to borrow a phrase from Richardson's manuscript poem, 'A Hymn to God', in his *Essay on Man*. Richardson there says he is 'Content, believing all that Is is Right', which becomes in Pope the abstracted statement 'Whatever IS, is RIGHT' (I.293–94).[13] Carol Gibson-Wood describes Richardson's art-theoretical project as a means of educating and modifying the taste of the British art-buying public, in part by rejecting continental authorities and pictorial modes in preference for a native British portraiture, and also by putting the theory of pictorial meaning on as firm a philosophical basis as Locke had put the theory of verbal meaning:

Another original feature of Richardson's introductory discussion is his replacement of the well-worn comparison of painting to poetry by a new linguistic model that was particularly meaningful to English readers at the beginning of the eighteenth century. Richardson abandons the rather forced parallel between the two art forms (which had been the subject of an essay by Dryden prefacing his 1695 translation of Du Fresnoy's *De Arte Graphica*) in favour of a Lockean conceptual scheme in which visual imagery takes its place alongside verbal language as 'one of the means whereby we convey our Ideas to each other'.... His re-framing of standard art-theoretical positions using contemporary English philosophical models, which is already evident here at the beginning of the *Theory of Painting*, is a distinctive feature of his art theory.[14]

In order to develop a sense of the context in which Pope compares the sister arts, I will look briefly at Richardson's comparisons of painting and language.

In the second of his *Two Discourses*, Richardson frequently describes painting as a hieroglyphic language whose signs represent their objects by resemblance rather than convention. In this sense, Richardson continues in the tradition of humanistic art theory, which throughout the seventeenth century had emphasised this natural relationship.[15]

> As the business of Painting is to Raise, and Improve Nature, it answers to Poetry; (tho' upon Occasion it can be Strictly Historical) And as it serves to the Other, more Noble End, this Hieroglyphic Language completes what Words, or Writing began, and Sculpture carried on, and Thus perfects all that Humane Nature is capable of in the communication of Ideas 'till we arrive to a more Angelical, and Spiritual State in another World.

> Thus History begins, Poetry raises higher, not by Embellishing the Story, but by Additions purely Poetical: Sculpture goes yet farther, and Painting Completes and Perfects, and That only can; and here ends, This is the utmost Limits of Humane power in the Communication of Ideas.[16]

The purpose of painting, as verbal language, is to externalise internal conceptions, or communicate ideas. Painting can produce highly verisimilar representations of people and things, whether historical or conjectural; it can represent people entertaining ideas and enduring passions, performing actions and being acted upon. By these means, Richardson argues, it is able to communicate more ideas more exactly than any other means of communication. The objects of painting, as for historical and poetical writing and sculpture, are not necessarily the very things that are seen in the world as they are seen in the world, but rather those things seen in their place in a divinely organised and significant world. As one of the most prominent art critics of the period says, genius is the ability to see images of nature that are 'not hinder'd by certain accidents'.[17] This form of Christian mimetic idealism is clearly expressed in Richardson's other works. In the *Essay on the Theory of Painting* he states that the Italian masters raise nature in their work (p. 161) and suggests that familiarity with great works of painting and literature can enable one to see the world as it is meant to be seen, not as it plainly presents itself: 'After having read *Milton*, one sees Nature with better Eyes than before, Beauties appear which else had been unregarded: So, by conversing with the Works of the best Masters in Painting, one forms better Images whilst Reading or Thinking' (p. 14). So to be able to read and write in the universal language of painting is to be closer to God, to achieve the highest form of knowledge available to people, by seeing the world as it should be rather than as it is. This view has enormous implications for the idea that descriptive and pictorial poetry relies on a pictorial theory of language, implications that I will look at a little later.

Familiarity with painting as a hieroglyphic language imparts social status and excludes the vulgar:

> Painting is but another Sort of Writing, but like the Hieroglyphicks anciently 'tis a Character not for the vulgar: To read it, is not only to know that 'tis such a Story, or such a Man, but to see the Beauties of the Thought, and Pencil; of the Colouring, and Composition; the Expression, Grace, and Greatness that is to be found in it: and not to be able to do This is a Sort of Illiterature, and Unpoliteness. (pp. 221–2)

Studying pictorial language is part of a didactic cultural project. But there are implications for the universality of pictorial language here. If the characters of this language are universal and refer to things by means of resemblance rather than convention, the language should be immediately evident to all people. It should not be an exclusive language that has to be learnt. The two contentions, that painting is a universal language constituted by natural signs and that it has to be learnt in the same way as any of the verbal languages, are contradictory. The implication is that failing to know how to read a picture is like failing to know how to read Latin. If one must learn to read and write the signs of this universal, natural and near-perfect language, then it must be because those signs are not entirely like the things in the world that they represent, but are like those things when seen as part of a divinely organised world in which everything, every object, action and passion, is seen as part of God's providence. Painting has a great ability to communicate ideas by employing natural signs that refer to things by resemblance rather than convention, but it turns out that the deviation of a painting from exact resemblance of the thing to which it refers is the most notable and important aspect of the painting. The certainty of Richardson's hieroglyphic language must be qualified.

A second claim made for the certainty of pictorial signs is that if verbal signs can be made to act more in the manner of natural pictorial signs, then verbal signs will acquire the certainty of pictorial signs. Simon Alderson suggests that the interest in what he calls iconic verse, and what I have been calling imitative versification, in the late seventeenth and early eighteenth centuries is an attempt to give verbal signs the certainty of pictorial signs. He notes the claim in art theory that painting was a universal language employing natural signs and suggests that iconic poetry is a reaction to this claim. Accepting Locke's view of language makes the contrast between verbal and visual signs particularly strong:

> The model of linguistic signification authoritatively established by Locke – with language as arbitrary, contractual, and consequently fundamentally unreliable – provided a tool for challenging the poetic image and asserting the difference between painterly isomorphism and the arbitrariness of the poetic (verbal) sign. . . . The images which are created [in poetry] are aroused via a system of arbitrary signification, so that the co-existence of the image in both content and form which is associated with painting is absent.[18]

Alderson's sureness of Locke's authority indicates that he believes Locke to be correct about the nature of language. Alderson does not claim to show that language is in fact iconic, or capable of producing as accurate a set of mental images as painting: 'What I am concerned with is not what *is* iconic about language, but what Pope and his contemporaries believed iconicity to be and do' (p. 19). Alderson is less interested in the philosophical than the historical aspect of claims about iconic language. He suggests that Pope and his contemporaries were attempting to make verbal signs more like pictorial signs by producing imitative or iconic effects in their writing, thereby communicating with greater certainty. His argument employs the idea that language depends on mental pictures of things: 'Poetry, utilizing the fact that language supposedly created sets of mental pictures, was concerned with finding ways to recall and to heighten such pictures using poetic language; and iconic form was, at least for Pope, one of the methods for achieving this end' (p. 117). So, when Pope begins his exemplary imitative passage in *An Essay on Criticism* he is attempting to give his language the certainty and universality of pictorial signs by achieving an emphatic vividness of description.

Interestingly, perhaps paradoxically, when Pope says the '*Sound* must seem an *Eccho* to the *Sense*' (l. 365), his effects are not to be thought of as sonic effects, but as pictorial effects.

I have been working towards several problems with the view that words refer to ideas that are pictures of things in the mind, and that words, if they do their utmost to evoke mental pictures, will communicate more clearly and effectively. If words refer to ideas that are mental pictures of things, there must be mental pictures of things. Strictly speaking, there can only be mental pictures of things that are evident to the sense of sight. It is difficult to see how one might have a mental picture of heat. One might associate the idea of heat with the mental image of fire, but this is not to have a mental image of heat. Similarly, one might associate the mental image of someone in pain with the idea of pain, but this is not to have a mental image of pain. The class of words that might be thought to refer to ideas that are pictures of things is remarkably small. If this kind of linguistic machinery operates in poetry that describes the world as it appears to the sense of sight, it cannot really operate in any other kind of poetry. So the claim that words refer to pictures of things in the mind must be strictly qualified. Furthermore, it appears from Richardson's writing and the tradition of art-theoretical thought from which it extends, that paintings should not refer to things as they are in the world, but things as they are in God's providential scheme, stripped of human accidence and revealed in something like their divine essence. So a masterful painting of a tree would not depict that tree as it exists in the world but in its full significance in God's providential scheme, and that might mean, for example, showing the nobility of the oak tree as a symbol of the Stuart monarchy, and its role in the divinely ordained restoration of that monarchy. In such a theory of painting, pictorial signs, although they are natural signs of things that refer by means of resemblance rather than convention, are significantly unlike the things in the world to which they refer, they refer to things by means of their unlikeness as much as their likeness.

Pictorial signs also refer to things that have never been seen, or at least, cannot have been seen by any spectator of the pictorial sign. No one who looks at a sixteenth-century painting of Christ has seen Christ in the most mundane sense of seeing. Even if they have seen Christ in other more mystical ways, the pictorial sign cannot work simply by looking like something in the world, because the reader of that sign has never seen the thing in the world to which it refers. Painting of course may depict a type of thing, a child or man in the case of Christ, and hope to show a viewer the specific man, Christ, by analogy with other men. The viewer must simply use his or her imagination. This is the power Addison describes in *Spectator* 416:

> When I say the Ideas we receive from Statues, Descriptions, or such like Occasions, are the same that were once actually in our View, it must not be understood that we had once seen the very Place, Action, or Person which are carved or described. It is sufficient, that we have seen Places, Persons, or Actions, in general, which bear a Resemblance, or at least some remote Analogy with what we find represented. Since it is in the Power of the Imagination, when it is once Stocked with particular Ideas, to enlarge, compound, and vary them at her own Pleasure.[19]

Yet precisely those qualities that Christ does not share with other men are what a painting of him should depict. The power of the imagination to store ideas as ideas of types of things, and to combine those ideas in ways that are not governed by what can be seen in the world, enables a spectator to identify certain things that do not exist, centaurs, for example.[20] A viewer could recognise a centaur in a picture by this operation of imagination, but could not recognise Nessus. Nessus would have to be identified by his customary props, an arrow in the chest, or a poisoned vest. This category of things, things that have never been seen by a reader of paintings and poems, are amongst the most frequently depicted in both visual and poetic art.[21] A reader of this kind of sign is only able to recognise Christ as Christ because of the conventions of depiction (adult expressions on a child's face, etc.) and the reference the painting or poem makes to a text (in this example, scripture). Rather than having a mental image of Christ, people able to recognise Christ in a painting or a poem, without him being named as Christ, have a mastery of the conventions employed when a painter or writer wants to depict or describe Christ.[22] Pictorial signs are only natural, certain and universal signs for certain things evident to sight (and here there are questions of cultural difference to think about too). For any more complex phenomena pictorial signs are highly dependent on conventions of representation. How, then, can one understand poetry as depending on a pictorial theory of language in order to achieve vividness and certainty in signification, when pictorial signs do not seem to refer to ideas that are pictures of things in a spectator's mind, or not, at least, pictures of things those spectators have ever seen? And if a spectator has never seen the thing a picture depicts, how can a pictorial sign of that thing be natural, certain and universal?

Walter Harte thought there was something pictorial about Pope's technique in general. He offers a characterisation of Pope's verse:

> So seems some Picture, where exact design,
> And curious pains, and strength and sweetness join:
> Where the free thought its pleasing grace bestows,
> And each warm stroke with living colour glows:
> Soft without weakness, without labour fair;
> Wrought up at once with happiness and care![23]

The imitative passage from *An Essay on Criticism*, to which Harte here alludes, may be considered iconic, that is, producing emphatic, vivid pictorial effects.[24] Pope's technique seems to bring an image of the things he describes before the reader's mind. Or at least that is one way of talking about the passage, about the imitative techniques Pope employs, and about successful poetry in general. Yet the imitative technique of the verse is at least as sonic as it is visual:

> *Soft* is the Strain when *Zephyr* gently blows,
> And the *smooth Stream* in *smoother Numbers* flows;
> But when loud Surges lash the sounding Shore,
> The *hoarse, rough* Verse shou'd like the *Torrent* roar.
> When *Ajax* strives, some Rock's vast Weight to throw,
> The Line too *labours*, and the Words move *slow*;
> Not so, when swift *Camilla* scours the Plain,
> Flies o'er th'unbending Corn, and skims along the Main.
> Hear how *Timotheus'* vary'd lays surprize,
> And bid Alternate Passions fall and rise!
> While, at each Change, the Son of *Libyan Jove*
> Now *burns* with Glory, and then *melts* with Love;
> Now his *fierce Eyes* with *sparkling Fury* glow;
> Now *Sighs* steal out, and *Tears begin to flow*:
> *Persians* and *Greeks* like *Turns of Nature* found,
> And the *World's Victor* stood subdu'd by *Sound*!
> *The Pow'r of Musick* all our Hearts allow;
> And what *Timotheus* was, is *Dryden* now.

(ll. 366–83)

I have already pointed out that Pope describes this technique in sonic terms, those of echo. Most of this passage describes and exemplifies the sonic qualities of things in the world: the smoothness of the stream, the crashing of waves, the music of Timotheus' lyre. Ajax throwing a rock and Camilla running over the battlefield are the only strong visual images in the passage, and it seems clear that even in those cases Pope is imitating the action each of those people performs by means of an analogy with the muscular effort required to pronounce the line of verse that describes the actions. One might say that the choice of words has a pictorial quality, that the submerged metaphor of Camilla scouring the plain calls up a detailed mental picture, but the scouring and skimming evoke as much by their combination of vowel sounds as by the images they call up (even if one can rid oneself of the picture of scouring pots). In these cases Pope seems to anticipate the strict rule that Johnson and Lessing would later formulate: poetry best imitates actions that take place over time, as poetry is in essence a temporal, not a spatial form of art.[25]

It is important to notice also that these two figures, Ajax and Camilla, are both characters from epic poems, the *Iliad* and *Aeneid* respectively. Of course, no reader of Pope's poem has ever seen Ajax or Camilla. If the reader is to have a mental picture of what these two characters do, it must be an image derived from having some idea of the type of action described. Yet both types of action are exceptional: Ajax is strong beyond anything people have seen, and Camilla faster. It is precisely what cannot have been seen in the same type of action as these two characters perform that makes them interesting: readers must conceive of these actions by a 'remote Analogy', in Addison's phrase. A reader's sense of these qualities, certainly the kind of reader Pope would have expected to have, would know what to think about these kinds of actions through having read the *Iliad* and the *Aeneid*. These pictorial effects are highly dependent on the knowledge of texts. Indeed, saying that these effects are pictorial might just be a way of saying that one is impressed by the sublimity and importance of the subject, and the vividness of the description.

Sublimity, importance and vividness are all attributes of the successful epic poem, at least as it was seen by Pope and his contemporaries. William Broome often uses a parallel between poetry and painting to help along the reader's understanding of a particular scene, episode or character in his notes to the *Odyssey*, which, together with Elijah Fenton, he translated with Pope. Broome regards Nausicaa as a painting, and refers to the tenderness of the character of Amphinomus and the details of the Ithacan landscape as painterly details.[26] Pope himself defends the *Odyssey* against the claim that it is inferior to the *Iliad* in painterly terms.[27] The defence is not based on single scenes and descriptions, but on a comparative analysis of both pieces in their entirety. The *Odyssey* is a work of maturity, and should not be expected to have the fire of the earlier poem, just as Raphael's *School of Athens* should not be expected to have the fire of *The Battle of Constantine*. Pope points out that Longinus approved of the poem precisely for 'those very *fictions* and *pictures of the manners*' of which Horace disapproved. He concludes that the poems are equal:

> it is certain we find in each, the same vivacity and fecundity of invention, the same life and strength of imaging and colouring, the particular descriptions as highly painted, the figures bold, the metaphors as animated, and the numbers as harmonious and as various.

The comparison to painting does not necessarily imply that the poem presents itself as a series of visual scenes and portraits. Vivacity and fecundity of invention, life and strength of imaging and colouring can be literary as much as pictorial qualities. Pope uses the language of painting to point out the vividness and impressiveness of the poem, to point out its moral and didactic function. He says that the '*pictures of the manners*' are 'the very essence of the work: But even without that regard, the fables themselves have both more invention and instruction, and the manners more moral and example, than those of the Iliad.'[28] It is not an end in itself that the poem is highly pictorial, but one of many means to the education of the reader in the moral of the poem, that the abuse of hospitality rites is one of the greatest crimes. Epic poetry corresponds to history painting: it is conventionally the highest of the genres. Pope uses the parallel between poetry and painting in his postscript, and Broome in the notes, to the *Odyssey*, in order to show that both epic poetry and history painting educate their audiences, that they show the world stripped of its accidental qualities and as it should be seen in God's divine scheme.

Where Pope does employ the parallel between poetry and painting in a more direct and obvious manner, he seems to blend iconic verse, verse that through its technique gives a reader the impression of pictorial vividness, with ekphrastic verse, verse that describes a work of visual art by giving it a voice. Whilst there are grounds for thinking that iconic verse has some relationship to a pictorial theory of language, there is no need for ekphrastic verse to do so. The convention is not that the verse seems to produce pictures, but that a picture produces verse. Pope's description of Achilles' shield is primarily ekphrastic verse, making a visual representation speak forth, but it also employs iconic techniques.

> Here, Herds of Oxen march, erect and bold,
> Rear high their Horns, and seem to lowe in Gold,
> And speed to Meadows on whose sounding Shores
> A rapid Torrent thro' the Rushes roars:
> Four golden Herdsmen as their Guardians stand,
> And nine sour Dogs complete the rustic Band.

(*Iliad*, XVIII.665–70)

Some of the qualities of this passage may be described as pictorial. There is an implicit spatial plane ('Here') and a number objects in the plane ('Oxen', 'Horns', 'Meadows', etc.) that occupy certain positions ('stand') in relation to one another ('high'). There are two references to the material in which these images are represented on the shield ('in Gold', 'golden'), indicating that the reader is not supposed to see the bucolic scene, but to see the bucolic scene as depicted in the shield. The reader must remain aware of the artificiality of the pictorial effect, rather than being led to see the things described as if they were actually present.

The verse is also iconic, making the reader feel with pictorial vividness that the things described are present to him or her with such evidence that he or she might be seeing them. The details that result in this accumulative effect include the lowing of the oxen heard in the assonance of 'lowe in Gold' and the imitation of the roaring of the torrent in the repeated *r*s of the second couplet quoted. These iconic effects are sonic, they are dependent on sound. Pope says that they merely 'seem' to take place (as the sound should 'seem' an echo to the sense), and so the reader is encouraged to think that the picture of the scene is so vivid, so pictorially verisimilar, it acquires sonic qualities, and, indeed, movement too, as the oxen 'speed' to the meadows. The pictorial effects of this passage are double, both ekphrastic and iconic, and in as much as they are iconic, that is, they attempt to give the poetry some of the certainty and universality of the natural signs of painting, they are dependent upon the sonic qualities of the words that should refer to the pictorial ideas of the things about which Pope is talking; with the further qualification that Pope is not talking about things, but about images of things, images of things seen on a mythical shield.

Pope's observations on Achilles' shield attempt to defend Homer from the accusation that the shield he describes is impossible to imagine. Pope undertakes 'to consider it as a Work of *Painting*, and prove it in all respects conformable to the most just Ideas and establish'd Rules of that Art' (*TE*, VIII, 358). But Pope shifts away from this line of defence, even though he goes to the trouble of providing a sketch of the shield to show that it is indeed possible to create a visual image based on Homer's description. By the opening of the third section of the observations Pope considers the description of the shield 'as a complete *Idea of Painting*, and a sketch for what one may call an *universal Picture*' (VIII, 363). The description is not a painting but an idea of painting, not an actual painting, but a description of what a painting might do. The description of the shield is perhaps not in the ekphrastic mode, but in the tradition of giving instructions to the painter, like Pope's *To a Lady*. That is, the poet does not give voice to images already there, but through words gives the painter a vivid idea of how the images should appear. In this case, the description is hardly pictorial at all, it merely shares with poetry the knack of choosing an important action to be imitated and setting that action out in the most fitting manner:

> The *Invention* is shewn in finding and introducing, in every Subject, the *greatest*, the most *significant*, and most *suitable* Objects. Accordingly in every single Picture of the Shield, *Homer* constantly finds out either those Objects which are naturally the Principal, those which most conduce to shew the Subject, or those which set it in the liveliest and most agreeable Light: These he never fails to dispose in the most advantagious Manner, Situations, and Oppositions. (*TE*, VIII, 364)

The vocabulary and critical procedure here is as much to do with the universality of epic poetry as the universality of the idea of painting. Pope's version of Homer's description of the shield is clearly pictorial, but it is difficult to discern how it is pictorial, of what it is a picture, how the vividness and evidence of that picture is produced in poetry, and whether the picture is not itself the product of verbal signs in the first place.[29]

The operation of Pope's pictorial verse is difficult to describe, but it cannot be described by saying that the words Pope uses refer to ideas that are pictures of things in the mind. Generalisations about the nature and popularity of pictorial poetry in the early eighteenth century based on this pseudo-Lockean position are unsupportable. The poetry itself does not sustain such a reading. I want to turn again to the 'Epistle to

Mr Jervas' to recapitulate the difficulties I have been describing. Pope in this epistle describes Rome, where he and Jervas see Raphael's monument, Virgil's urn, Cicero's grave, some ruins, sculptures, frescos and the paintings of Raphael, Guido Reni, Annibale Caracci, Correggio, Paulo Veronese and Titian. The reader, I suggested above, is supposed to form mental images of the things Pope describes, creating as it were a vista of Rome, and a tour of a collection of paintings.

> Together o'er the *Alps* methinks we fly,
> Fir'd with ideas of fair Italy.
> With thee, on *Raphael*'s Monument I mourn,
> Or wait inspiring dreams at *Maro*'s Urn:
> With thee repose, where *Tully* once was laid,
> Or seek some ruin's formidable shade;
> While fancy brings the vanish'd piles to view,
> And builds imaginary *Rome* a-new.
> Here thy well-study'd Marbles fix our eye;
> A fading Fresco here demands a sigh:
> Each heav'nly piece unweary'd we compare,
> Match *Raphael*'s grace, with thy lov'd *Guido*'s air,
> *Caracci*'s strength, *Correggio*'s softer line,
> *Paulo*'s free stroke, and *Titian*'s warmth divine.

> (ll. 25–38)

The reader may imagine a picture of Raphael's monument, Virgil's urn and so on, but cannot, at least not by means of the poem, have any more specific idea of the visual objects (their size and whereabouts in Rome, for example). One may have a picture of an urn, but no specific idea of its being Virgil's urn – one might imagine one of Sir Thomas Browne's urns, just in Rome not in Norfolk. And having this kind of image is no guarantee of having the same kind of image as the writer of the poem or as any other reader of the poem. The mental image is nothing like a painting in the verisimilar tradition as it is the point of verisimilar painting to provide those details that must be lacking in the verbal description.

These objections are becoming obtuse and even perverse, and merely amount to saying that poems are not paintings, but it is worth pursuing them to absurdity because they show just how little the theory of language that supposes that words work by pointing to ideas that are pictures of things can contribute to the achievements of a specific poem it is reasonable to describe as pictorial. Pope knows an awful lot about Rome, but, as he never left Britain, he knows it through pictures and through texts.[30] This passage is about his image of Rome, the image that he conjures up through artistic conversation with Jervas, not the real Rome. It is an image that is dependent on Pope's knowledge of artistic images and texts. If his words picture anything, they picture pictures and words, not things. The picture of Rome that Pope gives his readers is the product of the complex of artistic relations, conversations and echoes that were outlined when I first looked at this poem, with Pope concerned to point out the artistic and literary genealogy that supports the poem. The things of which ideas are pictures disappear from the pictorial account of language that is supposed to support pictorial effects in poetry, and the reader's imagination occupies itself with itself rather than any outside object. The things a reader sees when he or she reads a poem never existed, or were never seen by either the author or reader, or cannot be seen, or can only be seen in a form in which they do not exist in reality (as they are depicted as part of a grand divine scheme that strips them of accidental qualities), and are depicted in their pictorial vividness by means of sound and syntax. The spectacular certainty that may have been derived from making verbal signs more like visual signs disappears amidst these difficulties. Rather than stopping here at this rather unhelpful juncture, I would like to go on to suggest that Berkeley's writing on vision provides an alternative way of thinking about the relationship between visual and verbal signs that prevents external reality from disappearing and spoiling a poetic effect by its absence.

2.3   Berkeley on vision

Berkeley, as I have already noted, removes the duality of the external world and its perception by identifying perception and reality. I will give a brief account of Berkeley's writing on vision before showing how it can alter the understanding of Pope's pictorial effects. In *An Essay Towards a New Theory of Vision* (1709) and *The Theory of Vision, or Visual Language, Shewing the Immediate Presence and Providence of a Deity, Vindicated and Explained* (1733), Berkeley deals with some fundamental questions in optics. His main concern is to show that magnitude, distance and other secondary visual phenomena are not perceived directly by the eye, but are inferences from primary visual phenomena such as colour and clarity. Berkeley suggests that primary visual phenomena are signs that tell people certain things, rather than being more or less accurate reflections of an external reality whose existence people may infer from perceiving the visual phenomena. In this respect the *New Theory* is related to Berkeley's work on immaterialism in the *Principles* and *Three Dialogues*, as he attempts to identify the dual worlds of perception and reality, and solve problems that their failure to correspond creates. Berkeley has a utilitarian understanding of the meaning of the visual world. Visual phenomena, as all other phenomena, tell people how to go about their business, what to seek and what to shun. Vision is particularly useful in this sense as it is, unlike touch, an auxiliary sense that is not the primary means of feeling pleasure or pain:

> We regard the objects that environ us in proportion as they are adapted to benefit or injure our own bodies, and thereby produce in our minds the sensations of pleasure and pain. Now bodies operating on our organs, by an immediate application, and the hurt or advantage arising there-from, depending altogether on the tangible, and not at all on the visible, qualities of any object: This is a plain reason why those should be regarded by us much more than these: and for this end the visive sense seems to have been bestowed on animals, to wit, that by the perception of visible ideas (which in themselves are not capable of affecting or any wise altering the frame of their bodies) they may be able to foresee (from the experience they have had what tangible ideas are connected with such and such visible ideas) the damage or benefit which is like to ensue, upon the application of their own bodies to this or that body which is at a distance. (*New Theory, Works*, I, 193, paragraph 59)

Berkeley here develops one of his main arguments in the *New Theory*, that visible and tangible ideas are not necessarily connected to one another, at the same time as suggesting that visual phenomena are a guide to how to behave in the world. Visual phenomena are signs, but signs whose meaning is the intention of God to instruct people (and animals) to behave in certain ways in relation to certain things. Fire does not just signify heat, but tells people and animals to avoid the fire because it will cause pain.

As God has created the world, and visual phenomena are one of the most important ways of showing people and animals how to go about in the creation, Berkeley says that '*Vision is the Language of the Author of Nature*' (*Theory of Vision Vindicated*, I, 264, paragraph 38). Visual phenomena are a means of showing people what the world is and how to behave in it, or how to divide up reality, as Plato says. One of

Berkeley's more surprising contentions is that the signs that constitute this visual language are as arbitrary as verbal signs, that there is no essential connection between the form of a visual sign and its meaning for humans in the language of God: 'A great number of arbitrary signs, various and opposite, do constitute a language. If such arbitrary connexion be instituted by men, it is an artificial language; if by the Author of nature, it is a natural language' (*Theory of Vision Vindicated*, I, 265, paragraph 40).[31] Berkeley acknowledges that it is easier to confuse the visual sign with what it signifies than a verbal sign, but says that this is simply because people cannot remember a time when the signs of the visual language did not have their meaning, and that they are found to be the same wherever one goes (*Theory of Vision Vindicated*, I, 229–30, paragraph 144). These meanings do, however, have to be learnt, things need to be distinguished and their capacity to cause a person pleasure or pain must be known by experience. Human infants go through the process of distinguishing things in their visual plane, of learning what things are. Berkeley suggests that this process is continuous, that every encounter people have with the visual world is part of the attempt to understand the language of God.

This approach to the visual world is radically different than the pseudo-Lockean approach. Ideas are not signs that pictorially resemble things in the world, because, in the immaterialist system, there is no distinction between the thing perceived and the idea derived from its perception. A visual idea is a sign, not of a thing but of a meaning, God's intention that people should act in certain ways. The meaning of a visual sign is not an idea, or a thing to which that idea is annexed, but a form of behaviour. These visual signs are arbitrary, and have to be learnt, but they are arbitrary in a natural way in that they do not seem to vary over time or cultures. As the stage of reference to an external thing has been abandoned in Berkeley's theory of vision, no great certainty can be derived from a word referring to an idea of gold that is a picture in the mind. The visual idea of gold is not a picture of gold, it is gold: there is no material substance beyond the idea to which the idea refers, but this does not prevent it being a sign. The visual idea of gold is associated through custom and experience with other ideas of gold, the tactile idea of gold, for example. The meaning of these signs is the place gold has in the providential scheme, not their reference to an external thing with strictly delimitable properties that is really gold. There is no ulterior order of reality to which visual ideas refer in Berkeley's theory of vision, there are just more signs of God's providence. The crux at which a critique of the pseudo-Lockean model arrives, in which words and ideas seem never finally to refer to a thing, is the position from which Berkeley begins to derive his customary utilitarian view of the meaning of the visual world.

The simplest and greatest difference between the pseudo-Lockean and the Berkeleian position is that the former claims language works by analogy with vision, the latter that vision works by analogy with language.[32] Berkeley brings his ideas about visual language to verbal language, suggesting that words work in the same way as visual ideas, that they are arbitrary in as much as there is no necessary connection between the form of the sign and its meaning, but not at all arbitrary in that they occupy positions in a system of meaning in which every element is related one to another:

> I observe that visible figures represent tangible figures much after the same manner that written words do sounds. Now, in this respect, words are not arbitrary, it not being indifferent what written word stands for any sound: but it is requisite that each word contain in it so many distinct characters as there are variations in the sound it stands for.... It is indeed arbitrary that, in general, letters of any language represent sounds at all: but when that is once agreed, it is not arbitrary what combination of letters shall represent this or that particular sound. I leave this with the reader to pursue, and apply it in his own thoughts. (*New Theory*, I, 229, paragraph 143)

The tangible idea does not mean the visual idea, nor *vice versa*, but both have a meaning that is a kind of behaviour. The association between visual and tactile ideas is like the association between written and spoken forms of a language. It seems that Pope took Berkeley at his word, and applied the idea of the arbitrary connection of letters to sounds in his own thoughts. His essay 'On the Origin of Letters', already quoted in the previous chapter, recognises that animals

> have some few ways of expressing the Pleasure and Pain they undergo by certain Sounds and Gestures; but Man has articulate Sounds whereby to make known his inward Sentiments and Affections, tho' his Organs of Speech are no other than what he has in common with many other less perfect Animals. But the use of Letters, as significative of these Sounds, is such an additional Improvement to them, that I know not whether we ought not to attribute the Invention of them to the Assistance of a Power more than Human.

Pope goes on to remark that the connection between letters and sounds is arbitrary and yet somehow universal:

> There is this great Difficulty which could not but attend the first Invention of Letters, to wit, That all the World must conspire in affixing steadily the same Signs to their Sounds, which affixing was at first as arbitrary as possible; there being no more Connexion between the Letters, and the Sounds they are expressive of, than there is between those Sounds and the Ideas of the Mind they immediately stand for: Notwithstanding which Difficulty, and the Variety of Languages, the *Powers* of the Letters in each are very nearly the same, being in all Places about Twenty Four.

This essay was printed 28 September 1713. Pope had given Berkeley a copy of *Windsor-Forest* on 6 March 1713, and both were seeing a lot of Steele, and writing for *The Guardian* during that year.[33] It seems highly probable that Pope had read the *New Theory* and even discussed some of Berkeley's ideas about the arbitrariness of relationships between different signifying systems when he wrote this piece. Pope goes on to compare writing with painting:

> Have any of any School of Painters, gotten themselves an Immortal Name, by drawing a Face, or Painting a Landskip, by laying down on a piece of Canvas a Representation only of what Nature had given them Originals? What Applauses will he merit, who first made his Ideas set to his Pencil, and drew to his Eye the Picture of his Mind! Painting represents the outward Man, or the Shell; but can't reach the Inhabitant within, or the very Organ by which the Inhabitant is revealed: This Art may reach to represent a Face, but can't paint a Voice.[34]

Pope here applies Berkeley's remarks in order to defend writing from the claims of painting to be a universal, natural language. Writing, not painting, most truly reveals human essence as part of the divine scheme. Pope uses Berkeley's writing on vision to defend verbal language (here specifically written language) from subordination to the supposedly universal language of painting.

Berkeley finds other ways to complicate the arbitrariness of the verbal sign, suggesting that verbal signs may develop the same kind of associative force as visual signs:

> No sooner do we hear the words of a familiar language pronounced in our ears, but the ideas corresponding thereto present themselves

to our minds: in the very same instant the sound and the meaning
enter the understanding: So closely are they united that it is not in
our power to keep out the one, except we exclude the other also. We
even act in all respects as if we heard the very thoughts themselves.
(*New Theory*, I, 190, paragraph 51)

Verbal signs refer to or are associated with ideas in the same way as
visual ideas refer to or are associated with tactile ideas. Ideas refer
continually one to another, whether they are verbal, visual or tactile
ideas, as they are all signs whose meaning is only to be found in the
providential organisation of the world, and the way in which that
organisation reveals itself to people through pleasure and pain.[35]
Berkeley believes that ideas only ever refer to other ideas: 'an idea can
be like nothing but an idea; a colour or figure can be like nothing but
another colour or figure. If we look but ever so little into our thoughts,
we shall find it impossible for us to conceive a likeness except between
our ideas.'[36] Berkeley's theory of the visual world, then, replaces an
emphasis on the evident resemblance between an idea and a thing in
the world, and replaces it with an emphasis on the arbitrary yet naturalised relationships between different kinds of signs, relationships that
people come to understand as part of the meaning of the world. Visual
phenomena become meaningful to people by means of a customary
tie, by means of accumulated associations that allow them to know
whether to seek or shun particular things, that tell them how to behave.
If Berkeley's writing on vision is taken as an alternative context for
Pope's pictorial writing, a reader need not be dismayed by the apparent
failure of Pope's pictorial effects ever to refer to the real things of the
world, and to refer circularly to one sign after another, one kind of sign
after another. The forms of customary experience that Pope represents
and valorises in these pictorial poems are just as important to their
painterly qualities as any purely pictorial theory of language.

2.4   Visual traditions in Pope's poetry

None of the preceding argument is intended to suggest that poetry does
not produce images that are pictorial. Both Pope and Berkeley clearly
believed poetry to produce pictorial images. When Berkeley writes to
Pope from Italy he says he admires the 'Painting' of Pope's poems. He
asks 'whether it might not be worth a Poet's while, to travel, in order
to store his mind with strong Images of Nature', and suggests that 'to
enable a man to describe rocks and precipices, it is absolutely necessary

that he pass the *Alps'*. In a later letter he sends Pope descriptions of images he thinks might please him.[37] Berkeley's writing on vision suggests that the visual world is meaningful because people learn about God's intentions through custom and experience, rather than being meaningful because it reflects an external reality. When reading Pope's pictorial poetry in the context of Berkeley's work on vision, a reader might look to the way in which Pope makes the visual world meaningful, rather than suggesting his poetry reflects the meaning already inherent in the visual world. Rather than looking for the pictorial accuracy of particular phrases or passages, a reader might look for ways in which custom and experience have made the visual world carry meaning (meaning in the sense of the direction to behave in particular ways). In this sense Berkeley's writing on vision might imply a rather conservative and traditional response to the visual world, in which customary modes of perception are admired, and in which traditions of artistic production are regarded as the repository of such modes of perception. If one were to extract a theory of visual art from Berkeley's theory of vision, it would probably suggest that visual art consists in the artefacts produced by people that imitate visual ideas (or, more simply, things) in order to produce similar effects to the visual language of nature, that is, to instruct people how to behave. This is a very straightforward and traditional view of art, that it imitates nature in order to instruct and delight, but with the very important distinction that it would work as well for abstract as for verisimilar art. It is by no means necessary that the visual ideas people produce should be imitations of visual ideas that occur in the language of nature, or in the same form as they occur in nature, as the aim of the art work is not to imitate, but to instruct and delight, to persuade, to argue people into the belief that certain things should be sought or shunned. As Berkeley says the connexion between the visual idea and its meaning is arbitrary, there is no reason to presume a verisimilar visual sign would be more effective or communicative than any other. To take an example from the more recent history of painting, there is no reason that Barnett Newman's *Stations* should say less about feelings of metaphysical and spiritual abandonment than verisimilar paintings of the Stations of the Cross. As these paintings are humanly instituted signs, they come to mean these things by custom and experience, but once the custom is introduced, there is no turning back. It is simultaneously a very radical and a very conservative visual theory.

When Pope writes in a visual mode he combines overt pictorialism with plain description. He does not strictly distinguish between the natural visual environment and the artificial visual environment, and he could not be expected to do so when so much activity in the visual arts involves manipulation of the natural visual environment: landscape gardening and architecture are the most obvious examples here, and those with which Pope was most personally involved.[38] There is no need to distinguish between the purpose of the natural and the artificial visual world, as they should both be a form of instruction in the language of nature. I want to close this chapter by looking briefly at some more of Pope's visual poems, and arguing that their presentation of custom, of traditions of seeing and crafting the visual environment, is as important as their purely pictorial qualities. I want to suggest that Pope's visual poems emphasise a visual conservatism, a reverence for and valorisation of classical traditions in the visual arts, and a political scheme based on this reverence for customary modes of seeing and acting upon the visual environment.

Pope's most visual poems, those that offer vivid descriptions of particular environments, those that talk about works of visual art and those that compare works of visual art and poetry are consistently concerned with history, historical reception, custom, tradition and accumulated experience. Most of Pope's work, indeed, is concerned with these themes. I want to suggest that the visual poetry takes its place in a broader discursive sweep in Pope's work, that it is not a separate category; indeed, that the context Berkeley's writing on vision provides for Pope's visual poetry implies certain cultural and political preferences that are intrinsic to Pope's entire poetical project. In the 'Epistle to Mr Jervas', poetry and painting have the task of preserving images of people after their death, a task Pope modestly feels they barely achieve: 'Alas! how little from the grave we claim? / Thou but preserv'st a Face and I a Name' (ll. 77–8). But the implicit argument of the poem is that poetry and painting are the repository of great international traditions that live through the complex of poetical and painterly relationships between people like Pope and Jervas, and back through them to Dryden and du Fresnoy, and back through them to the great masters and writers mentioned in the poem, Zeuxis, Raphael, and Titian, Cicero and Virgil. The implicit argument of the poem is that by preserving the traditions of seeing the world and creating art that they inherit from the great masters of the past, Pope and Jervas preserve the best of the political circumstances in which those great masters lived and to which they contributed.[39] This argument is truly implicit, surviving only in the shades of a vocabulary used to describe artistic practice. Pope suggests that the best British artists (if the Irish Jervas can be a called British) understand the spirit of the great art of the classical past and the Renaissance, but do not follow it slavishly, in the same way as the (ideal) British political system acknowledges the great models of the past but asserts its own liberty. So Jervas strikes out 'some free design' (l. 3), has a 'free stroke' (l. 64), and Dryden has 'native fire' in contrast to du Fresnoy's more continental 'close art' (l. 8). The British artist takes what is best from the past and preserves its spirit in his own independent creative work, thus ensuring the survival of classical artistic and political traditions without compromising native British liberty. The reflection of images from art to art contributes to this conservative political independence.

Similar things can be said about Pope's other heavily visual poems. In his epistle 'To Mr Addison', Pope tries out a line that ends up in the poem to Jervas, saying that 'Art reflected images to Art' (l. 52). In this poem, Pope praises Addison's *Dialogues Upon the Usefulness of Ancient Medals*.[40] He says that the grand achievements of Rome have been ruined and have disappeared, leaving the history of that culture to survive by means of the medals, or coins, that record and celebrate political and imperial achievements: 'As soon as an Emperor had done any thing remarkable, it was immediately stamped on a Coin, and became current throughout his whole Dominions.'[41] The poem is remarkably similar to the poem to Jervas, if slightly more explicit, reconstructing the glories of Rome through a series of relationships between poets interested in the visual heritage of Rome: Addison becomes like Virgil through his interest in antiquities (l. 62), as he has resurrected Roman ideals in Britain – 'again Rome's glories shine' (l. 45). This poem calls openly on Britain to achieve the political ideals that the cultural inheritance maintained by poets and artists makes available: 'Oh when shall Britain, conscious of her claim, / Stand emulous of Greek and Roman fame?' (ll. 53–4). *Windsor-Forest* and *The Temple of Fame* similarly call on the British to recognise and make use of the cultural inheritance preserved for them by the work of poets and artists.[42] The referential quality of Pope's work, its depiction of certain real things in the world, is not as important as the fact that it forms a set of connections between people over time that enshrine particular ways of understanding and behaving in the world. Pope's poems are allowed to reflect images continually from art to art without ever arriving at a thing in the world distinct from the description, because it is their purpose to encourage certain modes of seeing and behaving in the world, rather than to depict it.

Associating artistic and political achievement is itself very traditional. Pliny suggests that the practice of painting in Rome was corrupted at the same time as political life was corrupted.[43] Palladio celebrates the power of architecture to resist periods of barbarism and decline through its sheer physical presence.[44] And the association of political and artistic achievement is central to the idea that Pope's time was Augustan, that it saw a similar coming together of art and politics as the reign of the Emperor Augustus in Rome. Pope's visual poems celebrate this combined artistic and poetical achievement by praising the political value of the visual world. Perhaps no poem in Pope's oeuvre makes clearer the connection between aesthetics and politics than the *Epistle to Burlington*.[45] Pope's praise of Lord Burlington, whom Colen Campbell called 'not only a great Patron of all Arts, but the first Architect', begins by noting his part in the Palladian architectural revival.[46] Burlington's building projects offer a contrast to the vain and foolish building of his contemporaries that Pope has just described (ll. 1–22): 'You show us, Rome was glorious, not profuse, / And pompous buildings once were things of Use' (ll. 23–4). Burlington's building project revives Roman practices not simply by visual similarity but also by functionality: his building is Roman in both architectural form and civic function. Burlington is able to build well, to embody the rules of Palladian architecture in beautiful and useful practice, because he has sense.

> Oft have you hinted to your brother Peer,
> A certain truth, which many buy too dear:
> Something there is more needful than Expense,
> And something previous ev'n to Taste – 'tis Sense:
> Good Sense, which only is the gift of Heav'n,
> And tho' no science, fairly worth the seven:
> A Light, which in yourself you must perceive;
> Jones and Le Nôtre have it not to give.

(ll. 39–46)

Sense is complex here, incorporating a basic insult levelled at the foolish and vain architects, telling them that they are senseless, saying that Burlington has the basic good sense to interpret the rules correctly, and also that he has that 'je ne sais quoi', the ability to choose just the right location for a building, and just the right amount of ornament for that building. It may even be that 'Sense' is the gift of God, an inner light, 'A Light, which in yourself you must perceive'. One could say that this sense is the sense to understand the visual world as the language of God, as a series of instructions to seek or shun certain things in the world. Burlington is a master of this language, and so, rather like the humanist painter, he is able to see things as they are in the providential scheme, not simply as they appear superficially to be.

Good architecture and landscape design, Pope suggests, is that which recognises God's utilitarian purpose in the landscape and imitates it. Pope depicts God's purposive landscape and human imitation of it in his iconic versification. His verse seems to picture forth the scene in its sound and syntax.

> Consult the Genius of the Place in all;
> That tells the Waters or to rise, or fall,
> Or helps th'ambitious Hill the heav'ns to scale,
> Or scoops in circling theatres the Vale,
> Calls in the Country, catches opening glades,
> Joins willing woods, and varies shades from shades,
> Now breaks, or now directs, th'intending Lines:
> Paints as you plant, and, as you work, designs.

(ll. 57–64)

The genius of the place here takes on the role of artificer, painting and designing as the architect goes to work. The arbitrary visual signs of the world are combined with arbitrary human interventions, both pointing up the utility of the world. Pope's verse imitates the visual world, the muscular effort required to pronounce l. 59 imitating the effort the hill makes to scale the heavens, the punctuation breaking and directing l. 63 imitating the outlines of the landscape as it breaks the poetic line. The economy and utility of Pope's verse imitate the purposiveness, the meaningfulness, of nature without in any clear way imitating it pictorially.

Without consulting the genius of the place, building is likely to become vain and ambitious. Pope gives 'proud Versailles' and 'Nero's Terraces' (ll. 71–2) as examples of buildings that fail to achieve a development of the natural genius. They are contrasted to Cobham's Opposition estate at Stowe (l. 70), with the clear implication that the political purpose of Stowe, its allegorisation of British political and cultural life, is far above the expression of autocratic power seen in the achievements of absolutist Rome or France.[47] Building is not useful if it serves just any political or cultural purpose: it is only truly useful if it emphasises the cultural and political purpose of land itself, in its function of uniting the responsibilities of proprietors and tenants, and of promoting customary experience and tradition as the best possible ways of occupying and improving the land.[48] The meaning of classical design is found in the function as much as the form of a building.

The poem moves on to its main negative example, Timon's villa. Timon is part of the economic argument of the poem, showing that vain expenditure can have its benefits.[49] He exemplifies expenditure on improving the land without sensitivity to the significance of the land in the civic order. In this respect, he is as much an aesthetic as a political example. The sustained use of antitheses in the description of Timon's grounds performs the inversion of nature described (l. 119), with half lines exemplifying errors of judgement:

> Grove nods at grove, each Alley has a brother,
> And half the platform just reflects the other.
> The suff'ring eye inverted Nature sees,
> Trees cut to Statues, Statues thick as trees,

(ll. 117–20)

Classical gestures are trivialised by their setting, providing a contrast to the revival and continuation of classical achievements in Burlington's contribution to the Palladian revival. Timon is an example of false tradition:

> Here Amphitrite sails thro' myrtle bow'rs;
> There Gladiators fight, or die, in flow'rs;
> Un-water'd see the drooping sea-horse mourn,
> And swallows roost in Nilus' dusty urn.

(ll. 123–6)

The management of the verse is a contrast to Timon's mismanagement of his land. Its performative qualities, such as the difficulty of ascent imitated in the monosyllables of l. 131, 'And when up ten steep slopes you've dragg'd your thighs', imply that Pope has achieved something of the sense of nature in his lines, in contrast to Timon. Timon is not merely a poor architect but lacks every other form of sense. His taste in books is false (ll. 133–40), he prefers ornament to doctrine in his chapel (ll. 141–50) and his entertainment is despicable (ll. 151–68). The last fault is seemingly trivial, but offends the epic requirement of hospitality. Timon's pride is not 'civil' at all (l. 166), as it indicates a disregard for the civic function of his land and its improvement.

Timon's failure is not disastrous, as it takes place in a providential scheme, and it provides employment and circulates wealth (ll. 169–72). The poem suggests that the restoration of classical utility to the land is inevitable, as 'laughing Ceres' will 're-assume' the land after Timon has gone (l. 176). Others will contribute more successfully to the development and ornamentation of a landscape that is full of aesthetic and political significance. The landowner who puts his grounds to use, aiding those dependent on the land, and contributing to wider political and imperial aims, is possessed of good sense (ll. 181–90). Burlington is to lead the innovation in architecture and development of the land, drawing on the customs and traditions of design in Jones, Palladio and Vitruvius, in order to create 'new wonders' (ll. 191–4). His aesthetic sense, it is implied, is capable of bringing peace to the land, improving the mercantile and civic potential of the country (ll. 195–202); 'These Honours, Peace to happy Britain brings, / These are Imperial Works, and worthy Kings' (ll. 203–4).

Pope presents in the *Epistle to Burlington* a visual world that is meaningful as it reveals certain things about the way God wishes people to inhabit the earth, and that has become meaningful through the inherited, customary experience of earlier generations and civilisations. The human signs that also populate this visual world, landscaped gardens, buildings, paintings and so on, do not imitate the form of the natural signs but their function – they aim to take their place alongside those natural signs. Pope's poem too aims to take its place alongside the signs in God's language by arguing that people should live in certain ways, that they should acknowledge the fact that their world is made meaningful through custom and experience by paying heed to custom in the organisation of society. The understanding of the visual world I have tried to draw from Berkeley gives rise to an aesthetic and political conservatism. I have tried to shift the emphasis in reading Pope's poems on the visual world away from pictorial imitation of a supposed real external world to an imitation of the function or utilitarian purpose of the signs that make up the language of the creation. The economic concerns upon which I have been beginning to touch are the subject of the next chapter.

3
Money and Language

I closed the last chapter by saying that the aesthetic argument of the *Epistle to Burlington* is also a political and an economic argument. As the visual world becomes meaningful only through customary experience, the mode in which people should intervene in that world should pay respect to custom and tradition. And as the visual world is a series of signs instituted by God that instructs people how to behave, then any intervention in the visual world ought to imitate God's utilitarian providence. So responses to and interventions in the visual world ought to be governed by a utilitarian regard for the way people have lived. Reading Pope next to Berkeley's writing on vision presents us with Pope as a visual, political and economic conservative, but of a rather radical and sceptical kind. I would like to pursue my account of Pope as a radical conservative with strong sceptical leanings in this chapter. It has a very similar trajectory to the preceding chapter. Having hinted at the dominant mode of reading Pope's poems on money and financial tokens, I will question the economic and philosophical groundwork of this dominant mode of reading.

Many recent literary critics and historians, such as Colin Nicholson and J.G.A. Pocock, have emphasised the way in which the financial revolution of the late seventeenth and early eighteenth centuries changed the way people thought about money and about language. The period is depicted in these accounts as one in which financial tokens become ever more removed from their referents, in which the gaps between monetary signifier, signified and referent become ever wider, as a result of the increased speculation in stocks and shares, the institution of national debt and so on. These critics and historians argue that the financial revolution has an analogue in language, that people in the early eighteenth century suddenly become much more aware of the gaps between the linguistic signifier, signified and referent because of the revolution in financial affairs, because value no longer seems to be about the amount of gold in the bank, but about various pieces of paper carrying various inscriptions whose relative value can increase and decrease greatly and quickly. Such historians and critics present Pope's writing on financial themes as a nostalgic retreat from this revolutionary moment. Pursuing an analogy with language, I will look at Locke's writing on money and suggest that his sustained attempt to demystify the relationship between the nominal value of coin and its weight, and to describe it as an arbitrary contractual relationship, has a fairly precise analogue in his writing on language. Locke's account of money shares problems with the analogous account of language, failing to acknowledge the power of use and convention in the attribution and maintenance of values, of use as a context in which the idea of value can make sense. Hoping to make the relationship between real and nominal value more certain by demystifying it, he opens it up to the vagaries of all human contractual relationships. This contractual relationship is open to all the abuses of those other contractual relationships in language that Locke describes in Book III of the *Essay Concerning Human Understanding*. The arbitrary and contractual view of the relationship between tokens and values is a significant part of the history of those highly manipulable forms of value that emerge during the financial revolution, and the reported contemporary crisis in financial and linguistic value, to which Pope is said to have a nostalgic reaction.

Following the pattern of the previous chapter, I would like to substitute Berkeley for Locke and suggest that adopting Berkeley's view of financial tokens provides readers of Pope's verse with a better idea of what Pope is trying to achieve in his poems on money and finance. Berkeley emphasises the arbitrariness of the financial token, but suggests at the same time that financial tokens should be regarded as a means of exerting power, that the value of any such token is its power. This power is only evident in use: it is not a question of the relationship between what is written on the token and its weight, or between what is written on the token and an amount of gold in the bank, but of what the token enables a person to do in the world, what it can be used to do. Berkeley's financial theory follows a general trend in his work away from reference and towards meaning. Pope's poems on finance, I suggest, follow the same pattern, aiming to show the reader how the expected reference of a financial token to a value is always a delusion, not only since the South Sea Bubble, but well before Horace cast doubts even on the certainty of property ownership. Certainly Pope condemns modern financial practices, arguing that paper credit 'lends Corruption lighter wings to fly' (*Epistle to Bathurst*, l. 70), and so is in large part responsible for the cultural decline of the Walpole years. This form of financial representation might seem flighty and unstable, but Pope presents the very possibility of property as uncertain and unstable: 'What's *Property*? dear Swift! you see it alter / From you to me, from me to Peter Walter' (Satire II.ii, ll. 167–8). In this chapter, I will focus on Pope's comments on use and the value of gold in an attempt to get beyond the accusation of nostalgia and provide an account of the complexity of Pope's attitude to financial tokens.

3.1   Pope's nostalgia

The story of the relationship between literature and finance in the early eighteenth century is now familiar. From the Revolution settlement of 1689, William III encourages investment in the government and anticipation of more than the following year's revenue by taxation, partly in order to fund his wars, and partly to give the monied classes an interest in the continuation of his regime; if it collapsed, they lost their money.[1] Thus national debt is established, and other financial institutions, such as the Bank of England, begin their lives. An enormous cultural and political divide develops, in which some believe in the new power of trade and speculation and the social forms that go along with it – urbanisation and class mobility – whilst others remain convinced that only possession of land gives one a true interest in the future of the country, and believe in older forms of paternalistic social organisation based on the civic obligations of the squire. Both sides of the debate recognise that progress has not necessarily led to virtue, thus separating the two concepts and shattering a previous understanding of the world.[2] Each of these factions has its writers. They continue relatively friendly until the bursting of the South Sea Bubble, in which many of the traditionalists are stung, at which point the opposition becomes rather more bitter and focused upon the figure of Walpole.[3] Those on the side of trade and speculation anticipate the development of modern economics, whilst those on the side of the land are gloomy, nostalgic Tories who want impossibly to revert to an older social order.[4] Pocock describes this nostalgic position, which has also been attributed to Pope in recent literary scholarship, as a position that Locke intended to demolish in his *Two Treatises of Government* (yet as

I shall show shortly, Locke was a great nostalgic with regard to the intrinsic value of coin):

> the civic or participatory ideal had come to be expressed in terms of an agrarian mode of property acknowledged to exist mainly in the past;...it employed a theory of social personality in which virtue was held to be civic and was grounded on material bases that could not be bartered away without the loss of virtue itself;...it recognized a modernity which looked very like corruption; and...it knew no theory of civic or moral personality which could easily be applied to the new society. (*Machiavellian Moment*, p. 436)

It is one of the quirks of literary history that the winning side in economic terms was the loser in cultural terms. Those who picked up the trading, monetary strain write bad poems and are forgotten; Pope and Swift write fascinating, biting indictments of the new regime, but their financial thought is backward. Those who wrote poems addressed to directors of the South Sea Company asking for subscriptions (a surprisingly large sub-genre in 1720) disappear.[5] Swift's assertions that credit is 'dangerous, illegal, and perhaps treasonable', and that 'the possessors of the soil are the best judges of what is for the advantage of the kingdom; If others had thought the same way, Funds of Credit and South-sea Projects would neither have been felt nor heard of', are readily to hand in a standard scholarly edition.[6] Although there is a lot of value and perhaps some accuracy in this narrative of the relationship between finance and literature in the early eighteenth century, I think it is flawed, at least in its presentation of Pope's economic thought as part of an impossibly nostalgic project. Pope's poems on financial themes are often read in this context of backwardness and nostalgia.[7] Modern financial innovation is said to be something Pope 'cannot successfully oppose'.[8] One might say that the sustained critique of mercantilist attitudes to economic life in the *Epistle to Bathurst* is an unfeasibly conservative approach to the financial revolution, doggedly sticking to the idea of intrinsic worth in the products of labour, without even being prepared to admit the possible benefits of a more speculative economy. Pope is troubled by the innovations of modern finance: they upset his idea of value, which should reside in land, and only in gold as an exchangeable commodity. His relationship to paper credit and speculation is soured by his being stung in the South Sea Bubble, and also by his dislike of the uncertainty that credit and speculation bring into language by allowing a form of words ('Equitable Life promises to pay you a pension of...' for example) to represent radically different values from one day to the next. It is the purpose of this chapter to question this strain in the reading of Pope, and to suggest that his writing on money and finance owes a lot to a rather more radical and sceptical tradition of thought than is presumed, a tradition that is exemplified by Berkeley's *Querist* (first published in 1735), and in which intrinsic value is abandoned in favour of an instrumental view of monetary tokens. Reading Pope's poems on finance next to Berkeley gives readers a more nuanced version of his satire than reading them in the context of an opposition between the new and the old forms of economic life.

An example from Pope may help to sketch the kinds of attitude he presents. In the *Epistle to Bathurst*, Pope says how easy it is to bribe politicians now that paper credit has taken the place of gold, which itself took the place of commodities.

> Oh! that such bulky Bribes as all might see,
> Still, as of old, incumber'd Villainy!
> In vain may Heroes fight, and Patriots rave;
> If secret Gold saps on from knave to knave.
> Could France or Rome divert our brave designs,
> With all their brandies or with all their wines?
> What could they more than Knights and Squires confound,
> Or water all the Quorum ten miles round?
> A Statesman's slumbers how this speech would spoil!
> "Sir, Spain has sent a thousand jars of oil;
> "Huge bales of British cloth blockade the door;
> "A hundred oxen at your levee roar."
>   Poor Avarice one torment more would find;
> Nor could Profusion squander all in kind.
>
> . . . .
>
> Shall then Uxorio, if the stakes he sweep,
> Bear home six Whores, and make his Lady weep?
> Or soft Adonis, so perfum'd and fine,
> Drive to St. James's a whole herd of swine?
>
> . . . .
>
> Blest paper-credit! last and best supply!
> That lends Corruption lighter wings to fly!
> Gold imp'd by thee can compass hardest things,
> Can pocket States, can fetch or carry Kings;
> A single leaf shall waft an Army o'er,
> Or ship off Senates to a distant Shore;

A leaf, like Sybil's, scatter to and fro
Our fates and fortunes, as the winds shall blow;
Pregnant with thousands flits the Scrap unseen,
And silent sells a King or buys a Queen.

(ll. 35–48, 59–62, 69–78)

The first thing to notice about this passage, and it has been noticed, is its distrust of the new forms of credit.[9] But Pope's satire goes further than the financial revolution. The nostalgic attitude to older forms of bribe that Pope presents is a joke. Pope sees that corruption is more possible in a modern speculative economy than in an economy of barter, but he is not nostalgic for any form of bribery. Pope ironises his own nostalgia, pointing out that it is ridiculous to think the past better than the present because people in the past had a less efficient mechanism of corruption. Pope does not deny that corruption existed in the past, he merely asserts that it has been facilitated in the present. Pope also makes the objects of older forms of exchange seem absurd by presenting them as if they were the new type of financial token, that is, he presents the objects involved in those transactions as counters rather than pledges. Indeed, neither counter nor pledge is required in barter. Pope presents objects of barter as financial tokens in order to moralise about the absurdity of corruption. It is absurd, no matter how corrupt one might be, to desire to possess a thousand jars of oil: the corrupt states-man here finds himself in the position of the small-time gangster who gets lumbered with a vast quantity of unsalable stolen goods. One aspect of corruption is the very old belief that one is able to acquire and store up more than one needs in order to be able to exercise power over others at some future point, and to do this without an interest in the general good.[10] This belief is made to appear absurd by presenting commodities as financial tokens, an inversion of the traditional absurdity of taking the token for the commodity; it merely remains absurd when the financial tokens desired are counters, not pledges, or the commodities themselves. Pope's poem is more than a nostalgia for older forms of financial representation: it is a thorough critique of the nature of financial representation altogether. And even though Pope presents the new world of finance as a threat to language, something that can pervert language, this possibility does not characterise modernity in opposition to the past. The bills of paper credit are like Sybil's leaves: they have great power despite their unreliability, they can bring about huge changes in world government despite being just flimsy leaves. These things are equally true of Sybil's leaves themselves: Pope does not legitimise the ancient practice when he satirises the modern, he criticises both. As in *The Rape of the Lock*, within the contrast of heroic and trivial, ancient and modern, there are straightforward similarities: Is Belinda's finery any less the spoil of defeated races than the Greeks' weaponry? Are Sybil's leaves any more reliable than paper credit? There has been a tendency to read Pope as a classicist, as a poet who raises the classical above the modern, and this tendency has masked an occasional use of the modern to illustrate the deficiencies of the classical world.[11] The wit in such moments as the comparison of credit notes and Sibyl's leaves is the sudden substitution of a relationship of comic similarity for one of comic dissimilarity in the parallel between the ancient and the modern. Pope recognises that seemingly trivial words can often cause enormous political revolutions, and that it is quite often the least reliable form of words that causes the greatest turmoil. Pope's satire uses a nostalgic response to financial innovation to imply a broader set of sceptical attitudes to value, and the ways in which value is represented and reproduced. Pope's poems on finance reveal him to be more of a sceptic than a nostalgic.

3.2 Signs of exchange

I will say a little more now about the kind of crisis that is supposed to have affected the opponents of financial revolution. The financial revolution of the late seventeenth and early eighteenth centuries is regarded as a cause of particular anxiety for poets and writers because it is said to alter the relationship between signs and what they signify, between various kinds of tokens and the things to which they refer. The financial revolution is said to introduce an instability into the relationship between signs and what they signify that is antipathetic to traditional poetic objectives of description, memorialisation and argument. Catherine Ingrassia says that 'Pope's attempts to contain and control paper credit with his textual representation indicate his aware-ness of not just its insubstantiality but its fundamental instability.' She recognises that purchasing stocks and bonds is a different kind of action than purchasing land, as the purchaser of stocks and bonds receives nothing but a receipt for the stock or bond, whereas most other earlier forms of purchase resulted in the acquisition of a thing (land, commodity, etc). 'Consequently, there was no apparent relationship between sign and signified, between the paper receipt and the value it represented.'[12] Paper credit, in Ingrassia's view, makes the relationship between signs and what they signify unstable and insubstantial. It makes all acts of signification into catachretic acts, because the signs employed refer to no fixed concepts.

Ingrassia is by no means unusual in wanting to read financial and linguistic practices in analogy with one another. Colin Nicholson says that he has studied 'the ways in which the languages and logics of political and economic activity merge and interact with those of imaginative production'. When discussing John Gay's use of financial metaphors in 'A Panegyric Epistle', he argues that the 'security of linguistic representation is itself undermined by speculative transactions, and that when optimistic fancy is submerged in fantasy then boundaries between hitherto accepted signifying systems must also and inevitably be brought into question'.[13] Nicholson envisages a world in which the wild inflation and deflation of the value of various stocks, bonds and notes has made all language look untrustworthy, has infiltrated the language of poetry and made it fluctuate in a manner analogous to the price of South Sea stock. Anne Hall Bailey has also argued that 'the philosophical and physical relationships between linguistics and economics were of particular interest to Alexander Pope' and that 'the convergence of linguistics and economics' is 'one aspect of the cultural degeneration Pope identifies' in the *Dunciad*. She compares the instability of linguistic and economic signs:

The relationship between the signifier and the signified does not carry embedded within it an inherent connection. Similarly, the operative signs of political economy are arbitrary. It is the subjective nature of the sign that serves to place linguistic and political economy in the same sphere: in both cases, the valuational representation of the sign is capriciously established.... Ultimately, the *Dunciad* warns its readers of the inherent corruption that exists in the formation of a capitalist market dependent upon the salability of thought.[14]

New financial practices reveal the capriciousness of the relationship between linguistic signs and their referents.

These recent critics are deeply indebted to Pocock and his account of the decline of civic virtue in a modern era of financial alienation and corruption. Speaking in a first person plural that is somewhere between an imaginative recreation of the intellectual world of the early eighteenth-century citizen and a recognition of the effect the financial revolution has had on twentieth-century finance Pocock says that gold and paper have become the symbolic medium in which we express our feelings and translate them into actions, so that at the same time they acquire a fictitious value of their own. The language in which we communicate has itself been reified and has become an object of desire, so that the knowledge and messages it conveys have been perverted and rendered less rational. And the institution of funded debt and public stocks have turned the counters of language into marketable commodities, so that the manipulators of their value...are in a position to control and falsify 'the intercourse of speech'. (*Machiavellian Moment*, p. 441)

This transition in eighteenth-century thought is of great importance to Pocock's grand narrative of British intellectual life. He says in a later work that he is 'contrasting a conception of property which stresses possession and civic virtue with one which stresses exchange and the civilisation of the passions, and thereby disclosing that the debate between the two is a major key to eighteenth-century social thought'.[15] He applies to the eighteenth-century Marc Shell's idea that innovation in the means of economic exchange brings about an alteration in the meaning of meaning: 'Whether or not a writer mentioned money or was aware of its potentially subversive role in his thinking, the new forms of metaphorization or exchanges of meaning that accompanied the new forms of economic symbolization and production were changing the meaning of meaning itself.'[16]

Regardless of the value of this transition to understanding eighteenth-century social thought, I would like to query the view of language that Pocock, Nicholson and Ingrassia employ when writing about the analogy between money and words.[17] The view insists that words are tokens that refer to things, whether those things are ideas of things or the things themselves. The relationship between the token and the thing becomes unstable, or is revealed to be unstable, by means of an analogy with money and less traditional forms of financial token. This view of language is a critique of Locke's view, but Pocock and Locke share the view that the relationships between signifier, signified and referent are the characteristic features of languages, and that they are liable to abuse. Both views subsume all the functions of language, meaning, under one of its incidental features, reference. I will look at some connections between this view of language and Locke's monetary theory before moving on to a discussion of Berkeley.

Locke's most serious contributions to economic thought relate not to credit and new forms of financial token but to money, and the recoinage crisis of 1696–98. Locke was not just the philosopher of the recoinage – he was actively involved in the process.[18] Locke's interest is in the denomination of silver coin, the possibility of raising the denomination of coin and the effect this might have, or rather might fail to have, on its value. I suggested above that Locke's writing on coin has an analogy in his writing on language. This analogy is to be found principally in his insistence that the denomination of coin is entirely arbitrary, and merely fixed by convention (as the reference of words is entirely arbitrary) and that adopting a clearer and more philosophical vocabulary would eliminate many of the problems encountered when discussing the value of money. I would like to suggest that this referential, contractual view of money lies behind the current understanding of the financial and linguistic crisis of the early eighteenth century, with a view to challenging that understanding.

Locke says that

> Mankind, having consented to put an imaginary Value upon Gold and Silver by reason of their Durableness, Scarcity, and not being very liable to be Counterfeited, have made them by general consent the common Pledges, whereby Men are assured, in Exchange for them to receive equally valuable things to those they parted with for any *quantity* of these Metals. (I, 233–4)

It is important to Locke that money is both a counter and a pledge (I, 233), that it is both the sign of an agreement between people and also the substance of that agreement. Locke distinguishes between coin and paper money in this respect. Coin is 'a pledge, which Writing cannot supply the place of': 'a law cannot give to Bills that intrinsick Value, which the universal Consent of Mankind has annexed to Silver and Gold' (I, 234). Locke is not an advocate of the new forms of paper money and credit that open up the nature of value to all sorts of sceptical questioning. He prefers to think that the intrinsic value of gold and silver has been settled by universal agreement, although he still refers to the value of gold as 'an imaginary Value'. Locke gives a complex account of intrinsic value, stating

> that one Ounce of Silver is always of equal value to another Ounce of Silver considered in its Intrinsick worth, or in reference to the universal Trade of the World: But 'tis not of the same value at the same time, in several parts of the World, but is of most worth in that Country where there is the least Money, in proportion to its Trade[.] (I, 267)

Locke is in a position that recalls his difficulties with language. He recognises that gold and silver are not equally valuable at different times and in different places, but at the same time holds that they have a form of intrinsic value that differentiates them from paper credit and other forms of modern financial token. This intrinsic value is fixed, strangely, by the universal consent of humankind: it is not just *acknowledged* by universal consent, but *fixed* by universal consent. So the intrinsic value of gold and silver is a matter of consent, but of a different kind of consent than that which fixes value on a piece of paper with writing on it ('The Governor of The Bank of England promises to pay the bearer on demand'...). The intrinsic value of gold and silver is imaginary, arbitrary, a matter of convention, but not the kind of convention that can be replicated in a deliberate act of fixing the imaginary value of paper money.

Locke wants to distinguish between denomination, the mere names attached to money, and its value. 'For Locke's opponents in the coinage controversy denomination was a real value, while for him it was merely an arbitrary name' (I, 88, editor's introduction). Indeed, Locke says that a 'penny is an arbitrary denomination no more belonging to 8 than to 80. . . . such like divisions being only Extrinsical denominations are every where perfectly arbitrary' (II, 396). Whilst defending the intrinsic value of gold and silver coin and distinguishing it from the nominal value of the words used to quantify value, and from laws imposed to give value to paper money, Locke comes very close to recognising a radical arbitrariness in intrinsic value. Applying to the 'universal Consent of Mankind' as a means of fixing the intrinsic value of gold and silver more or less does away with the idea of intrinsic value. Locke's editor attempts to clarify Locke's idea of universal consent: 'Consent, for Locke, is concurrence in a mutually beneficial course of action, arising as it were in the form of spontaneous intellectual assent once the advantages of an arrangement become apparent' (I, 87–8). This phenomenological consent may well help to distinguish between the historical adoption of a practice (such as using money) and the institution of a practice by law (such as using paper money), but it does so with false confidence. What was once instituted by law becomes practice, just as paper money, and electronic money, have become no less acceptable than coin. Locke's view privileges old laws and calls them consent.

Locke has the same problems with the nature of universal consent in relation to money that I identified in his discussion of the arbitrariness of the relationship between words and the ideas they signify. Locke in the *Essay* calls upon common consent and use as a means of judging the propriety of speech, and says that even the Emperor Augustus recognised he did not have the power to coin a new Latin word. Yet he refuses to acknowledge common conversation and use as criteria for knowing that language has successfully performed its function of externalising internal conceptions: he refuses to let use prove that reference has taken place, or even to acknowledge it as the best available proof.[19] Similarly with money, Locke insists on common consent as the means of giving intrinsic value to gold and silver, but will not let it do the same for paper money. He insists that there is an indescribable but authentic relationship between a token and a thing that can be abused and perverted without the users of the token knowing how to prevent the abuse and perversion. He does not accept that the intrinsic value of the gold or silver is not in its weight, but only in the fact that people will accept it as a counter, that people will use it.

Locke's response to both of the crises he identifies, those concerning the nature of money and the nature of language, is to blame language. He calls upon people to 'consider things beyond their Names' (I, 247) and says that his writings should make things clear 'throughout this whole (as it is thought) mysterious Business of Money, to all those, who will but be at the easie Trouble of stripping this Subject of hard, obscure and doubtful Words, wherewith Men are often misled and mislead others' (II, 403). Locke believes that an effort of concentration that takes one beyond the delusory qualities of signifying systems will clarify thinking on money and language. He does not acknowledge that one cannot think about money and language without thinking of the tokens that constitute money and language, whatsoever they may refer to, if, indeed, they refer to anything at all: to think about money and language without thinking about signification is to put aside the very thing that is essential to both money and language. Locke believes that coin is valuable because it refers to itself, it refers to its own weight and purity, and thereby gives a perfectly reliable account of its own value.[20] Yet he says that value is dependent on the consent of humankind: there is nothing in the gold and silver itself that is valuable other than their acceptation in an international system of exchange. Locke does not take the next step and suggest that the gold and silver refer to the consent of humankind to recognise the tokens as a means of alienating their labour, as a means of exercising power. Berkeley does make this step, and I will shortly give an account of his work on the subject.

Locke's monetary theory is referential in that it emphasises the reference any financial token must make to the quantities of gold and silver that humankind decide are the prices of various goods and services. He is concerned that modern financial tokens do not have the referential certainty of coin, as they are not at the same time counter and pledge. These two aspects of Locke's money, its work as both counter and pledge, are like his duplicate worlds of reality and of ideas: why does one need a counter of something for which one already has a pledge? Why does one need a real world if the world of ideas (perceptions, experiences, reflections, thoughts, etc.) is perfectly adequate? The literary critics and intellectual historians I mentioned above have identified the weakness that the double life of financial tokens introduces into financial affairs: if money is regarded as a token that refers to something else, there will be all sorts of problems with that reference – more problems, the more the counter becomes detached from the pledge. The process of abstracting the counter from the pledge is the process of financial and linguistic crisis these critics and historians identify. I will go on to say why I think Locke is simply wrong to think that financial tokens, in his case money, are both counters and pledges. I will use Berkeley's *Querist* to try to argue that a financial token can only ever be a counter, never a pledge. I will suggest that Berkeley's instrumentalist view of financial tokens, that they are the means of transferring power, and that, if they have reference, they have reference to human conventions of transferring power rather than to some other intrinsically valuable thing, offers a way out of some of Locke's difficulties. I suggest that this parallels Berkeley's solution of Locke's difficulties with the reference of words by means of custom and convention.

3.3   Pope's lost gold

Before moving on to Berkeley's writing on finance I want to look at a few examples of gold in Pope's work, showing in each case how the presumed intrinsic value of the gold disintegrates and is replaced by ethical and cultural values, an emphasis on use, custom and convention. I hope that my discussion of Locke's description of gold and silver, contrasted with Pope's presentation of gold in the *Epistle to Bathurst*, will inform my argument here: Pope only refers to real gold, the physical and fiscal properties of the metal, in order to show that these supposedly real properties are nothing but incidental features of the way in which the metal is used. I will look at rust and gold in relation to classical antiquity, and dross for duchesses in the *Epistle to a Lady*.

On at least three separate occasions in his writing, Pope suggests that the world has lost its sense of what is truly valuable by esteeming the rust on a coin more than the coin itself. The idea is found in 'To Mr Addison':

> With sharpen'd sight pale Antiquaries pore,
> Th'inscription value, but the rust adore;
> This the blue varnish, that the green endears,
> The sacred rust of twice ten hundred years!

(ll. 35–8)

Here the antiquary loses sight of what should be most valuable to him – the historical evidence the medal can provide through its inscription – becoming pre-occupied with the rust as a sign of the age of the coin. The antiquary, who is charged with reviving the glory of Rome and providing a cultural and political example to the British, is distracted. Pope describes the veneration of classical authors in similar terms in a note to the *Iliad*:

> Fame is a Debt, which when we have kept from People as long as we can, we pay with a prodigious Interest, which amounts to twice the Value of the Principal. Thus 'tis with ancient Works as with ancient Coins, they pass for a vast deal more than they were worth at first; and the very Obscurities and Deformities which Time has thrown upon them, are the sacred Rust, which enhances their Value with all true Lovers of Antiquity. (XVI.1032n)

In both these passages the rust becomes sacred. In the note to Homer, Pope writes in more explicitly economic terms. The debt of fame that is paid to ancient authors is the product of a credit system, and is made to look almost unsavoury: contemporary readers only pay so much now because their predecessors were profligate enough to incur the debt in the first place by not acknowledging the greatness of a writer. There is also a reasoned call to recognise the fallibility of the ancients: just as Homer sometimes nods, so his readers should realise that his market value is sometimes inflated. Works of ancient literature are like ancient coins, which, although they contain only a certain amount of precious metal, and thus have a definable intrinsic value, are still exchanged for much more than that definable value. Pope implies that there is an absurdity in valuing the age of the coin like that, just as he implies that there is absurdity in valuing just the age of a literary work.

Pope's economic vocabulary bears more scrutiny than this. As in the comparison of gold to silver, virtue to gold in *Imitations of Horace*, Epistle I.i that I will discuss later, Pope is not saying that what one should really value about an ancient coin is its intrinsic value as defined by the weight and fineness of the metal in the coin. Pope's irony is double: the value of the coin is neither its rust nor its metal, but its function in Roman society, which Addison, as remarked in the previous chapter, notes to be the recording, reproducing and advertising the achievements and glories of the republic, in order to develop and maintain patriotic feeling in its citizens. Such is the real function and value of the coin, and such is the real function and value of a literary work, recording, reproducing and advertising glorious achievements in order to rouse patriotism – certainly that is one of Pope's main aims throughout his career. Pope adopts a forlorn tone in these passages because contemporary Britons fail to recognise the value of this cultural function. The same world-weariness of tone is found in *Imitations of Horace*, Epistle II.i, in which 'Authors, like Coins, grow dear as they grow old; / It is the rust we value, not the gold' (ll. 35–6).[21] (Pope does not take this comparison of authors and coins from Horace.) The value of the coin is not the amount of gold it contains, neither is the value of the work definable by means of looking simply at what it contains. The literary work, like the coin, must be active in the process of exchange between literate individuals and groups that leads to national betterment. The work's being written in an ancient dialect and containing striking images, for example, is not valuable in itself. Value is found in those things when the ancient dialect inspires a people to deal with one another in straightforwardness and simplicity, and when the images inspire people to see the world in its primitive authenticity. The ancientness of the work is only valuable if it inspires the British to imitate the political and cultural virtues of the ancients. The intrinsic value of the gold in the coin to which the ancient literary work is compared disintegrates in a close reading of Pope's economic vocabulary.

Literary work also has a relationship to gold in the *Epistle to a Lady*. This poem begins with the famous condemnation of female character-lessness that Pope puts in Martha Blount's mouth:

> Nothing so true as what you once let fall,
> 'Most Women have no Characters at all'.
> Matter too soft a lasting mark to bear,
> And best distinguish'd by black, brown, or fair.

(ll. 1–4)

Character is here a distinguishing personal trait, but also the impression left on metal, in a derivation from the primary meaning of the Greek χαρακτήρ.[22] Women are not sufficiently durable to support the marks that make gold and silver suitable means of exchange, in the way that men are able to maintain their characters in the exchange economy of early eighteenth-century life. The implied image here of women's heads printed on coins leads into the body of the poem that represents various women in various portrait postures. This variety of posture demonstrates their fundamental inconsistency of motive and action, in a gender-specific attack that replicates the form of the *Epistle to Cobham*, which, in the collected editions of the *Moral Essays*, immediately precedes the *Epistle to a Lady*. Money appears incidentally in the main body of the poem: Papillia is bought a park (l. 39), Narcissa pays a tradesman and gives alms (ll. 56–7), Atossa's will is dispersed in the absence of an heir (ll. 149–50). Gold comes back into the poem at its close, when Pope is praising Martha's blend of male and female qualities.

> Be this a Woman's Fame: with this unblest,
> Toasts live a scorn, and Queens may die a jest.
> This Phoebus promis'd (I forget the year)
> When those blue eyes first open'd on the sphere;
> Ascendant Phoebus watch'd that hour with care,
> Averted half your Parents simple Pray'r,
> And gave you Beauty, but deny'd the Pelf
> That buys your sex a Tyrant o'er itself.
> The gen'rous God, who Wit and Gold refines,
> And ripens Spirits as he ripens Mines,
> Kept Dross for Duchesses, the world shall know it,
> To you gave Sense, Good-humour, and a Poet.

> (ll. 281–92)

Phoebus, the god of poetry and of the sun, refines wit and gold (the sun was thought to ripen gold in the earth). He reserves for Duchesses just the dross, the excess metal produced in the process of smelting, as in the production of coins. Now, if metal has an inalienable intrinsic value based on weight and fineness, then the metal in dross is as valuable as the metal in the coin. But the metal in the coin is sanctioned by the characters impressed upon it and the exchanges in which it is used, in a way that the metal in the dross is not. It cannot be the intrinsic value of the metal that is valuable. Dross here is being used in a metonymic way to describe all gold, indeed all material goods, and Pope continues in the satirical line of thought that if the unworthy great are rewarded with material goods, those material goods cannot be a true reward. So, Pope implies all material goods are dross, and all intrinsic values are nothing but what character and exchange make them. Material goods are reserved for Duchesses, whilst Martha receives sense, good-humour and a poet, Pope himself. All gold is dross, not just the excess from smelting. The character that ladies lack is not so valuable after all, as the gold which carries imprints or characters is itself of little value. Martha's sense and good humour, and the fact that she knows someone capable of recognising and depicting them, are the things of true value. So these qualities, and Pope himself, stand in for the value of gold now that it has disintegrated: the intrinsic value of gold against which women's characters (or lack of them) were seen to be valueless is now redescribed as dross for Duchesses. Pope implies that this dross is also the execrable writing that one is presented with if one pays for compliments, the dull writing of patronised poets. Pope's writing is the true characterful exchange, the true gold. Pope and his poem take the place of gold because they are truly valuable. They are conferred upon Martha as a gift, and confer upon her, and memorialise, those qualities they themselves identify, her sense and good humour. If the readers of the poem are convinced that these qualities are more important than social status, then common esteem, or consent, has taken the place of intrinsic value. The exchange economy, or rather gift economy, of which Pope and his poem become part is not based on intrinsic value, especially not that of gold, but on the use of words, on putting the words that take the place of gold to good use.

I said earlier that the gold imped by paper credit in the *Epistle to Bathurst* was perhaps no less reliable or more prone to corruption than the commands spelt out by Sybil's leaves, or the physical commodities that had previously been used to bribe people. I tried to suggest that Pope's nostalgia for an older form of bribe was itself, quite clearly, a joke, and a joke that pointed out the potential for corruption in any system of exchange when the people involved in exchange believe it possible to make a profit without ever having to hand back what is gained at another's expense. I have tried to show here how solid gold dissolves in Pope's writing and is replaced by the esteem with which cultural artefacts and words are exchanged. I will turn now to Berkeley's writing on money to draw parallels with Pope.

3.4   Signs of use

Berkeley, in his writing on money as in his writing on language, places a much greater emphasis on use than Locke. Berkeley's economic writings relate to a different set of concerns than Locke's, those of thirty or forty years after the recoinage controversy, and those of Ireland rather than England. The general concerns of writing on money had changed: 'The theory of money moved away from an emphasis on the nature, or even the value, of money as such to the problems of monetary circulation and the larger issues of the relationship between money and the working of a monetary economic system.'[23] Yet the general remarks each philosopher makes about the nature of financial signs are comparable, and serve to illustrate my general argument, that Berkeley's writings provide a more rewarding philosophical context for the interpretation of Pope's work than Locke's. Indeed, it has been said that 'Berkeley's arguments against Locke's theory of the meaning of money were rooted in a rejection of Locke's semantics, his theory of abstraction, and his materialism. His critical program formed the basis of the Querist's confidence in his defetishization of gold and constituted something of an unspoken Prolegomenon of *The Querist*.'[24] Berkeley's monetary philosophy is part of a sustained critique of Locke that works itself out of a central concern with language.

In 1713 Berkeley emphasises the referential function of money and words:

And the same Weakness, or Defect in the Mind, from whence Pedantry takes its rise, does likewise give Birth to Avarice. Words and Mony are both to be regarded as only Marks of Things. And as the Knowledge of the one, so the Possession of the other is of no Use, unless directed to a further End. A mutual Commerce could not be carried on among Men, if some common Standard had not been agreed upon, to which the Value of all the various Products of Art and Nature were reducible, and which might be of the same use in the conveyance of Property, as Words are in that of Ideas. Gold, by its Beauty, Scarceness, and durable Nature, seems designed by Providence to a Purpose so excellent and advantageous to Mankind. Upon these Considerations that Metal came first into Esteem. But such who cannot see beyond what is nearest in the Pursuit, beholding Mankind touched with an Affection for Gold, and being ignorant of the true Reason that introduced this odd Passion into Human Nature, imagine some intrinsick Worth in the

Metal to be the Cause of it. Hence the same Men who, had they been turned towards Learning, would have employed themselves in laying up Words in their Memory, are by a different Application employed to as much purpose in treasuring up Gold in their Coffers. They differ only in the Object; the Principle on which they act, and the inward frame of Mind, is the same in the *Critick* and the *Miser*.[25]

The utility of gold as an instrument of commerce is lost when people regard it as the substance of commerce. The referential account of money here in Berkeley's *Guardian* essays hints at the ethical purpose he develops in the *Querist*: when distinguishing between real and fantastical pleasures, Berkeley makes it clear that 'a Desire terminated in Mony is fantastical'.[26] Even when thinking of money in terms of reference rather than use Berkeley's emphasis is on the ethical purpose of wealth.

Berkeley's *Querist* was first published in 1735, well after the South Sea Bubble, and well into the period that has been identified as the financial revolution. One might well expect an economic treatise written at this date to be more at ease with innovations in the representation of economic value than Locke's dislike of paper money suggests he was. Berkeley is more familiar with these methods of representing money, but he seems in many ways less modern than Locke, almost refusing to acknowledge the existence of a monetary economy altogether. Berkeley writes with the aim of establishing the best economic policy for Ireland at the time, given its perennial problems of vicious economic oppression by the English and a lack of suitable small denomination coinage with which to conduct day-to-day business. He is also concerned about the financial problems facing the Church of Ireland, particularly in relation to tithe gathering.[27] His emphasis is on the necessity of industry to wealth and on the moral imperatives that should inform all economic decisions. Patrick Kelly, also the editor of *Locke on Money*, regards *The Querist* as 'a major contribution to the development of monetary theory in English prior to Hume's essays', noting that Berkeley believes all financial tokens are entitlements to power rather than tickets for exchange.[28] He also recognises the Christian moral force behind Berkeley's insistence that only the general well being of the population is to be regarded as wealth, and that money is only to be regarded as wealth if it promotes industry (pp. 15–16). Kelly finds in Berkeley's economic theory a nostalgia similar to Pope's in his *Moral Essays*: 'For Berkeley it would seem that commercial society, as gradually conceived in the eighteenth century, was ultimately incompatible with the exercise of virtue and with the divine plan for man' (p. 23). I think Berkeley has a philosophical rather than a nostalgic objection to the modern world, and that if one dwells upon his objection it seems as radical as it is conservative.

Berkeley does not object to new forms of financial token and credit in the way that Locke does. He is not concerned that financial tokens should be pledges as well as counters. He expresses this point of view in his response to the South Sea Bubble, *An Essay Towards Preventing the Ruin of Great Britain*:

> Money is so far useful to the public as it promoteth industry, and credit having the same effect is of the same value with money; but money or credit circulating through a nation from hand to hand without producing labour and industry in the inhabitants, is direct gaming.[29]

This view is maintained in *The Querist*, which is written as a series of provocative questions. The Querist asks 'Whether any other means, equally conducing to excite and circulate the industry of mankind, may not be as useful as money.'[30]

Whilst Locke recognises that money is 'the *instrument* of commerce', and so must promote commerce, he is unwilling to detach himself from the idea that money is also the '*measure* of Commerce' (*Locke on Money*, II, 374). Berkeley retains only the instrumental part of Locke's thought, and sets about attacking the idea of money having an intrinsic value. He asks

> Whether money is to be considered as having an intrinsic value, or as being a commodity, a standard, a measure, a pledge, as is variously suggested by writers? And whether the true idea of money, as such, be not altogether that of a ticket or counter?... Whether power to command the industry of others be not real wealth? And whether money be not in truth tickets or tokens for conveying and recording such power, and whether it be of great consequence what materials the tickets are made of? (VI, 106–7, Q23, Q35)

Berkeley is not interested in the opposition between money and credit, between old and stable, new and unstable forms of financial token. One reader of *The Querist* notes that, in Berkeley's thinking, 'credit is logically prior to the institution of the things called money, and is an essential element in every exchange economy'. He goes as far as to say that 'Ultimately, for Berkeley, there is no real distinction between metallic money and credit, since each is a means of commanding the services of others in the community or the economy, and the mere increase of money in either of its forms increases only the monetary expression of the liability to render such services to the owners of the money.'[31]

Berkeley suggests that economic problems are not so much to do with the value of money itself, or the form it takes, as with the way in which people who use money think about it, asking:

> Whether it be not the opinion or will of the people, exciting them to industry, that truly enricheth a nation?...Whether reflection in the better sort might not soon remedy our evils? And whether our real defect be not a wrong way of thinking? (VI, 107–8, Q31, Q48)

Misunderstandings about money are moral and philosophical problems, not just linguistic problems, as Locke suggests. If people thought of money merely as a means of circulating power, of facilitating industry, then the problems of Ireland would be diminished. Berkeley does not believe even that a store of bullion is needed to validate the amount of money circulating in the form of various tokens (Q26). His idea of money is as a means merely of circulation, not a means of reference, neither the reference of the counter aspect of a coin to its pledge aspect, nor of the writing on a bank note, bill, or receipt for stocks and shares to some bullion, some goods, or some notional 'part' of a trading enterprise. As Constantine George Caffentzis notes, 'It is not that money represents nothing in *The Querist*, but rather that money does not represent at all.'[32]

Berkeley casts doubt on Locke's idea that the relationship between a certain weight of gold or silver and a certain commodity or service is fixed by universal human consent, and that, although the relative value of gold and silver might vary in one place over time, their value in relation to world trade is constant. Berkeley is perfectly aware that gold and silver vary drastically in value, and that it is precisely because different people set different values on gold and silver that they are a profitable means of exchange. Living in Ireland, and having Irish prosperity at heart, Berkeley knows that absentee landlords had been drawing coinage out of the country into England. His friend Thomas Prior wrote on the problems created by small coinage leaving the country to pay the excess rent on lands rented from absentee landlords when payment in kind was not sufficient.[33] This removal of currency creates a rate of exchange between the two countries, an inequality of circulating currency giving greater value to coin in Ireland than in England, and enabling the English to sell coin to Ireland at a profit.[34] This fact, combined with the fact that Ireland already had by the seventeenth century a notional currency of its own that employed English coinage at a lower nominal value (there were, for example, sixteen Irish pennies to the shilling, twelve English pennies, despite the fact that the two coins used, the penny and the shilling, were the same on both sides of the water),[35] must have made it obvious that money was not a means of facilitating equal exchange, but a means of facilitating unequal exchange.[36] The reference a pound of silver has to world trade considered in the abstract and apart from the fluctuations of relative value in silver from one country to another on the same day is a delusion proposed merely to enforce a particular set of economic power relations. Money only makes sense to Berkeley if it does what people say it should do, that is, enable the exchange of equal amounts of labour or a particular commodity. He sees that the claim that money enables this equal exchange is false, and that the claim is used to facilitate the exchange of unequal amounts of labour or a particular commodity. The illusion of intrinsic value in coin facilitates unequal exchange. The illusion of intrinsic value, and the illusion of a financial token gaining its value by referring to some quantity of bullion or the like, is an illusion of reference. It is an illusion of reference that allows one country, England, to maintain its wealth apparently by the circulation of credit in the absence of industry, what Berkeley calls 'direct gaming', but in fact by the economic oppression of other countries, whether Ireland, the East Indies, the West Indies or any other unfortunate place. Berkeley hopes that by removing this referential stage in people's thinking about money, he can disillusion them, and simultaneously prevent the defrauding of the Irish, and presumably other oppressed peoples of the world. Thinking about money is not merely a linguistic problem: it is a linguistic problem with immense moral and political consequences.[37]

Berkeley's thought here is, of course, far removed from the actual history of economic development in Britain and Ireland. His thought on money is not, however, purely nostalgic: he is as sceptical about the nature of value in coin as he is about the nature of value in credit, if not more so. He is more interested in the use of these different kinds of financial token. As his writing on language, Berkeley's writing on money emphasises the use of tokens in a signifying system rather than their reference to something beyond that system. And, as in his writing on vision, his sense of the structure and purpose of that system is inseparable from his sense of God's providence, and human ethical obligations. I suggest that Pope shares with Berkeley this emphasis on the role of money, credit, indeed any token representing value, in an ethical system governed by God's providence in which the use of the token is not just more important than its reference, but, in an important sense, *is* its reference. That is, using the token makes one aware of one's ethical obligations to other users. This kind of systematic exchange necessarily includes a moral and social obligation. Berkeley is distinguished from Locke by this overtly moralistic approach to economics. Locke has been praised for being one of those thinkers who had 'forcefully suspended all judgments of theology, morality, and justice, [and] were willing to consider the economy as nothing more than an intricate mechanism, refraining for the while from asking whether the mechanism worked for good or evil'.[38] Both Pope and Berkeley, I suggest, are deliberately pre-monetary thinkers in that they deny what Marx identifies as the transformational quality of money, going alongside every commodity and transforming its value by doing so, giving everything a price (see note 17). I tried to show how Pope makes the idea that money and paper credit might transform commodities into some more accessible form appear absurd. The use to which words are put is Pope's ultimate concern, not whether bills of credit or Sybil's leaves actually refer to something palpable or real, but how the inscriptions they present are put to use. I will try to advance this view of Pope a little through a discussion of use in the *Imitations of Horace*.[39]

The *Imitations* are comparable to the *Moral Essays*: whilst evincing an evident dislike of modern financial policy and practice, they extend their scepticism to all forms of wealth, and their satire to all forms of economic greed and excessive appetite. Pope emphasises use in the *Imitations* as a contrast to the instability of all forms of property, whether in land, money, stocks or bonds. He also emphasises use in language, as a criterion of literary success. Pope's treatment of use in the *Imitations* is informed by a world-weariness that acknowledges political disappointment and the philosophical appeal of retirement from public life. Pope uses the vagaries of modern finance, the instability of value in the new world of stocks and shares, to cast equal doubt back on the value of property. Pope's nostalgia becomes a form of historical scepticism in which he doubts there ever was a time of fixed and reliable value in property. Pope's presentation of use in the *Imitations* is also closely related to his concern in the *Moral Essays* with the inscrutability and unreliability of human motivation. Pope introduces use as a common-sense means of working out the value of an object or practice in the failure of any more abstract criteria, and in doing so he follows a similar trajectory to Berkeley in his economic writing, and, indeed, in his writing on vision.

In Epistle I.i, addressed to Bolingbroke, Pope suggests that he will retire from writing frivolous poetry, and concentrate instead on philosophical themes, a common claim in Pope's poems of this period. Pope condemns the avarice that has recently gripped the nation.

> Well, if a King's a Lion, at the least
> The People are a many-headed Beast:
> Can they direct what measures to pursue,
> Who know themselves so little what to do?
> Alike in nothing but one Lust of Gold,
> Just half the land would buy, and half be sold:
> Their Country's wealth our mightier Misers drain,
> Or cross, to plunder Provinces, the Main:
> The rest, some farm the Poor-box, some the Pews;
> Some keep Assemblies, and wou'd keep the Stews;
> Some with fat Bucks on childless Dotards fawn;
> Some win rich Widows by their Chine and Brawn;
> While with the silent growth of ten per Cent,
> In Dirt and darkness hundreds stink content.

(ll. 120–33)

The people fail as badly as the king to show any directed purpose, or any ability to govern. The people are united in their love of gold, but that expresses itself in radically different ways, in miserliness and plunder, in flattery and pimping. Some of this activity is designed falsely to secure inheritances, to win property, land, by bribing and flattering the dying and stupid. This activity is certainly no better than stinking on in the unproductive profit arising from interest, but probably no worse. Wealth, in land or money or credit, perverts the unity of purpose the people need if they are to have an elective monarch, if they are to save themselves from the corrupting influence of a court cabal.[40] The pursuit of wealth, or love of gold, results in the changefulness of fashion:

> Did ever Proteus, Merlin, any Witch,
> Transform themselves so strangely as the Rich?
> "Well, but the Poor" – the Poor have the same itch:

(ll. 152–4)

The power of modern financial tokens to transform one thing into another has taken root in the people themselves, so that they are transformed along with their desires for the consumer objects into which their money can be so easily transformed, and they retain no coherent purpose.

Questioning this transformability is an important part of Pope's argument. He represents Wisdom crying out in opposition to the City.

> Here, Wisdom calls: "Seek Virtue first! be bold!
> "As Gold to Silver, Virtue is to Gold."
> There, London's voice: "Get Mony, Mony still!
> "And then let Virtue follow, if she will."

> (ll. 77–80)

There is a clear opposition between the imperative of Wisdom and the imperative of London, but once that is recognised, the oppositions within the imperative of Wisdom stand out. Gold and silver can be exchanged one for another, a certain mass of gold for a certain greater mass of silver. Gold is not an order of good that is intrinsically higher than silver, as virtue is to gold. One cannot exchange any amount of gold for any amount of virtue. Wisdom, it seems, is tainted by the acquisitive desire displayed by London, unable to express the appetite for virtue other than as financial ambition. Pope picks away at the idea of philosophical wisdom throughout this poem, asking, in the lines that immediately precede those quoted, if the addressee (not Bolingbroke here) will do nothing 'To stop thy foolish views, thy long desires, / And ease thy heart of all that it admires?' (ll. 75–6). This line of critique culminates in the description of Bolingbroke clouded by vapours at the end of the poem. Philosophical detachment is not successful in this poem, as the philosopher's claim to tranquillity of mind is unsupportable, and the philosophical admiration of virtue has been tainted by the avarice of City commerce.

Although Epistle I.i concentrates its satire on the new forms of wealth, it also satirises those who seek wealth in land. The *Imitations* in general do not spare those who seek wealth in land. Pope points out the virtues of self-sufficient existence on a small plot of land withdrawn from the City:

> South-sea Subscriptions take who please,
> Leave me but Liberty and Ease.
> 'Twas what I said to Craggs and Child,
> Who prais'd my Modesty, and smil'd.
> Give me, I cry'd, (enough for me)
> My Bread, and Independency!

So bought an Annual Rent or two.
And liv'd – just as you see I do;
Near fifty, and without a Wife,
I trust that sinking Fund, my Life.
Can I retrench? Yes, mighty well,
Shrink back to my Paternal Cell,
A little House, with Trees a-row,
And like its Master, very low,
There dy'd my Father, no man's Debtor,
And there I'll die, nor worse nor better.

(Epistle I.vii, ll. 65–80)

Yet Pope cannot enjoy the virtues of retired property ownership because, as a Catholic, he could not own property: he could never be in a position to enjoy the old stable value of property to which he is said to look back with such nostalgia. The virtue of self-possession that Pope displays and enacts in these *Imitations*, and that allows him to satirise with free rein any group of people in the country, is gained despite property, not because of it.[41] Pope works through this position more fully in Satire II.ii, most of which purports to be a transcription of the wise words of Pope's abstemious friend Hugh Bethel.[42] Bethel outlines a life of *mediocritas* that contrasts with the lives of the rich who either keep their wealth to themselves, or lend it to the government for private profit (ll. 111–22). Pope says his life accords with Bethel's advice: although his home is rented, it is open to his friends, and although his food is basic, it is still nourishing. Pope responds to Swift's self-destructive comment that

'you'll enjoy it only all your life.' –
Well, if the Use be mine, can it concern one
Whether the Name belong to Pope or Vernon?
What's *Property*? dear Swift! you see it alter
From you to me, from me to Peter Walter,
Or, in a mortgage, prove a Lawyer's share,
Or, in a jointure, vanish from the Heir,
Or in pure Equity (the case not clear)
The Chanc'ry takes your rents for twenty year:
At best, it falls to some ungracious Son
Who cries, my father's damn'd, and all's my own.
Shades, that to Bacon could retreat afford,

> Become the portion of a booby Lord;
> And Hemsley once proud Buckingham's delight,
> Slides to a Scriv'ner or a City Knight.
> Let Lands and Houses have what Lords they will,
> Let Us be fix'd, and our own Masters still.
>
> (ll. 164–80)

Property in the form of land ownership seems to be as reliant on unstable forms of words as the new forms of credit and financial token: Vernon has the name of the property and that name can be transferred from one person to another with ease, playing havoc with the social order as it is transferred, even seeming to obliterate the distinction one merits through literary and philosophical work, as with Francis Bacon's estate passing to other less worthy occupants.[43] Property in the land seems inherently unstable, based on the notoriously slippery wording of legal documents. Pope's solution to this instability is a turn to use, the use of the property, the value that is derived from the land by occupying it in a sensitive and purposeful manner, by occupying the land with an eye to what God intended people should do when occupying the land – in this case, live a life of Horatian mediocrity. Pope is less interested in the reference the land has to some abstract ownership, to the name that marks the land as Vernon's, than in its use. He is not interested in a relation of reference (that of the right of ownership to the land, of the legal document to the land, say, something Blackstone queries – 'there is no foundation in nature or in natural law, why a set of words upon parchment should convey the dominion of land'), but in the function of the land, its relationship to a certain way of life.[44] As Pope cannot own the land, he is aware of the radical instability of land ownership. He is not prevented from being of the Country party, nor from being nostalgic for the times before the South Sea scheme, by this awareness, but it does make him more of a radical sceptic in terms of economic and proprietary theory than I think is generally allowed.

Pope presents use both as a proprietary, legalistic concept, and as a linguistic concept in Epistle II.ii. His response to a request for a poem from the addressee of the Epistle is to recount his early life, drawing attention to the loss of privileges for Catholics that prevented his father from owning property or holding public office (ll. 58–61). Pope says that he learnt to read Homer at home, as he was denied a university education (ll. 52–7). Pope makes himself financially independent through the translation of Homer, so, through his early home education, he inherits something as valuable and also more solid than land from his father, a literary inheritance that happens to be both symbolically and literally valuable (ll. 68–9), as Pope made his fortune by translating Homer. Pope's literary production takes the place of conventional forms of wealth, land or money, as a mode of political and economic existence.[45] When Pope comes to discuss the use of words, then, there is a sense in which words have actually, rather than metaphorically, supplanted economic tokens of other kinds. Pope here discusses the intense labour undertaken by a poet wishing to produce verse of quality.

> But how severely with themselves proceed
> The Men, who write such Verse as we can read?
> Their own strict Judges, not a word they spare
> That wants or Force, or Light, or Weight, or Care,
> Howe'er unwillingly it quits its place,
> Nay tho' at Court (perhaps) it may find grace:
> Such they'll degrade; and sometimes, in its stead,
> In downright Charity revive the dead;
> Mark where a bold expressive Phrase appears,
> Bright thro' the rubbish of some hundred years;
> Command old words that long have slept, to wake,
> Words, that wise *Bacon*, or brave *Raleigh* spake;
> Or bid the new be *English*, Ages hence,
> (For Use will father what's begot by Sense)
> Pour the full Tide of Eloquence along,
> Serenely pure, and yet divinely strong,
> Rich with the Treasures of each foreign Tongue;
> Prune the luxuriant, the uncouth refine,
> But show no mercy to an empty line;
> Then polish all, with so much life and ease,
> You think 'tis Nature, and a knack to please:
> "But Ease in writing flows from Art, not Chance,
> "As those move easiest who have learn'd to dance."

(ll. 157–79)

Here the good poet, the poet whose works one can bear to read, distinguishes himself from the courtier by refusing to use cant words, and also by exhibiting charity towards older English that has fallen out of use. This poet is capable of reviving the language of Bacon and Ralegh (in the preferred modern spelling), that is, reviving the lives of two authors, one whose estate was sustained in his life by incredible borrowing, and dissolved after his death, and one who was stripped of his estates at the change of monarchs.[46] Poetry has the ability to restore property to those who lost their land, but only through use, through the renewed employment of a vocabulary, through a new engagement with that author's words. Use fathers what is begot by sense: using language, and making one's own language the English of the future, is to stand in a paternal relationship to language and to later users of the language, giving to others what Pope's father gave him in an early literary and moral education that was ultimately more profitable than land or money, both literally and symbolically. These literary and linguistic applications of the idea of use go along with a developed sense that use is a more valuable criterion than ownership. Pope points out that 'Estates have wings' (l. 248) and can be gained or lost in an hour. He resorts to a glib interpretation of law: 'If there be truth in Law, and *Use* can give / A *Property*, that's yours on which you live' (ll. 230–1). The argument is not legal but moral: one ought always to be content with the temporary and transitory nature of material goods, because they can never be more than temporary and transitory. The moment in the development of natural law that attributes property in something beyond the period in which it is being used to the person who exerts the labour required to use it or occupy it initially appears flimsy in the simplicity of Pope's legal paraphrase, thereby questioning the endurance of property.[47] To desire property beyond use is to enter into the absurdity Pope makes Swift voice in Satire II.ii. Pope suggests that literature is one of the only ways of having a property in something beyond the grave, but suggests also that property is only to be found in use, in the revived engagement with and imitation of particular literary works.

Pope and Berkeley both present a more radically sceptical attitude to the nature of value in tokens than Locke, and, indeed, than some recent critics and historians of eighteenth-century economic and literary thought and practice. Pope and Berkeley probe the very notion of intrinsic value until it disintegrates, leaving nothing but use as a criterion for judging the value of a certain object, financial token, piece of land, word and so on. Pope and Berkeley move from a referential account of value, in which gold is valuable as a pledge because it refers to its own function as a counter, and in which paper money, stocks and bonds and so on are valuable because they refer to some bullion in the bank, some part of a company, some obligation; they move from this account to an instrumental account of value, in which a token only ever has a value in use, in what it enables people to do, rather than having value by referring to something beyond itself. Pope and Berkeley are clear that this use has a place in a grand providential scheme, and that it is governed by ethical obligations, rather than the lesser economic imperatives of the marketplace. Both Pope and Berkeley are attempting to get their readers to rethink the idea of value in order to disillusion and so politically and ethically re-educate them.

Reading across the *Imitations of Horace* and Pope's other mentions of gold shows that even the intrinsic value of gold, its weight and fineness, appears to be without value when employed in exchanges that are not governed by ethical and religious obligations. Pope's engagement with economic ideas is more sophisticated, and more radically sceptical, than the current critical emphasis on his nostalgia indicates. His engagement is with the ethical and religious obligations that go along with using signs in a system, rather than with the referential function of the signs and the things to which the signs might refer. Pope explores the use to which a signifying system is put, the ethics of the customs and conventions that govern that system, and suggests that if people were only to have the right ideas about what was valuable, there would be far fewer problems with the economy than currently there are. In these respects his writing on economic issues is better understood in relation to Berkeley's writing on money than Locke's, better understood in relation to an ethics of wealth than a theory of intrinsic monetary value.

4
Providence as the Language of God in *Alciphron* and *An Essay on Man*

Joseph Spence reports Pope talking about an episode in the evolution of his philosophical masterpiece *An Essay on Man*: 'In the Moral Poem I had written an address to our Saviour, imitated from Lucretius' compliment to Epicurus, but omitted it by the advice of Dean Berkeley.' Spence's editor adds that Joseph Warton said the address was excluded 'because the Christian dispensation did not come within the compass of his plan', and remarks himself that the 'significance of the fact that Pope got Berkeley, one of the greatest philosophers of the age, to pass judgement on parts (at least) of the *Essay on Man* has not been generally realised'.[1] Although this anecdote has become part of the common wisdom surrounding the composition of the *Essay on Man*, particularly with regard to the limitations of its religious argument, the significance of Berkeley's relationship to Pope and his philosophical *magnum opus* has still not been generally realised. William Bowman Piper has recently suggested that Berkeley's writing on perception forms the appropriate background for a reading of the *Essay on Man*, and Pope's attempt to present the perceptual world as a coherent whole.[2] I would like to take Piper's suggestion on, and suggest that Berkeley's Christian apologetics are also important to Pope by looking at some points of contact in argument and subject between the *Essay* and *Alciphron*. In this chapter, I will suggest that Pope and Berkeley were working on very similar projects in the early 1730s and offer a reading of *An Essay on Man* that adds *Alciphron* to the vast set of works to which Pope might have turned or of which he may have been thinking whilst composing his poem. I will be contrasting Berkeley to Shaftesbury and Hutcheson more than Locke, the main point of comparison in previous chapters, as Shaftesburian philosophy is one of the main targets of *Alciphron*.

116

My argument in this chapter concerns different ways in which the creation is aestheticised, different ways in which the creation comes to be known as an object of human perception. In Berkeley, root perceptions of pleasure and pain allow people to familiarise themselves with the language of God, allow them to find meaning in perceptual experience and finally to make moral choices on the basis of that experience. In Shaftesbury and Hutcheson people have instinctive drives towards the beautiful and the moral that are, specifically, to be distinguished from a desire for the pleasurable: rather than learning the language of the world, one exercises taste upon the world; rather than learning moral behaviour, one has a taste for it. I suggest that Pope's emphasis on pleasure and pain as the basis of Christian utilitarian ethics allies him with Berkeley more than Shaftesbury and Hutcheson. To make this case fully I will have to touch on several large issues in eighteenth-century philosophical and religious thought, such as the nature of providence; the identification of self-interest and social (including ideas of common sense and other people as ends in themselves); the limits of human reason. In relation to many of these issues I shall be arguing that Pope presents a phenomenological view that the meaningful human moral world is a product of culture (at its most fundamental), and that this view is closely related to Berkeley's work. I will remark on agricultural and horticultural metaphors in *Alciphron* and *An Essay on Man*, suggesting that they offer a useful field of analogy for writers who want to naturalise acquired virtues and social institutions. I will look also at the recurrence of financial and visual vocabulary discussed in the two previous chapters.

Berkeley and Pope must have been in close correspondence in order for the philosopher to advise the poet on such an important aspect of the composition of the *Essay*. From Pope's remark to Spence on the address to the saviour, it must be presumed that Pope and Berkeley were in correspondence as soon as Berkeley returned from America, perhaps also whilst Berkeley was in America. Berkeley published *Alciphron* as soon as he returned:

> It must have been completed when he landed in England in October 1731, for it was published in London in February 1732. On the 27th of this month Viscount Percival recorded in his journal that the book 'was the discourse of the Court, and that yesterday the Queen publicly commended it at her drawing-room.'[3]

Pope and his circle read the book soon after its publication. In a joint letter with Bolingbroke to Swift, Pope prefers *Alciphron* to Patrick Delany's

Revelation Examined with Candour: 'Dr D——'s Book is what I can't commend so much as Dean Berkeley's.' Swift asks Gay if he has read the book and Gay responds: 'I have not seen Dean Berkeley, but have read his Book, & like many parts of it, but in general think with you, that it is too Speculative, at least for me.'[4] Pope recommends the book and seems to approve it more than some of his acquaintance. Pope had completed three of the four epistles of the *Essay* by August 1731, but those four epistles 'were published successively on 20 February, 29 March, 8 May 1733, and 24 January 1734'. Pope, then, had a year in which to digest *Alciphron* as he revised the *Essay on Man*, and he must have been in contact with Berkeley during this period to have asked his advice concerning the address to the saviour.[5] Pope must have thought his philosophical scheme close enough to Berkeley's to ask his advice about the content of the poem.

Pope must also have been thinking about Berkeley's work over a slightly longer period. I want to examine the *Essay* and *Alciphron* as discourses on providence. Pope says in a footnote to an early edition of *Epistle I* that its lines 15–16 allude 'to the subject which runs through the whole design, – the justification of the methods of Providence'.[6] As Pope was writing a long poem on providence he may have tried to read works that explicitly engage with this subject. The English Short Title Catalogue lists fifty-one works published 1724–34 that contain the word 'providence' in the title (excluding references to Providence, Rhode Island and the use of formulaic expressions such as 'by divine providence' when noting an author's clerical position). Ten of them are escape narratives or occasional sermons that announce their occasion; seven of them are editions of Charles Johnson's *History of the Pyrates*; six of them are editions of Edward Young's *A Vindication of Providence*; four of them are editions of Stephen Duck's poem on providence; two of them are editions of William Sherlock's *A Discourse Concerning the Divine Providence*; two of them are editions of Jean Balguy's *Divine Rectitude*. If one deducts the narratives, occasional sermons and further editions, there remain twenty-four separate works. Berkeley is the only author to appear with two separate works, the 1725 edition of *Three Dialogues* and the 1732 edition of the *Theory of Vision*. One might say, therefore, that Berkeley published one twelfth of the literature that explicitly announced its treatment of providence in the years leading up to and including the publication of *An Essay on Man*. Keeping up with literature on providence would have meant, for Pope as for anyone else, keeping up with Berkeley.

Although *Alciphron* is not explicitly described as a work on the nature of providence it has much to say on the subject, and in its first three editions it was published with the *New Theory of Vision*. *Alciphron* is a philosophical dialogue in seven sections that records the arguments of the free-thinkers Lysicles and Alciphron and their right-thinking opponents Euphranor and Crito. The defence of the Christian religion in *Alciphron* is a defence of God's providence, the element of linguistic design that is evident to Berkeley in the creation, and had been evident to him since his first publication of the *New Theory of Vision*. Berkeley may well have been engaged in a programmatic vindication of providence throughout his philosophical career, an unusual vindication that identifies providence with the linguistic structure of the phenomenal world. Pope seems to share the desire to engage in a programmatic vindication of providence in the 1730s, and asks Berkeley's help in this project. There seem to be strong grounds for a comparative reading of *Alciphron* and the *Essay*, and it seems very unlikely that Pope would not have comprehended the importance of Berkeley's divine language to his own vindication of providence. I will argue in the rest of this chapter, then, that Berkeley provides some very interesting and acute responses to philosophical concerns about the relationship between divine providence and the created world, responses to which his earlier work on the linguistic structure of the phenomenal world is of great importance. I will suggest that Pope, having followed Berkeley's philosophical career, understands how important the concept of the phenomenal world as a divine language is to the vindication of providence, and that his Christian utilitarian ethics are founded on a vision of the world as a language rather than as an object of taste. That is, the world is not a pre-existent object or artefact upon which people exercise an instinctive taste that is evidence of the existence and benevolence of God; rather, the world comes into meaningful existence for people through their customary experience of phenomenal signs that make up the language of the created world, which is itself evidence of the existence and benevolence of God. In both systems, people are drawn towards what is good, but there is a distinction between having a conversation with the world and exercising one's taste upon the world. Berkeley involves the human mind in creating the reality that in Shaftesbury and Hutcheson is merely an object for the exercise of mental faculties. I will mention in the course of this chapter other writers in whom Pope and Berkeley may have taken an interest in the early 1730s, and who have not been much discussed in relation to their work.

4.1 Analogy and *Epistle I*

I would like to begin by discussing Pope's limitation of human reason in relation to Berkeley's account of analogy. Pope's account of a restricted, humble human reason in the first epistle is a piece of first philosophy that sets out a specifically human phenomenal world in Lucretian terms, a world that exists in and because of the specifically human capacity to perceive, as distinct from the perceptive capability of any other creature. This phenomenal world is not the world of providence but has nonetheless an analogical relationship to the world of providence. Berkeley's right-thinking Crito, in the fourth dialogue of *Alciphron*, explains the analogical relationship between terms in human language and their application to attributes of God when he defends theological language from the free-thinking attack that such terms are meaningless. This argument is completed in the seventh dialogue, in which the atheism of the free-thinkers is directly connected to the mistaken belief that words must stand for ideas: as no one has a clear and distinct idea of God, all religious language must be meaningless. Berkeley employs the instrumentalist account of language that he also used in the *Principles* to show that 'the true end of speech, reason, science, faith, assent, in all its different degrees, is not merely, or principally, or always, the imparting or acquiring of ideas, but rather something of an active operative nature, tending to a conceived good' (VII.14, p. 307). The purpose of religious language is not to describe a state of affairs, but to incline people towards doing good.[7] The purpose of the human phenomenal world in the first epistle of the *Essay* is not to reflect the world of providence, but to incline people to do good.

Crito argues that terms applied analogically to God are meaningful, that it is possible to have 'a true and proper notion of attributes applied by analogy' (IV.21, p. 169). Perhaps he uses 'notion' here in its technical sense: one may not have ideas of the attributes of God in the way that one has the idea of a visual object, but one can extract by inference a *notion* of the attributes of God by comparison with those attributes in people and animals. Crito says that the Greek term 'analogy' originally referred to a mathematical ratio but is now used loosely to imply any kind of relationship. He focuses on metaphorical language: if one says that something is performed by the hand of God one does not imply that God has hands, but that God has means of executing active will. He closes by comparing knowledge of God to knowledge of the phenomenal world.

We may, therefore, consistently with what hath been premised, affirm that all sorts of perfection which we can conceive in a finite spirit are in God, but without any of that alloy which is found in the creatures. This doctrine, therefore, of analogical perfections in God, or our knowing God by analogy, seems very much misunderstood and misapplied by those who would infer from thence that we cannot frame any direct or proper notion, though never so inadequate, of knowledge or wisdom, as they are in the Deity; or understand any more of them than one born blind can of light and colours. (IV.21, p. 170)

The person who experiences the world is not in the same position with regard to the attributes of God as a blind person is with regard to light and colour. There is nothing from which the blind person can infer light or colour, but every sign in the visual language allows people to infer God's providence, to have a notion of God, even if they have no clear and distinct idea of God. Analogy enables people to have notions, to infer the existence of other beings like themselves and infinitely better than themselves.

Euphranor, who speaks the arguments closest to those in Berkeley's other philosophical works, is 'inclined to think the doctrine of signs a point of great importance and general extent, which, if duly considered, would cast no small light upon things, and afford a just and genuine solution of many difficulties' (VII.13, p. 307). The doctrine of signs is of great importance in the part of Berkeley's justification of providence that concerns the knowledge of God by analogy. The free-thinker Alciphron initiates the seventh dialogue by arguing that 'Words are signs: they do or should stand for ideas, which so far as they suggest they are significant. But words that suggest no ideas are insignificant' (VII.2, p. 287). People who do not 'distinctly perceive the ideas marked by the terms, so as to form a mental proposition answering to the verbal, cannot possibly have knowledge' (VII.3, p. 288). People cannot have faith in or assent to things of which they have no clear idea. Alciphron attacks grace as the basis of the Christian dispensation:

when it denotes an active, vital, ruling principle, influencing and operating on the mind of man, distinct from every natural power or motive, I profess myself altogether unable to understand it, or frame any distinct idea of it; and therefore I cannot assent to any proposition concerning it, nor, consequently have any faith about it; and it is a self-evident truth, that God obligeth no man to impossibilities. (VII.4, p. 290)

Alciphron argues that religious language is meaningless because it refers to no clear and distinct ideas. Euphranor responds with an instrumentalist emphasis on knowledge based on signs rather than ideas, and inquires into the use of words to see 'if we can make sense of our daily practice' (VII.5, p. 291). Recapitulating arguments against abstract ideas from the *Principles*, Euphranor argues that theological terms such as grace are every bit as precise as mathematical terms such as force. Faith, for example, is not a clear and distinct idea, 'not an indolent perception, but an operative persuasion of mind, which ever worketh some suitable action, disposition or emotion in those who have it; as it were easy to prove and illustrate by innumerable instances taken from human affairs' (VII.10, p. 301). The argument of the entire book rests on there being languages that are meaningful without having to refer to clear and distinct ideas. Such languages produce dispositions in people rather than clear and distinct ideas. Berkeley, as I mentioned in Chapter 1, uses a quotation from Plato's *Cratylus* on the frontispiece of the second volume of the first edition of *Alciphron*.[8] Socrates here says that self-deception is the worst kind of deception, and then goes on to deconstruct the mimetic etymologies he had just given, and enters into the argument that names are instruments given in order to instruct. This quotation on the frontispiece comes from a moment in Plato's argument when he moves from talking about language as a system of reference, to talking about language as an instrument. Berkeley is entering into a similar phase in his argument, emphasising the value of words as creators of dispositions and propensities to act in people. I would like here to turn to Bolingbroke to demonstrate the relevance of these arguments concerning analogy to the first epistle of the *Essay*.

Bolingbroke's *Letters or Essays Addressed to Alexander Pope, Esq* and *Fragments or Minutes of Essays* were, according to Bolingbroke himself, 'thrown upon paper in Mr. POPE's lifetime, and at his desire. They were all communicated to him in scraps, as they were occasionally writ.'[9] Both sets of essays probably record some parts of the philosophical conversations Pope and Bolingbroke had whilst Pope was writing his *Essay*, and both probably add to those conversations in the light of the publication and reception of the *Essay*. Brean Hammond has noted that both works contain references to the Bishop of Cloyne, and that this must date the published form of Bolingbroke's works later than 19 May 1734, when Berkeley was made a bishop, and months after the publication of the final epistle of Pope's *Essay*.[10] More interesting in the current context than the contribution this mention makes to the dating of the *Essays* is the pronounced presence of Berkeley in these texts. I suggest that Berkeley is worked into these texts, in which he is an object of avowed fondness as well as satirical attack, as a response to Pope's request for the advice of Berkeley regarding the *Essay*. The negative response to Berkeley in Bolingbroke might be taken as evidence that Pope and Bolingbroke sat together and laughed at the eccentricities of the philosopher, but this does not fit very well with Pope's open admiration of *Alciphron* (it is in a joint letter with Bolingbroke to Swift that Pope commends *Alciphron*) and his request for Berkeley's advice. When Bolingbroke writes alone to Swift, however, he says that Berkeley is too metaphysical to be read through, and says he will 'reconcile [Swift] to Metaphysics by shewing you how they may be employed against Metaphysicians', perhaps referring to arguments against Berkeley he was drafting in the *Letters* and *Fragments*.[11] Bolingbroke, I suggest, sets out in these works to eradicate the influence that Berkeley had on Pope, to cover up the interest Pope took in Berkeley.[12] He aims to reclaim the *Essay on Man* as the product of predominantly his own philosophical inspiration. Bolingbroke's rejection of Berkeley is centred on analogy and the reference of words to ideas, two areas in which I think Berkeley is particularly important to Pope.

Two ideas closely associated with Berkeley make their way into Bolingroke's *Letters or Essays* and *Fragments or Minutes*. Bolingbroke says of ideas that 'their esse is percipi, to have them we must perceive that we have them' (III, 363). Here Bolingbroke is applying Berkeley's vocabulary to Locke's idea that sense perceptions are involuntary, and that having sense perceptions is necessarily to perceive that one has them. Bolingbroke also borrows Berkeley's thinking on abstraction, suggesting that the real quality shared by various objects cannot be abstracted from them: 'I have no perception of a general idea of white abstracted from every particular idea of this sort. The idea I have, when this word is used, is always that of some particular white extension, or of several such whose ideas rush confusedly into the mind together' (III, 434). This opinion is recapitulated in the *Fragments or Minutes* (V, 17). But these are the only concessions to and developments of Berkeley's thought in these works by Bolingbroke. All other references to Berkeley contest his ideas about the analogy between human and divine attributes, about the use of words that do not refer to clear and distinct ideas or indeed any ideas at all, and about the visual world as the language of God.

Bolingbroke writes against thinkers who 'absurdly and presumptuously... reason upon a supposed analogy of the human with the divine mind, whilst they scorn to look downwards, and to observe the real analogy that there is between the mind or soul of the whole animal kind, the human species included' (IV, 175). Analogy between the human and the divine is presented merely as a means of explaining paradoxes that cannot be explained by any other means: 'Analogy is employed in this case as it is in the other, and indeed in every case where theological paradoxes, which are not a few, are to be defended' (V, 522). This attack on analogy is specifically an attack on Berkeley: 'It may be said, you know it has been said by one I love and honour [a footnote clearly indicates Berkeley] that God has ideas, and that we can imagine God's perfect intellectual processes by comparison with our own imperfect' (V, 34). It might be suggested on this evidence that Pope and Bolingbroke explicitly discussed Berkeley's account of analogy whilst Pope was at work on the *Essay*. Bolingbroke argues consistently against any system in which God is said to have ideas in the same way that people have ideas, and he parcels Berkeley up together with some idealists of a very different kind:

> Have the authors of such systems, from PLATO down to that fine writer MALEBRANCHE, or to that sublime genius, and good man, the bishop of CLOYNE, contributed to make us better acquainted with ourselves? I think not. They have done all that human capacity can do in a wrong method; but all they have done has been to vend us poetry for philosophy, and to multiply systems of imagination. (III, 360 Note that Bolingbroke's manner of describing Berkeley is echoed exactly by Warton as quoted in n1 above.)

Bolingbroke exaggerates Berkeley's account of visual language and analogy to provide a parodic explanation of prophecy. He asks Pope to consider the 'hypothesis of a philosopher, whom you and I love and honour':

> could I comprehend that visual language in which 'the author of nature constantly speaks to the eyes of all mankind;' I might be able perhaps to comprehend how God may speak to prophets and apostles in visions, or else I might deduce by analogy that as we think we see when we do not really see, but only receive ideas through the eye from an immediate action of God, so prophets and apostles might think that they employed the faculties of their own excited and illuminated minds, and signified their own thoughts by the words they pronounced, when they neither thought nor spoke, but when the breath of God articulated in their organs. (III, 471–2)

Bolingbroke unfairly implies that Berkeley's God is interventionist, personally responsible for the existence of all visual ideas in all people. The degree of antagonism here is indicated by the fact the John Hervey used the same quotation from *Alciphron* (IV.11, p. 155) when attacking the theory of visual language, in a work in which *Alciphron* is called 'an inexhaustible Fund for Ridicule and Objection'.[13]

Behind Bolingbroke's objection to Berkeley's use of analogy is an objection to Berkeley's writing on language and not just visual language but the relationship between words and ideas that Berkeley investigates with such originality throughout his career. At first it seems that Bolingbroke is sympathetic to Berkeley's claim that a word is frequently used without any reference to an idea, let alone a clear and distinct idea: 'We are sometimes obliged in philosophical, as well as in common discourse, to make use of words that have no determinate, nor indeed, properly, any ideas or notions at all annexed to them' (IV, 473). Bolingbroke distinguishes this fact about language from the deliberately obscure use of words in metaphysical and theological arguments conducted in bad faith. He gives 'chance' as an example of a word to which no idea can be assigned. It becomes clear, however, that Bolingbroke thinks Berkeley argues in bad faith.

Bolingbroke clearly thinks that he himself has found a distinction between the uses of the words 'force' and 'grace' that bankrupts Berkeley's argument. Bolingbroke suggests that 'force' is used to describe the as yet unknown cause of some event, whereas 'grace' is used to describe a cause that cannot be known. Bolingbroke regards this as a philosophical triumph over Berkeley: 'I could wish that ALCIPHRON and LYSICLES had made this observation to EUPHRANOR, and had applied it to shew him why they admitted the word force, and rejected the word grace' (III, 484–5). Bolingbroke refines his argument:

> The disparity and impropriety do not arise from our having no idea of grace, for it is true that we have none of force; but they arise from hence, that there is not the same possibility of believing a cause whereof we have no idea, and which cannot be ascertained by its effects, as there is of believing one whereof we have no idea indeed, but which may be ascertained by its effects. (III, 486–7)

Bolingbroke here chooses to ignore Berkeley's contention that grace can indeed be distinguished by its effects. As with faith, grace is 'not an indolent perception, but an operative persuasion of mind, which ever worketh some suitable action, disposition or emotion in those who have it; as it were easy to prove and illustrate by innumerable instances taken from human affairs' (*Alciphron*, VII.10, p. 301). Grace, as faith, can be distinguished by its effects. Grace can be known by looking at those things of which people say it is an attribute (a gait, a musical performance, a movement, an act of charity) and establishing by analogy that attribute of God known as grace. Berkeley's contention is that the description of 'force' in the physical sciences is no more precise than the language of ethical and theological discrimination used to define faith and grace. Bolingbroke refuses to admit human behaviour as effects of a cause, effects that can be used to talk about that cause. Bolingbroke will not even allow what Hume in his *Abstract* to the *Treatise of Human Nature* allows, that words such as 'force' and 'energy', even if they correspond to no clear ideas, 'mean nothing but that determination of the thought, acquir'd by habit, to pass from the cause to its usual effect'.[14] Hume takes from Berkeley the idea that a word might refer to habits of the mind rather than contents of the mind. Even if the cause that is described by the general term 'force' is never to be known, the word can describe a habit of mental association that may well be analogous to other habits.[15]

Bolingbroke turns away from the idea that words can be used without reference to clear and distinct ideas in a summary dismissal of Berkeley:

> It must not be imagined, that he who reasons, or seems rather to reason closely and consequentially, has therefore truth always on his side. To be sure of this, we must be sure that his words have ideas and notions perceivable by us, attached to them; we must be sure that all these are steadily employed, and we must be able, by a careful analyse of the ideas and notions, where there is the least room for doubt, to discern whether they are fantastical or real, and adequate and complete, clear and distinct, or the contrary, relatively to the subjects about which they are employed.... If we neglect this, not only MALEBRANCHE, or the bishop of CLOYNE, those excellent poets, may lead us agreeably 'per ambages deorumque ministeria,' through such mazes of error as none but the brightest genii are able to contrive[.] (IV, 159)

Bolingbroke suggests that someone even less scrupulous in the manipulation of language than Berkeley might lead the unwary reader astray, and again accuses Berkeley of poetry.[16] Bolingbroke refuses to see the argument in Berkeley that words in the physical sciences are used no differently than words in theology, to refer to a group of attributes in observable phenomena that allow the observer to infer the existence of a motivating force, power or divinity. The way in which these words are used tells people all that can be known of 'force' or the attributes of God. Bolingbroke rejects Berkeley's instrumental, theological language and the theory of divine analogy that goes with it. Despite an apparent interest in the Berkeleian arguments concerning the impossibility of abstraction, and that to be is to be perceived, Bolingbroke refuses the idea that the way in which people use language may allow them to know something of the divine attributes by analogy with the phenomenal world. In his essays on first philosophy, on natural theology and natural ethics, Bolingbroke attempts to write Berkeley out of the range of views that support the argument in *An Essay on Man* that God's providence is evident in the phenomenal world. Bolingbroke has been unfortunately successful in removing Berkeley from commentary on Pope's *Essay*.

Gregory Holingshed has suggested that 'what Berkeley's theory of signs has in common with his understanding of analogy is a sense of human language as being, like physical reality itself, a means of access to consciousness of a larger plan, a divine context for human action'.[17] I will move on now to the limited world of human reason that Pope presents in the first epistle of the *Essay* and suggest that this world is a language that should put people in a certain disposition rather than giving them clear and distinct ideas. People do not have a clear idea of the divine scheme that governs the world, but if they follow the evidence presented to their senses they should find themselves disposed to submit to providence. The task of the first epistle is to demonstrate that the language of human rational enquiry is analogous to providence, and whilst it can never give people a clear and distinct idea of providence, it can be 'like physical reality itself, a means of access to consciousness of a larger plan, a divine context for human action'.

Following the opening exhortation of Bolingbroke (I.1–16), the epistle begins its main task of limiting the ambition of human reason. The circumscribed picture of human reason that emerges through the course of the epistle is not offered as a complete account of reason: it is not an epistemology, but a statement of method, suggesting that if one is to proceed rationally, one must first recognise the limitations of rational inquiry. It is part of Pope's first philosophy.[18] Pope's poetry questions the meaning of such words as 'reason', constantly refining its terminology. The series of questions, imperatives and examples running from I.17 to I.91 distinguishes between the partial reason of man and the complete reason of God, and also strives to point out the importance of the analogical relation in which they stand to one another. Man might only be able to reason from what he knows and what is evident to him (I.17–34), but this fact should hardly be surprising, as there is no evidence from which to reason other than what is evident. It is more surprising that God's complete reason is evident to the limited reason of man, that the poet can observe God observing 'how system into system runs' (I.25).[19] Complete reason in the divine world is recognisable through and by analogy with the limited reason of human intellect. For human reason to function properly it must be recognised as part of an analogically conceived complete rationality. Even if the complete reason of God is only recognised in a hypothetical clause ('Of Systems possible, if 'tis confest / That Wisdom infinite must form the best,' I.43–4), the hypothesis is one that secures the proper function of human reason in the poem.[20]

The limitation of human reason does not seem to be such a terrible limitation at all. Pope aligns himself with a sceptical tradition that sees a recognition of human limitations as the basis of human divinity.[21] And such a recognition is not a complete refusal to employ reason, but an introduction to the appropriate use of reason. The methodological retreat to a form of limited reason culminates in advice on how to proceed in intellectual inquiry, in specifically poetic vocabulary: 'Hope humbly then; with trembling pinions soar; / Wait the great teacher Death, and God adore!' (I.91–2). Poets and philosophers soar on pinions, but they also tremble, as Pope himself in *An Essay on Criticism* calls for the aid of earlier bards to inspire the 'last, the meanest of your Sons', '(That on weak Wings, from far, pursues your Flights; / *Glows* while he *reads*, but *trembles* as he *writes*)' (ll. 196–8). The earlier *Essay* goes on to castigate pride (ll. 201–14), as *An Essay on Man* will do also ('In Pride, in reas'ning Pride, our error lies', I.123). Pope offers not just a philosophical methodology in the first 90 lines of the first epistle, but also authorial advice as to how one should go about writing philosophy and poetry.

The epistle moves on to discuss the physical bases of perception. Life is not passive but active: 'ALL subsists by elemental strife' (I.169). God, however, has framed the human and animal creation appropriately, so that each creation is fit for its particular sphere. Pope then puts nature in the place of God, beginning a line of argument that will distinguish the world seen as the contingent product of natural forces from the world seen as the necessary product of God's providence. Pope presents interpretative possibilities to the reader that allow him or her to see the world of the poem as the product of chance or the product of providence: the reader is faced with the same ethical and spiritual decisions in interpreting the poem as in interpreting the world. Pope tries to get his readers to see the world as the product of providence, or the evidence on the basis of which a notion of God's providence may be established by analogy.

'Nature' to all the brute creation 'without profusion kind, / The proper organs, proper pow'rs assign'd' (I.179–80). 'Kind' here could qualify either 'Nature' or 'profusion'. In both cases, the generosity of nature is limited, in the first case to strict economy, being kind without being profuse, in the second to a moral indifference, without kind profusion. In the latter case, the creation is more like that of Lucretius' *De Rerum Natura*, in which 'No *Light* before the *Eye*, no *Speech* was found / Before the *Tongue*, before the *Ears* no *Sound*.'[22] The fit of the senses to the world is a matter of chance that happens to produce the phenomenal world of each creature. The kindness of nature or of profusion also emphasises an element of kinship: nature could be kind to the creation in the sense that it is of the same kind as nature. If, however, the kindness of profusion is lacking, the creation is formed by a nature neither like the creation, nor profuse to it. If nature lacks kind profusion, the sense of 'proper' in the following line is altered. The organs of each creature in that case are not perfectly appropriate, the organs inherent in the perfect state of the creature, but merely adequate, appropriate in the circumstances. The syntactical ambiguity suggests that the organs of perception are the product of either mere chance or complete necessity.[23] Just so the syntactical ambiguity might be a contingent product of the language or a carefully devised statement, the poem presenting the two interpretative possibilities simultaneously. The ambiguity asks the reader to consider the providential government of the poem as analogous to God's providence. The signs presented to people in the phenomenal world seem to be the product of perfect contingency or perfect rationality, either a simple chance or God's beneficent design to fit the appropriate creature with appropriate organs of perception and the capacity to interpret natural signs. Berkeley presents his readers with an argument for providential design based on the meaning of the phenomenal world in human sensory experience. Pope presents his readers with an interpretative choice between seeing the human phenomenal world as the product of chance or the product of providential design, a choice analogous to that they face when thinking about the phenomenal world.

God returns to take the place borrowed by nature when the poet asks if only humankind in all the creation is badly served by its sensory apparatus: 'Is Heav'n unkind to Man, and Man alone?' (I.186). Heaven is kind to the brute creation and to man by forming all creatures appropriately to their position in the creation. God's providence is seen in the attribution of appropriate powers to each creature, creating incidentally a specifically human phenomenal world: 'Who finds not Providence all good and wise, / Alike in what it gives, and what denies?' (I.205–6). In recognising that the work of an unknowable providence that sometimes appears to be sheer chance is actually, or at least must be considered as, the product of complete rationality, Pope follows his own epistemological and literary advice. If nature created the world, the phenomenal world of each creature may be seen as the product of chance. If God created the world then the phenomenal world of each creature is the product of providence. It is peculiarly the place of man to make such a reflection, and one that governs the procedure of the entire poem and its modes of producing meaning. The specifically human phenomenal world is presented in stock vocabulary that suggests part of the appropriateness of this world is its existence in literary language. Man, if given the senses of any other creature, would wish for 'The whisp'ring Zephyr, and the purling rill' (I.204). These objects of perception are not simply external objects, a breeze and a stream, but objects which have been accepted into a meaningful repertoire of cultural associations, specifically poetic associations, as, perhaps, are all objects of human perception.[24]

Whilst running through the gradations of the animal creation the epistle emphasises the activity of the world: 'See, thro' this air, this ocean, and this earth, / All matter quick, and bursting into birth' (I.233–4). The strong independence of matter is suggested, as if autogenetic, yet at the same time its providential organisation is apparent. God's place at the head of the creation is affirmed, but strangely as a principle of indifferentiation rather than differentiation: 'To him no high, no low, no great, no small; / He fills, he bounds, connects, and equals all' (I.279–80). The creation may be seen as complete and just gradation or as entirely level. Any perceived chance, discord or evil is really direction, harmony and good (I.290–2). The creation may be seen as either arbitrary or directed, but it is somewhere between the two: human perception is limited by its arbitrary position and function in the creation, but the consciousness of this arbitrary position elevates human perception to the capacity for seeing providential care in its very limitation. By retreating to a position of limited rationality, the poet reclaims his reason and sets out the manner of intellectual inquiry available to him, simultaneously redefining terms with subtlety and clarity. The tension between limited human reason and providence creates the poem's vocabulary, and its tendency to appear contingent and necessary at once. The human phenomenal world is the product of providence, and the principles of organisation apparent in it allow people to infer by analogy the existence of a complete and perfect rationality governing the world. Pope nowhere says that this human phenomenal world is God's language and the clearest indication of God's providence, as Berkeley does, but he does suggest that the human phenomenal world exists in language, the language in which that world is received. Pope also duplicates the conditions for interpreting the phenomenal world as providence in the technique of his poem, offering possible readings of lines that present the world either as perfect design or as perfect chance. Pope makes analogies, as Bolingbroke suggests, between the human and animal creation; but he does this in order to establish a further analogy between human and divine intellect and powers of disposition and organisation. I will go on in the rest of this chapter to look at ways in which Pope and Berkeley derive social and ethical obligations from their assumptions about the providential organisation of the phenomenal world.

4.2   Self-love and the providential debate

One of the fundamental questions in the debates about providence in the early eighteenth century is how God induces people to act morally. Douglas White identifies two schools of thought on this question, the first suggesting that God implants an innate love of the beauty of morality in people, the second suggesting that self-love leads ultimately to moral behaviour.[25] Shaftesbury and Hutcheson are of the first school, Berkeley and Pope of the second. Shaftesbury posits a taste in morality that is equivalent to a taste in music and poetry and that requires the individual (an author) to appreciate the 'interior numbers' that constitute 'moral truth'.[26] Without this appreciation of moral beauty, one can be good, but not virtuous:

> The case is the same in the mental or moral subjects as in the ordinary bodies or common objects of sense. The shapes, motions, colours and proportions of these latter being presented to our eye, there necessarily results a beauty or deformity, according to the different measure, arrangement, and disposition of their several parts. So in behaviour and actions, when presented to our understanding, there must be found, of necessity, an apparent difference, according to the regularity or irregularity of the subjects.... And in this case alone may we call any creature worthy or virtuous, when it can have the notion of a public interest and can attain the speculation or science of what is morally good or ill, admirable or blameable, right or wrong. ('An Inquiry Concerning Virtue or Merit', pp. 172–3)

Hutcheson shares the insistence that for an action to be moral it must be removed from the consideration of personal interest, and based instead on the conformity to a sense of what is morally beautiful: 'MORAL GOODNESS, denotes our Idea of *some Quality apprehended in Actions, which produces Approbation, and Love towards the Actor, from those who receive no Advantage by the Action.*'[27] The dissociation of self-interest and morality is important to writers wishing to free God from accusations of constructing the world on the principle of eudaimonism, the desire for personal happiness. John Balguy suggests that 'as much *Happiness* was produced, and provided for, as was consistent with the *Order* and Perfection of the Universe... then *vice versa*'.[28] It is considered somehow to detract from God's perfection that self-interest, the pursuit of personal pleasure and happiness, should be the principal drive for moral actions.[29] In order to derive moral actions from something other than self-interest, these thinkers suggest that taste, an intuitive sense of fitness, is the criterion for an action's being moral.[30]

Berkeley and Pope belong to the second school of thought, deriving moral actions from self-love or self-interest. They see no problem with God using self-love and self-interest as the means of educating people into moral action: the use of self-interest and self-love to indicate providential design and to enjoin people to act sociably does not taint God's pedagogy. One of Pope's achievements in the *Essay* is to smooth over the distinction between self-love and social by means of compressed conjectural histories of human development: the way God has ordered the human moral world makes self-love and social the same. Berkeley, in *Alciphron* as in his earlier writings, makes the principle of self-love, the desire to avoid pain and seek pleasure, the means by which people come to live in a meaningful world. I will spend some time on the role of pleasure and pain, or self-interest, in Berkeley's attempt to prove God's providence and benevolence from the phenomenal world, before showing how Pope might have picked up on Berkeley's work.

If a large part of Berkeley's philosophical project up to and including the publication of *Alciphron* concerned proving the providence of God, Berkeley argued for providence from the availability of phenomena to interpretation, the meaningfulness of the evidence of the senses. The works on vision and immaterialism both suggest that the world becomes meaningful to people if they engage in a conversation with God through the language of the world, through the phenomena presented to them by their senses. Pleasure and pain are the basis of this language of phenomena. As early as the *Philosophical Commentaries*

Berkeley notes that 'Sensual Pleasure is the Summum Bonum'.[31] Berkeley goes on in his career to distinguish between the way that this statement is true for a Christian utilitarian such as himself and the way that it is true for a free-thinker. As I have said in relation to the writing on vision, Berkeley has a utilitarian understanding of the meaning of the phenomenal world. Phenomena instruct people what to seek and shun by means of pleasure and pain: 'We regard the objects that environ us in proportion as they are adapted to benefit or injure our own bodies, and thereby produce in our minds the sensations of pleasure and pain' (*New Theory*, *Works*, I, 193, paragraph 59). Pleasure and pain enable people in a very basic way to get on in the world. Berkeley takes this thought further in the *Three Dialogues*. It is not just that sensations of pleasure and pain exist in order that people become able through experience and custom to get on in the world, but that, as all things are sensations, or perceptions, then there are no things in the world but what are intended by God for the instruction of people. There are no neutral or inert objects. Philonous asks Hylas to try 'if you can conceive a vehement sensation to be without pain, or pleasure ... Or can you frame to yourself an idea of sensible pain or pleasure in general, abstracted from every particular idea of heat, cold, tastes, smells? &c' (*Works*, II, 176–7). He is not only pressing the argument that there are no grounds for assuming the existence of some external heat distinct from a perception of pain, but also the argument that every such perception is part of the language of God, the medium of instruction by which people are enabled temporarily to survive the world. Pleasure and pain, the two general terms under which, it seems, all perceptions are classifiable, are the means by which the world becomes evident and interpretable to people, and so the strongest proof of the providence of a benevolent God. Pleasure and pain are perceptions, they are in some sense aesthetic, concerned with the response of the human mechanism to the world. The form of aesthetic response seen in Berkeley's utilitarian project is always interpretative, always involves an active conversation with the world, a coming to terms with the world through custom and experience. It is unlike Shaftesbury's aesthetic response to the world, a response that can be educated, but that is granted to a greater or lesser extent from the beginning of human life or an individual human's life.

In *Alciphron* Berkeley takes the utilitarian principle he has employed in the works on vision into the sphere of public life, and attempts to work out a utilitarian ethics. He does this by employing the Socratic argument that immediate pleasures are not always the greatest. He presents a slightly more advanced form of the utilitarian argument of the writings on vision to dismiss the Mandevillian suggestion that private vices need not be discouraged as they lead on to public benefits:

Lysicles: Happiness is the end to which created beings naturally tend; but we find that all animals, whether men or brutes, do naturally and principally pursue real pleasure of sense; which is therefore to be thought their supreme good, their true end and happiness. It is for this men live; and whoever understands life must allow that man to enjoy the top and flower of it who hath a quick sense of pleasure, and withal spirit, skill, and fortune sufficient to gratify every appetite and every taste. Niggards and fools will envy or traduce such a one because they cannot equal him. Hence all that sober trifling in disparagement of what every one would be master of if he could, a full freedom and unlimited scope of pleasure.

Euphranor: Let me see whether I understand you. Pleasure of sense, you say, is the chief pleasure?

Lysicles: I do.

Euphranor: And this would be cramped and diminished by virtue?

Lysicles: It would.

Euphranor: Tell me, Lysicles, is pleasure then at the height when the appetites are satisfied?

Lysicles: There is then only an indolence, the lively sense of pleasure being past.

Euphranor: It should seem therefore that the appetites must be always craving, to preserve pleasure alive?

Lysicles: That is our sense of the matter.

Euphranor: The Greek philosopher, therefore, was in the right, who considered the body of a man of pleasure as a leaky vessel, always filling, and never full. (*Works*, III, 83–4)

Lysicles, the free-thinker, here picks up on the phrase of Hylas, the materialist, from the same passage of the *Three Dialogues* in which Hylas wants to suggest that there are some perceptions that are not accompanied by or classifiable into pleasure and pain and that this state is 'an *indolence*. It seems to be nothing more than a privation of both pain and pleasure. And that such a quality or state as this may agree to an unthinking substance' (*Works*, II, 178). Berkeley denies indolence, the neutral state of unperceived perceptions and gratified appetites. He denies that the human mechanism is an indolent mechanism, as it must always interpret its painful and pleasurable perceptions. Faith, as Berkeley argues, is not an 'indolent perception' but an 'operative persuasion' (*Alciphron*, VII. 10, p. 301): any virtuous state of mind recognises that the world is a constant interpretative problem. Indolence is a refusal to enter into conversation with God through the phenomenal world. *Alciphron* is Berkeley's sustained defence of self-love or self-interest, the basic utilitarian reliance on pleasure and pain, as the language of God, as evidence of God's providence, played out in the public sphere rather than in the *sensorium*.

Pope introduces two balancing principles in human life in the second epistle of the *Essay*:

> Two Principles in human nature reign;
> Self-love, to urge, and Reason, to restrain; . . .
> Self-love and Reason to one end aspire,
> Pain their aversion, Pleasure their desire;

(II.53–4, 87–8)

Reason makes the kind of utilitarian calculations that prevent the individual from merely giving in to the most immediate pleasures, and becoming a leaky vessel.[32] The language Pope uses to describe the relationship between self-love and reason may echo Berkeley's language of mediate and immediate objects of sight, and his distinction between tangible and visual ideas. Pope says that self-love is the stronger impulse:

> Self love still stronger, as its objects nigh;
> Reason's at distance, and in prospect lie:
> That sees immediate good by present sense;
> Reason, the future and the consequence. . . .
> Pleasures are ever in our hands or eyes,
> And when in act they cease, in prospect rise;
> Present to grasp, and future still to find,
> The whole employ of body and of mind.

(II.71–4, 123–6)

Self-love acts as perception, reason as the interpretative faculty, comparing tangible and visible perceptions, deriving mediate from immediate perceptions, deriving possible future goods from sure present goods. The interpretative power of these balancing human principles is evidence of God's providence. Both principles, however, are concerned with utilitarian calculus, not taste. Pope's writing on self-love and social love can be derived from a Berkeleian utilitarian principle distinguished from others in that it interprets sensations of pleasure and pain as the language of God, that which makes the world meaningful and temporarily survivable.

Pope spends much of the second and third epistles finding a way to demonstrate that sociability and morality are derived from self-love. He argues that the entire creation is mutually supportive, that as God's perfection requires the plenitude of creation, so it also requires its harmony: 'Look round our World; behold the chain of Love / Combining all below and all above' (III.7–8). The sexual instinct draws each species together:

> Not man alone, but all that roam the wood,
> Or wing the sky, or roll along the flood,
> Each loves itself, but not itself alone,
> Each sex desires alike, 'till two are one.
> Nor ends the pleasure with the fierce embrace;
> They love themselves, a third time, in their race.

> (III.119–24)

Whilst all the other animals tend their young only a short while, the extended period of human child-rearing generates social love:

> A longer care Man's helpless kind demands;
> That longer care contracts more lasting bands:
> Reflection, Reason, still the ties improve,
> At once extend the int'rest, and the love;
> With choice we fix, with sympathy we burn;
> Each Virtue in each Passion takes its turn;
> And still new needs, new helps, new habits rise,
> That graft benevolence on charities.
> Still as one brood, and as another rose,
> These nat'ral love maintain'd, habitual those:
> The last, scarce ripen'd into perfect Man,
> Saw helpless him from whom their life began:
> Mem'ry and fore-cast just returns engage,
> That pointed back to youth, this on to age;
> While pleasure, gratitude, and hope, combin'd,
> Still spread the int'rest, and preserv'd the kind.

> (III.131–46)

Pope's vocabulary presents the bond between parent and child as artificial and natural at once. The extended period of child-rearing allows habits of love to form, so that single acts of charity prompted by the love of self are extended into a disposition towards benevolence. The transition from the single act to the disposition is a 'graft', the horticultural image catching the artifice introduced into natural relations by protracting them and regularising them over time. The vocabulary opens out from the ripening of children into the economic calculations those children make when confronted with the question of what to do with their parents. The child remembers the love expressed in rearing and repays it to the parent, whilst aware that he or she will require such help in old age also. The 'interest' paid on the parent's investment is spread, as the child paying the parent back also accumulates credit against his or her old age. This interest, then, is a calculated interest, but also the natural interest of love for other people, the natural love of child for parent. Pope argues that calculating and natural love are not just compatible but necessary to one another.

Berkeley employs a similar metaphor when arguing against Alciphron, who asserts that human nature includes only those things that appear in all people at all times and in all places immediately from the beginnings of society: 'These limitations of original, universal, and invariable, exclude all those notions found in the human mind which are the effect of custom and education.... if upon a plum-tree, peaches and apricots are engrafted, nobody will say they are the natural growth of the plum tree' (I.14, p. 55) Euphranor responds by pursuing the idea of cultivation, asking if the blossom and fruit of trees, although they do not appear immediately, are no less natural to the tree. He complicates matters by discussing climate: 'The plant being the same in all places doth not produce the same fruit – sun, soil, and cultivation making a difference ... things may be natural to men, although they do not actually show themselves in all men, nor in equal perfection; there being as great difference of culture, and every other advantage, with respect to human nature, as is to be found with respect to the vegetable nature of plants' (I.14, pp. 56–7). Euphranor demonstrates that the natural is not always the same in all places, and that it sometimes incorporates the artificial.

Although self-love seems prior to social love, in that it leads people to love their likeness in others and desire to recreate themselves in their offspring, as well as prompting the utilitarian calculation that it is good to love one's parents, Pope heralds it as coeval:

> Nor think in NATURE'S STATE they blindly trod;
> The state of Nature was the reign of God:
> Self-love and Social at her birth began,
> Union the bond of all things, and of Man.

> (III.147–50)

Self-love is only analytically or metaphysically prior to social love. Both kinds of love are present from the beginning of human existence, but when Pope presents the arguments for the necessity of both kinds of love, given the nature of God and of the creation, he decides to posit a conjectural priority of self-love over social. What was always natural or essential to being a person only elaborates itself over the course of a human existence. The close of the *Epistle* presents self-love and social as identical not just coeval: 'Thus God and Nature link'd the gen'ral frame, / And bade Self-love and Social be the same' (III.316–17). This cannot be a perfect identity, as self-love and social must already exist, and must exist distinctly, if they can be bidden to be the same. The poetry identifies the two kinds of love, has God and nature identify them, but in the same line holds them apart. The couplet dramatises a moment of divine creation, the calling forth of a human world bound together by self-interest that must always also be social interest: it dramatises the emergence of the natural world from God's will. A synthesis is presented analytically, an event out of time is presented as a compressed conjectural history. The lines argue that people can see God's providence in the manner in which self-love leads on as if by nature to social love, the way nature makes utilitarian calculation work for others as well as the self.

4.3   Common sense

Shaftesbury's thought is by no means exclusively centred on private individuals responding to the moral world as an aesthetic object. A sense of common good complements the taste for morality. There is no historical derivation of social love from self-interest in Shaftesbury, but on the contrary an insistence that social feelings must pre-date any moment of social contractual agreement. Common sense is defined with reference to commentators on Juvenal's eighth satire:

> They make this common sense of the poet, by a Greek derivation, to signify sense of public weal and of the common interest, love of the community or society, natural affection, humanity, obligingness, or that sort of civility which rises from a just sense of the common rights of mankind, and the natural equality there is among those of the same species. (*Characteristics*, 'Sensus Communis', p. 48)

Shaftesbury prefers a sense of common good to the derivation of social from private interest found in many accounts of the emergence of contractual society. He suggests that if people have no inherent sense of common interest it is impossible that they should acquire one at the moment of promise, simply by becoming contracted. If people have not the natural virtues of justice, faith and so on, how can they be expected to acquire them simply by making a self-interested promise? The moment at which social virtues are acquired by making the contract seems permanently to recede: 'A man is obliged to keep his word. Why? Because he has given his word to keep it. – Is not this a notable account of the original of moral justice and the rise of civil government and allegiance?' (p. 51). Shaftesbury identifies an absurdity in the development of social love from self-love, the absurdity of such a development occurring at a single co-ordinated moment in human history.

Shaftesbury, however, refuses to accept the kind of historical thought practised in such moments of conjectural reconstruction. These moments are conjectural, they present synthetic facts, such as God's identification of self-love with social, as analytical processes; they present a metaphysical priority as a historical priority. Such historical thought only appears absurd if it is read as an accurate, factual chronology of the development of human society. It is necessarily conjectural, but attempts to connect the emergence of social forms with probable stages in the material conditions of pre-historic society. In my final chapter I will discuss Hume's account of the emergence of artificial virtues such as justice in relation to *An Essay on Man* at greater length. Such accounts ask a reader to presume that material conditions, such as population growth, are connected to the development of human virtues; this is a lesser presumption than that all the virtues are innate. Accounts such as Hume's also make more room for the failure of certain virtues to emerge in certain conditions, for the failure of humanity to be characterised by common sense. Even one of Shaftesbury's admirers, Bernard Mandeville, disagrees with him on the innateness of senses of virtue and common good, their existence unmediated by modes of life and custom, and the notion that human life must always have been sociable:

> I differ from My Lord *Shaftsbury* entirely, as to the Certainty of the *Pulchrum* & *Honestum*, abstract from Mode and Custom: I do the same about the Origin of Society, and in many other Things.[33]

Mandeville here is trying to distinguish himself from Shaftesbury and step to the side of Berkeley's attack in the second dialogue of *Alciphron*. Berkeley denies that moral sense and common sense alone are the basis for an ethical life through a satirical exposition of the unrestrained self-interest he detects lurking beneath the jargon of taste and sense. Berkeley puts in place of these tastes and senses his notions and spirits, the means of identifying other people as part of the language of God in the phenomenal world.

The possibility that Berkeley might have thought of human contractual society as an intrinsically linguistic state is indicated by passages he includes in *The Ladies Library*, the anthology of literature for women he produced for Richard Steele. Human social instincts are distinguished from those of other animals by the capacity for speech that makes true society possible:

> *Man*, of all sublunary Creatures, is most adapted to *Society*; for tho' the greatest part of other Creatures do covet Society as well as he, yet he alone is furnish'd with that Gift of Nature which renders Society the most pleasant and useful, and that is the Gift of *Speech*: By means of which we can express our Thoughts, maintain a mutual Intelligence of Minds one with another, and thereby divert our Sorrows, mingle our Mirth, impart our Secrets, communicate our Counsels, and make mutual Compacts and Agreements to supply and assist each other. And in these things consists the greatest Pleasure and Use of *Society*.

The writer from whom Berkeley extracts this passage presents the constant use of words, the implicit promise that all words, and not just the words of a promise, will be used honestly, as the true indication of social life:

> *Words* being instituted for no other end but to signify our Meaning, and to be the Instrument of our Intercourse and *Society* with one another, every one who is a Member of human *Society*, has a Right to have our Meaning truly signify'd to him by our Words; and whosoever lies or equivocates to another, does injuriously deprive him of the natural Right of *Society*.[34]

Berkeley might have thought of human social life as life in language. But he also thinks of social life (in the basic sense of knowing that other people exist and co-ordinating behaviour towards them) as something only possible because of the linguistic structure of the world. Language is not just the expression or mark of social love, but the medium in which society becomes possible.

The existence and importance of other people is a more analytical question in Berkeley than Shaftesbury. Berkeley compares gravity and social love as natural laws in an early essay: 'as the attractive Power in Bodies is the most universal Principle which produceth innumerable Effects, and is a Key to explain the various *Phenomena* of Nature; so the corresponding Social Appetite in Human Souls is the great Spring and Source of Moral Actions'.[35] Berkeley works out the mechanics of human social interest in *Alciphron*, analysing the social appetite. The existence of other people is inferred from visual signs: 'I do not see Alciphron, *i.e.* that individual thinking thing, but only such visible signs and tokens as suggest and infer the being of that invisible thinking principle or soul' (IV.5, p. 147). Of that which is inferred one has a notion rather than an idea, as one cannot have ideas of agents:

> Such is the nature of *spirit* or that which acts, that it cannot be of it self perceived, but only by the effects which it produceth. . . . so far as I can see, the words *will, soul, spirit*, do not stand for different ideas, or in truth, for any idea at all, but for something which is very different from ideas, and which being an agent cannot be like unto, or represented by, any idea whatsoever. Though it must be owned at the same time, that we have some notion of soul, spirit, and the operations of the mind, such as willing, loving, hating, in as much as we know or understand the meaning of those words.[36]

The argument that not all words need refer to ideas is tied up with the argument that one can have no idea of agents, but one can have a notion of them. Euphranor makes the connection:

> An agent therefore, an active mind or spirit, cannot be an idea, or like an idea. Whence it should seem to follow that those words which denote an active principle, soul, or spirit do not, in a strict and proper sense, stand for ideas. And yet they are not insignificant neither; since I understand what is signified by the term *I*, or *myself*, or know what it means, although it be no idea, nor like an idea, but that which thinks, and wills, and apprehends ideas, and operates about them. (VII.5, p. 292)[37]

Words can be meaningful even if they do not refer to ideas, and one such way in which they can be meaningful is to refer to agents, of which other agents may only have notions, not ideas. Agents have notions of other agents by inferring from visual signs the existence of something parallel to their own agency, the existence of other people. These signs operate in the same way as all other signs from God: they show people what to seek and what to shun, 'informing us more distinctly of those objects whose nearness and magnitude qualify them to be of greatest detriment or benefit to our bodies, and less exactly in proportion as their littleness or distance makes them of less concern to us' (IV.15, pp. 160–1). The existence and value of other people is almost as evident from the language of phenomena as the existence and benevolence of God.

From this aesthetic utilitarian approach to other people a sophisticated ethics can be developed. Another text Pope probably read in the period of the *Essay*'s composition comes close to defining other people as ends in themselves by elaborating basic utilitarian principles. John Gay, fellow of Sidney Sussex college in Cambridge and later a vicar in Bedfordshire, wrote a preface for Edmund Law's translation of William King's *De Origine Mali*, a text Mack recognises as a possible source for Pope ('Introduction', xxviii–xxix).[38] Berkeley had been in trouble with King in 1710 for taking holy orders without the permission of King, then archbishop of Dublin. David Berman also suggests that early interaction with King helps to form aspects of Berkeley's theology and linguistic theory, particularly his emotive theory of religious terms.[39] It seems likely then that both Pope and Berkeley would have looked at the English translation of King, as they were both at work on vindications of providence at the time of its publication; it is likely that they would both have read Gay. Gay is an opponent of moral sense. He notes that Hutcheson has

> supposed (without *proving*, unless by shewing the insufficiency of all other Schemes) a *Moral* Sense to account for the former [the will to virtue], and a *public* or *benevolent Affection* for the latter [concern for others]: And these, *viz.*, the Moral Sense and Public Affection, he supposes to be implanted in us like *Instincts*, independent of Reason, and previous to any Instruction.[40]

Gay argues that pleasure and pain are the true source of moral ideas, that they represent the will of God, the ultimate criterion of virtue, to people – an idea not far removed from Berkeley's divine language. He acknowledges that personal happiness is dependent on other people:

> That there will arise different means of Happiness, is evident from hence, *viz.* that Rational Agents, in being subservient to our Happiness, are not passive but voluntary. And therefore since we are in pursuit of that to obtain which we apprehend the concurrence of their Wills necessary, we cannot but approve of whatever is apt to procure this

Concurrence. And that can be only the Pleasure or Pain expected from it by them. And therefore, as I perceive that my Happiness is dependent on others, I cannot but judge whatever I apprehend to be proper to excite them to endeavour to promote my Happiness, to be a means of Happiness: *i.e.* I cannot but *approve it*. And since the annexing Pleasure to their Endeavours to promote my Happiness is the only thing in my power to this end, I cannot but approve of the annexing Pleasure to such Actions of theirs as are undertaken upon my account. Hence to approve of a Rational agent as a means of Happiness, is different from the Approbation of any other means; because it implies an Approbation also of an Endeavour to promote the Happiness of that Agent, in order to excite him and others to the same concern for my Happiness for the future. (p. xxiv)

Gay puts forward the seemingly contradictory argument that the self-interested selection of other people as means to personal happiness is not at all self-interested, because the selection necessarily implies that the happiness of other people is of concern to any agent who makes it. The selfish choice is the sociable choice. Choosing other people as a means to personal happiness is a recognition of those people as ends in themselves. Regarding others in this seemingly transcendent, Kantian fashion as ends in themselves is, paradoxically, only possible by regarding them in a very untranscendental manner as the means to personal happiness. Gay demonstrates one possible mode of God's identification of self-love and social, one way in which a benevolent system of public ethics can be elaborated from self-interest. Recognising and valuing other people is one part of the aesthetic experience of the world, one aspect of moral perception.

Throughout the second epistle of the *Essay* Pope employs the language of art and aesthetic experience to describe the balance and proportion of reason and self-love, the balance and proportion of present and future goods. Indeed, God's providence as a work of visual art is a governing metaphor in the *Essay*. 'Passions, like Elements, tho' born to fight, / Yet, mix'd and soften'd, in his [God's] work unite:' (II.111–12) the various instincts of the human mind are harmonised as colours in painting.

> These mix'd with art, and to due bounds confin'd,
> Make and maintain the balance of the mind:
> The lights and shades, whose well accorded strife
> Gives all the strength and colour of our life.

> (II.119–22)

The confines of the line also confine the mixture of the passions; the balance of the mind is echoed in the balance provided by the second line of the couplet, the equilibrium of the rhyme. Pope employs similar techniques to those of the epistles to Burlington and Bathurst to suggest performatively that his verse imitates God's management of the mind. Moral phenomena are the object of aesthetic appreciation just as the verse is the object of aesthetic appreciation. Moral life is a matter of seeing meaning in visual phenomena. Vice and virtue mix in the human mind 'As, in some well-wrought picture, light and shade' (II.208). Divine benevolence is seen in the aesthetic properties, the meaningfulness of the visually conceived phenomena of the moral world. It is by the artful contrivance of God that 'Ev'n mean Self-love becomes, by force divine, / The scale to measure others wants by thine' (II.291–2). Here the aesthetic balance has reverted to the economic balance, the need to balance investment and return. People have an aesthetic response to the moral world that involves considering other people as analogous to themselves. This response is not intuitive; it is based on customary, habitual experiences of pleasure and pain that come to have the force of a language. The aesthetic worlds of the poem, of morality and of phenomena run in parallel.

I would like to conclude this chapter by looking at the fourth epistle, and Pope's reconciliation of the human phenomenal world, the world of the poem, and providence. The nature of happiness in the fourth epistle is tautological. Pope suggests that no one to whom one might turn for a definition of happiness is able to provide one: 'Who thus define it, say they more or less / Than this, that Happiness is Happiness?' (IV.27–8). Happiness is obvious and elusive, just as providence is obvious and elusive. As God has been a principle of indifferentiation as well as differentiation earlier in the *Essay*, so happiness functions now. 'Equal is Common Sense, and Common Ease' (IV.35).

> Heav'n to Mankind impartial we confess,
> If all are equal in their Happiness:
> But mutual wants this Happiness increase,
> All Nature's difference keeps all Nature's peace.

> (IV.53–6)

The hypothesis is made indisputable by the only possible objection to it being incorporated into it: even lack of happiness is happiness (as the unhappiness caused by want of material possessions prompts social contact through labour and trade). Heaven provides each person with the means to happiness: 'Heav'ns just balance equal will appear' (IV.69). Unhappiness is similar to chance: if both are seen as part of a completely rational providential scheme, they must be redescribed as happiness and necessity respectively. It is the peculiar place of people to perform this act of redescription and see happiness in unhappiness. Happiness is dependent on this poetico-philosophical reconsideration of terms, on the ability to see the world as a language that makes sense.

The fourth epistle progresses through a series of satirical expositions in which the desire for riches, fame and power are ridiculed as in no way leading to true happiness, and works towards the notion that virtue is its own reward. In concluding this section Pope again adopts financial vocabulary, this time having very recently denigrated the desire for riches:

> Bring then these blessings to a strict account,
> Make fair deductions, see to what they mount.
> How much of other each is sure to cost;
> How each for other oft is wholly lost;
> How inconsistent greater goods with these;
> How sometimes life is risq'd, and always ease:
> Think, and if still the things thy envy call,
> Say, would'st thou be the Man to whom they fall?

> (IV.269–76)

Financial vocabulary is here employed in order to put off the pursuit of goods, and it seems as if in this epistle simply nothing is admirable or estimable, that God's equalisation of human happiness is in danger of levelling it. However, true

> Merit constant pay receives,
> Is blest in what it takes, and what it gives;
> The joy unequal'd, if its end it gain,
> And if it lose, attended with no pain:

> (IV.313–16)

The pay of merit is not financial: the vocabulary is easily reclaimed from the financial world and applied to the intellectual rewards of virtue. The state of merit is also equalised in that it cannot result in loss, yet its reward is 'unequal'd joy', a surplus seeming to arise from the impossibility of pain. Merit defies economy by offering a gain with no possibility of loss. Pope's state of merit seems comparable to Temple's description of *ataraxia*, the peace of mind aimed at by all philosophical schools.[41] Yet this merit depends on a revision of terms, a questioning of the vocabulary used to describe values and rewards, a redescription which is itself the achievement of merit.

The introduction of the idea of true merit restores Pope's vocabulary. The person of merit, 'Slave to no sect' (IV.331), shares attitudes with Pope in the *Imitations of Horace*: 'Sworn to no Master, of no Sect am I' (Ep.I.i, l.24). He or she shares an indifference with the poet, an indifference towards apparent values and beliefs which is itself a value and a belief. The person of merit

> sees, why Nature plants in Man alone
> Hope of known bliss, and Faith in bliss unknown:
> (Nature, whose dictates to no other kind
> Are giv'n in vain, but what they seek they find)
> Wise is her present; she connects in this
> His greatest Virtue with his greatest Bliss,
> At once his own bright prospect to be blest,
> And strongest motive to assist the rest.
>   Self-love thus push'd to social, to divine,
> Gives thee to make thy neighbour's blessing thine.

$$(IV.345-54)$$

This person is a rational agent who approves of the happiness of other people as a means to his or her own happiness in a selfless way, and as a criterion of the will of God. The impetus for social as well as self-love dictates that the 'human soul / Must rise from Individual to the Whole' (IV.361–2).

The course of questioning and revising vocabulary throughout the *Essay* is completed, with chance redescribed as the result of providential wisdom, reason and passion serving the same end, self-love and society identified, and misery becoming happiness. Recognition of the limited position of reason, the function of pleasure and pain and the necessity of community makes the world of the *Essay* meaningful, and therefore replete with happiness for the person capable of making such reflections as the *Essay* performs. The poem closes with a summary of the terms investigated in the *Essay*. Pope hopes to be able to claim

That urg'd by thee [Bolingbroke], I turn'd the tuneful art
From sounds to things, from fancy to the heart;
For Wit's false mirror held up Nature's light;
Shew'd erring Pride, WHATEVER IS, IS RIGHT;
That REASON, PASSION, answer one great aim;
That true SELF-LOVE and SOCIAL are the same;
That VIRTUE only makes our Bliss below;
And all our Knowledge is, OURSELVES TO KNOW.

(ll. 391–8)

Poetry has been turned from 'sounds to things', but it remains 'the tuneful art': it has not abandoned its artifice, it has not moved from *words* to things, but seen meaning in things, something not found in the mere signifying sonic qualities of words. Walter Harte's *Essay on Reason*, which Pope helped to revise, and was happy should be mistaken for his own, states that true reason sees how 'meaning *lives* in things': Pope's conclusion to his *Essay* makes a similar argumentative turn, finding meaning in a language of phenomena.[42] The primary sense of IV.393 is that Pope substituted 'Nature's light' for 'Wit's false mirror', but there is a residual sense that *because* 'Wit's false mirror held up Nature's light', Pope was able to enter into a poetic discourse which revealed the appropriate conduct of human life. True wit is reclaimed from the improper sense of fanciful conjunction and embellishment to become a tool of discrimination and discernment, without abandoning the poetic and philosophical artifice necessary to achieve happiness. That is, the poet and philosopher of the essay has come to find a way of seeing and talking about the phenomena of the world that recognises their place in a providential scheme that has the structure and force of a language; the management of the poem itself, its redefinition of terms, its redescription of every event as a product of God's providence, is enacted in the vocabulary, syntax and lineation of the poem itself. The poet has come to see the world as meaningful not because he has practised his taste on the world, nor even educated his taste by practising it upon the world, but because he has entered into a conversation with the world. By imagining other people who feel pleasure and pain in a similar way to himself, by imagining a God who has knowledge infinitely greater than himself, by seeing how that God created all phenomena that are evident to people, including the evidence of the existence of other people and of the existence of God, as meaningful phenomena, the poet is equipped to talk about the world, and enter into conversation with the world through benevolent and yet self-interested action, and become happy. On these grounds I think the poem is comparable to *Alciphron* as a Christian utilitarian discourse on providence.

Reading Pope next to Berkeley, I hope to have shown how the sound can seem an echo to the sense of poetry by expanding on Berkeley's account of a phenomenal world that has the structure of a language, an artificial structure that is naturalised by use and custom, and a structure that is shared by human languages. The sound can seem to echo the sense because poetic language is analogous to the divine language of nature. Berkeley and Pope are conservatives of a radical kind, conservatives who question such certainties as the resemblance of a pictorial sign to that which it represents, and the intrinsic value of the precious metals. They put practical, ethical life before abstract solutions to such lines of questioning, because they recognise that these questionings only ever exist in practical, ethical human life: consideration of these questions beyond the realm of human phenomenal and linguistic experience is entirely hollow and pointless, leading to free-thinking and minute philosophy. Pope's poetic language imitates the language of nature instituted by Berkeley's God, and plays constantly on its own emergence as a natural artifice. I will close this study by looking at the ways in which Pope and Berkeley might live on in Hume.

Epilogue: Pope, Berkeley and Hume

In this brief chapter, I will attempt to show where the connection I have traced between Pope and Berkeley might lead. In the broadest sense I want to suggest a connection between Pope, Berkeley and Hume, based on their presentation of the world as something that has to be learnt through habit and custom, like a language, or indeed as a language. All of these writers present the human world as a world produced at the point where nature and custom meet. I will discuss Hume's conjectural history of the virtues in his *Treatise of Human Nature* in relation to Pope's treatment of the origins of society and kingship in the *Essay on Man*. Berkeley always turns to God as the ordering and organising principle of the world, the author of the language of the world. Hume does not rely so heavily upon God, and puts custom in God's place as the guarantor of meaning.[1] Hume develops a desacralised version of Berkeley's providentially meaningful world: 'Although he is opposed to any *a priori* account of standards, values, laws, or institutions, Hume gives to conventions, in terms of which all social phenomena are defined, an authority which might be called "the secular *a priori*".'[2] There is a large theological difference then between Berkeley and Hume, and I would like to suggest that Pope does something to resolve this difference, rather than to exemplify it: Pope's *Essay on Man* connects the two philosophers, offers a means of interpreting the ambiguous way in which Hume's reading in Berkeley becomes evident in Hume's work.

The connection of these three figures may seem improbable. It has indeed been argued that Pope's *Essay* belongs to the world of Locke, and that Hume's *Treatise* and *Enquiries* mark a change in thinking about the self and external reality that makes later eighteenth-century poetry very different from Pope: the shift from Pope to Hume is a shift from a solid belief in external reality, the existence of other people and the benevolent

providence of God, to a doubt about the kinds of impressions people
have of external reality, an introspective mode of enquiry and no particular conviction about the benevolence of God.[3] There are, however,
strong grounds for reading Pope and Hume together. That Hume read
Pope is very uncontroversial. Hume refers to Pope several times in his
correspondence, saying in 1754 he had recited the 'Elegy to the Memory
of an Unfortunate Lady' to Blacklock twelve years previously, quoting
from the 'Epistle to Mr Jervas', discussing Pope's spelling and reminiscing
on Pope's connections with a place he is staying.[4] When Hume remembers
the reception of the *Treatise of Human Nature*, saying it dropped still
born from the press, he quotes from the poem by Pope that also praises
Berkeley, the second dialogue of the *Epilogue to the Satires*.[5] It is less
frequently noted that Hume presented a copy of his *Treatise* to Pope,
inscribed (not by Hume), with errors corrected.[6] I suggest Hume sent this
edition to Pope as an acknowledgement of the influence of Pope's work
on the *Treatise*. One critic has previously noted the existence of the
presentation copy and suggested that the *Treatise* 'is an ambitious if
sometimes awkward working out in philosophic prose of the major
assumptions of *An Essay on Man*'.[7] Another writer on the connections
between eighteenth-century philosophical writing and poetry identifies
similarities between Pope's and Hume's writing on ruling passions.[8] The
following discussion is a contribution to the study of Hume's reading of
Pope, and so also an attempt to improve understanding of the place of *An
Essay on Man* in European intellectual life of the mid-to late eighteenth
century.

Hume had read Berkeley, but how much Berkeley he had read and the
importance of Berkeley to his philosophical career are contested issues.
I will just mention here some of Hume's references to Berkeley, and
suggest that Berkeley is a useful figure for Hume, because Hume can
point out similarities between the positions he and Berkeley hold and
claim the support of a Church of Ireland divine whilst maintaining
his own radical views. Hume does this in his *Letter to a Gentleman in
Edinburgh*, his letter of protest at accusations levelled against him when
he applied for a professorship at Edinburgh. Hume defends his rejection
of abstract ideas, 'after the present pious and learned *Bishop of Cloyne*',
arguing that denial of an abstract idea of existence is not necessarily
denial of the existence of God, nor indeed of the existence of anything.[9]
Hume, however, may have provoked rather than placated his antagonist.
William Wishart, the Principal of the University, who had attacked
Hume's *Treatise* and undermined his application for the Professorship,
is also the author of an attack on Berkeley's *Alciphron*, despite having been

a founder member of the Rankenian Club, the group of intellectuals that is said to have done most to popularise Berkeley's views in Scotland. M.A. Stewart has shown how Wishart turned against Berkeley following the latter's attacks on Shaftesbury and his presentation of the argument from design solely through the concept of visual language.[10] Hume's invocation of Berkeley is likely to have backfired. His own allusions to *Alciphron* in some very close verbal parallels in the *Dialogues on Natural Religion* show Hume reversing some of Berkeley's points. Hume gives Cleanthes, his devoted theist, the words of Berkeley's free-thinker Alciphron, attributing to a believer the slovenly habits of mind displayed by Berkeley's unbeliever.[11]

Hume writes to Michael Ramsay, listing the *Principles* as one of the texts one should read in order to be able to understand the metaphysical aspects of his arguments, and on another occasion stating what a pleasure it is to reread Berkeley in the library he is using in Rheims, France.[12] The *Treatise* has recently been included in a selection of responses to Berkeley's *Principles*, and the same volume records Hamann's comment that 'the new scepticism owes more to the older idealism than this casual, single occasion [Hume's praise of Berkeley's critique of abstraction] would incidentally give us to understand, . . . without Berkeley Hume would scarcely have become the great philosopher which criticism, in unanimous gratitude, makes him out to be.'[13] One brief discussion of Hume's reading in Berkeley also mentions Pope. M.A. Box runs through the history of the dispute concerning Hume's reading in Berkeley, and suggests a textual echo between Hume and Berkeley saying sensitive people feel things as if their skin has been stripped off. Box suggests that Pope's lines on the man 'tremblingly alive all o'er' who agonizes 'at ev'ry pore' (*Essay on Man*, I.197–8) could be a common source for these passages.[14] There has been little speculative writing on the discursive parallels between Pope, Berkeley and Hume, despite the evidence of these references and textual echoes. I will trace some parallels in argument and theme between the *Essay* and the *Treatise*, and suggest that they demonstrate ways in which Hume's philosophical project comes into contact with Berkeley's, a contact that some historians of philosophy have doubted.[15] I will be covering parts of the second and third epistles of *An Essay on Man* already discussed in the previous chapter, attempting to present them in a more Humean light.

At the beginning of the second epistle Pope concludes the methodological discussion of the first epistle with a statement of the true object of intellectual inquiry: 'Know then thyself, presume not God to scan; / The proper study of Mankind is Man' (II.1–2). Again, the study is 'proper' as it is either necessarily limited by human reason or provided as an adequate object by God, as the 'proper organs' and 'proper pow'rs' assigned by God to the creation in the first epistle (I.180, discussed in the previous chapter). Hume echoes Pope: 'Human Nature is the only science of man; and yet has been hitherto the most neglected.'[16] Hume's statement concludes a long discussion of the relative worth of philosophical reasoning and the common superstitions of human life. Philosophical reason might be limited, and its conclusions dissatisfactory (searching for some external principle, the philosopher finds only the operations of his or her own mind to be the causes of actions and events in the world), but it is always preferable to the false levity of superstition. The science of human nature is proper for Hume in the same balanced manner as for Pope. The sequence of contrasting half-lines in which Pope describes the medial position of man ends by describing him as the 'Sole judge of Truth, in Endless Error hurl'd: / The glory, jest, and riddle of the world!' (II.17–18). There is no judgement of truth without the existence of man, but the judgement of truth cannot be the aim of man's existence as it is unattainable in any complete form. It is perhaps easier to see in these lines the encouragement of an attitude rather than an epistemological claim.[17] It is an attitude in which if there is a proper object of study it is the prescribed human mind, itself the instrument of study.

Pope moves on to the dual principles of humanity, passion (or self-love: 'Modes of Self-love the Passions we may call', II.93) and reason, the main topics of the epistle. Reason has recovered from its occasional subservience to pride in the first epistle, and is here reason limited to appropriate objects:

> Two Principles in human nature reign;
> Self-love, to urge, and Reason, to restrain;
> Nor this a good, nor that a bad we call,
> Each works its end, to move or govern all:
> And to their proper operation still,
> Ascribe all Good; to their improper, Ill.

(II.53–8)

Hume is again very close to Pope. 'I shall endeavour to prove *first*, that reason alone can never be a motive to any action of the will; and *secondly*, that it can never oppose passion in the direction of the will' (*Treatise*, II.iii.3, p. 413). That which Pope calls self-love Hume calls passion, but both terms indicate the cause of human volition. Passion may be called self-love as it too attempts to avoid pain: 'when we have the prospect of pain or pleasure from any object, we feel a consequent emotion of aversion or propensity, and are carry'd to avoid or embrace what will give us this uneasiness or satisfaction' (*Treatise*, II.iii.3, p. 414).[18] Passion is the cause of volition on utilitarian principles. Hume, in stating that 'Reason is, and ought only to be the slave of the passions,' (II.ii.3, p. 415) is not as far from Pope as it might appear. Pope recommends the practice of reason, which through habit and experience restrains self-love effectively: 'Attention, habit and experience gains, / Each strengthens Reason, and Self-love restrains' (II.79–80). Hume notes that causes and effects of objects which cause people pleasure or pain are 'pointed out to us by reason and experience' (II.iii.3, p. 414). He goes on to note that 'The moment we perceive the falshood of any supposition, or the insufficiency of any means our passions yield to our reason without any opposition' (II.iii.3, p. 416).

Pope is also in agreement with Hume concerning the fundamentally utilitarian purpose of reason and passion or self-love.

> Self-love and Reason to one end aspire,
> Pain their aversion, Pleasure their desire;

> (II.87–8)

The previous chapter deals at greater length with Berkeley's utilitarian providentialism that presents the world as the language of God. Neither Hume nor Pope mention God as the creator of the meaning of pleasure and pain, but both introduce pleasure and pain as essential to a meaningful world in which objects may be desired and actions judged. Pope and Hume, in very different ways, desacralise Berkeley's divine language theory and its utilitarian, customary foundations.

Having discussed the causes of human action, Pope goes on in the third epistle to affirm the union of self and social love in a conjectural prehistoric society:

> Nor think, in NATURE'S STATE they blindly trod;
> The state of Nature was the reign of God:
> Self-love and Social at her birth began,
> Union the bond of all things, and of Man.

> (III.147–50)

Self-love is metaphysically prior to social love, but as observable phenomena they are coeval. There follows a depiction of the golden age, in which there was neither slaughter, betrayal nor corruption, and the section closes by showing man 'from Nature rising slow to Art' (III.169) by imitating the behaviour of other animals. Hume's writing on justice (*Treatise*, III.ii.1–2, pp. 477–501) provides a close commentary on Pope's account of the origin of society that I touched on in the previous chapter. Hume attempts to show that just actions are not the product of unreflective nature. He calls justice an artificial virtue.

> To avoid giving offence, I must here observe, that when I deny justice to be a natural virtue, I make use of the word, *natural*, only as oppos'd to *artificial*. In another sense of the word; as no principle of the human mind is more natural than a sense of virtue; so no virtue is more natural than justice. . . . Tho' the rules of justice be *artificial*, they are not *arbitrary*. Nor is the expression improper to call them *Laws of Nature*; if by natural we understand what is common to any species, or even if we confine it to mean what is inseparable from the species. (III.ii.1, p. 484)

What Hume says here is related to Berkeley's argument in *Alciphron* that some qualities are natural to a species even if they do not immediately or always manifest themselves:

> The plant being the same in all places doth not produce the same fruit – sun, soil, and cultivation making a difference . . . things may be natural to men, although they do not actually show themselves in all men, nor in equal perfection; there being as great difference of culture, and every other advantage, with respect to human nature, as is to be found with respect to the vegetable nature of plants (*Alciphron*, I.14, pp. 56–7).

The virtues are a matter of natural cultivation in both of these arguments. Hume wants to pursue the manner in which these virtues develop. He has already stated that an 'affection betwixt the sexes is a passion evidently implanted in human nature' (III.ii.1, p. 481). The sexual instinct is a necessity that makes people aware of the advantages of society by raising them above other animals:

> This necessity is no other than that natural appetite betwixt the sexes, which unites them together, and preserves their union, till a new tye takes place in their concern for their common offspring. This new concern becomes also a principle of union betwixt the parents and offspring,

and forms a more numerous society; where the parents govern by the advantage of their superior strength and wisdom, and at the same time are restrain'd in the exercise of their authority by that natural affection, which they bear their children. In a little time, custom and habit operating on the tender minds of the children, makes them sensible of the advantages, which they reap from society, as well as fashions them by degrees for it, by rubbing off those rough corners and untoward affections, which prevent their coalition. (III.ii.2, p. 486)

Beginning with the sexual instinct, Hume traces the development of social affection through principles that are artificial but not arbitrary, based on the peculiar animal nature of man. He points out the selfish love of parents for each other and for their children, and the way in which this love leads, through custom and habit also peculiar to people, to a sense of mutual interest.

Hume is very close to the passage from Pope that I previously described as an attempt to identify natural and calculated affection:

> Not man alone, but all that roam the wood,
> Or wing the sky, or roll along the flood,
> Each loves itself, but not itself alone,
> Each sex desires alike, 'till two are one.
> Nor ends the pleasure with the fierce embrace;
> They love themselves, a third time, in their race. . . .
> A longer care Man's helpless kind demands;
> That longer care contracts more lasting bands:
> Reflection, Reason, still the ties improve,
> At once extend the int'rest, and the love;
> With choice we fix, with sympathy we burn;
> Each Virtue in each Passion takes its turn;
> And still new needs, new helps, new habits rise,
> That graft benevolence on charities.
> Still as one brood, and as another rose,
> These nat'ral love maintain'd, habitual those:
> The last, scarce ripen'd into perfect Man,
> Saw helpless him from whom their life began:
> Mem'ry and fore-cast just returns engage,
> That pointed back to youth, this on to age;
> While pleasure, gratitude, and hope, combin'd,
> Still spread the int'rest, and preserv'd the kind.

(III.119–24, 131–46)

Hume recapitulates Pope's account in his history of human conventions, finding something radical in Pope's perhaps conventional account, and finding something radical in the idea of convention itself. Hume's remarks on parental authority will also be of relevance to my account of Pope on the origin of kingship. Hume goes on to describe the human need for a form of justice that guarantees the stability of external goods as a convention:

> This convention is not of the nature of a *promise*: For even promises themselves, as we shall see afterwards, arise from human conventions. It is only a general sense of common interest; which sense all the members of the society express to one another, and which induces them to regulate their conduct by certain rules. . . . In like manner are languages gradually establish'd by human conventions without any promise. In like manner do gold and silver become the common measures of exchange, and are esteem'd sufficient payment for what is of a hundred times their value. (III.ii.2, p. 490)

Justice, words and money all rise out of conventions without the interposition of a promise through the habit and custom of self- and social-love. Hume's vocabulary here recalls Shaftesbury's common sense. Yet at the same time the argument is close to Berkeley's account of the development of a meaningful phenomenal world which is the language of God, and also of the proper use of financial tokens that can never be more than the representatives of human ethical obligations. Hume is indebted to Berkeley's presentation of the world as a language.

Given the rise of justice through customs, habits and conventions without promises, Hume dismisses the notion that the state of nature is one of unrestricted indulgence of the passions: "'tis utterly impossible for men to remain any considerable time in that savage condition, which precedes society; . . . his very first state and situation may be justly esteemed social' (III.ii.2, p. 491). The state of nature is to be regarded as a philosophical fiction, just as the golden age is a poetic fiction. Hume's depiction of the golden age is very similar to Pope's. Hume, again veering towards Shaftesbury, says that philosophers have been surpassed by poets, who 'have been guided more infallibly, by a certain taste or common instinct, which in most kinds of reasoning goes farther than any of that art and philosophy, with which we have been yet acquainted' (III.ii.2, p. 494). In giving a complex account of the rise of human social love, which is recognised as artificial yet not arbitrary, and which although perhaps metaphysically posterior is chronologically simultaneous with self-love or passion, in recognising a similar natural artificiality in the use of language and of money, and in preferring a golden age to a state of nature, Hume is here very close to Pope, and perhaps his best reader and interpreter. Moreover, Hume is close to Pope at points where Pope is close to Berkeley. Hume is reconciling the position of Shaftesbury, that 'faith, justice, honesty and virtue must have been as early as the state of nature or they could never have been at all' (because one cannot make a promise that obliges one to keep promises), and his insistence on taste, with Pope's conjectural history of the rise of social obligation through self-interest and the desire for pleasure.[19]

The origin of civic or political society is the next topic of the third epistle of *An Essay on Man*. Pope describes the inequality of natural resources in different tracts of land as the origin of aggression and commerce, with commerce and a love of society limiting aggression:

> Converse and Love mankind might strongly draw,
> When Love was Liberty, and Nature Law.
> Thus States were form'd; the name of King unknown,
> 'Till common int'rest plac'd the sway in one.
> 'Twas VIRTUE ONLY (or in arts or arms,
> Diffusing blessings, or averting harms)
> The same which in a Sire the Sons obey'd,
> A Prince the Father of a People made.

(III.207–14)

Pope's comparison is a little odd. Obedience to recognised superiority makes the king the father of the people as it makes a father the king of his son. Yet fatherhood is simultaneous with the existence of offspring, and kingship seems to follow some while after society and the existence of different gradations of virtue amongst people. It is as if being a father depends on being more virtuous than one's children instead of merely having them. There seems to be a compressed argument that as fathers must be virtuous, so societies must have kings. Both the authority of the father and the virtue of the king are naturalised. Pope's miniature conjectural history is imperfect. The point at which the king is recognised as more virtuous than his people is the same as the point at which a father is recognised as a father. The conjectural history is presented as what Hume calls a philosophical fiction, demonstrating that the virtue of kings is artificial, but artificial in Hume's qualified sense of something that follows from the physiological and early social conditions of the species. The virtue of kings is artificial compared to the natural virtue and authority of fathers, but not arbitrary. The contractual moment which, if questioned in such writers as Hobbes and Locke, must be a moment of origin rather than a moment of culmination is here recognised as a fiction, and a convention without promise is put in its place.[20] The comparison also implies an imperative: a real king, as a real father *should* be more virtuous than his people. Pope's history of the origin of kingship is conjectural and imperative, and Hume draws on it to describe the natural authority and restraint of parents: 'parents govern by the advantage of their superior strength and wisdom, and at the same time are restrain'd in the exercise of their authority by that natural affection, which they bear their children'.

Pope traces the degeneration of a natural state of virtuous rule until a more familiar exposition of the function of self-love in forming contractual society is reached:

> Forc'd into virtue, thus by self-defence,
> Ev'n Kings learn'd justice and benevolence:
> Self-love forsook the path it first pursu'd,
> And found the private in the public good.

(III.279–82)

Kings are no longer simply the most virtuous of men. These kings are those of the opening of the first epistle of the *Essay*, whose pride is disdained. Even for them, however, social love comes to be preferable to unrestrained self-interest. In the same way that kings have been defined and redefined, so that there is the true king of superior virtue, and the factual king of corruption, so have self- and social-love been defined and redefined: unrestrained self-interest was not the path first pursued, as from the beginning of the epistle it has been noted that passions cause the need for human society, and self-love and social have already been partly identified. Pope presents two origins of benevolent monarchy; in the first of these, kings demonstrate artificial virtues that arise out of the physiological and social conditions of primitive humanity; in the second, kings, after having given in to the corruptions attendant on their position in developed society, make a utilitarian calculation concerning the benefits of social love, and again demonstrate the virtues.

Pope goes on almost to identify this utilitarian benevolence in monarchs with the activity of the poet: both the monarch and the poet look back to a nature that contains within it the directions for appropriate human behaviour. The poet, patriot and monarch are obliged to point out to other people those artificial ways to behave that are dependent on the natural origins of the species. The poet and patriot restore concepts of justice, loyalty and legality as the benevolent monarch restores the idea of kingship:

> 'Twas then, the studious head or gen'rous mind,
> Follow'r of God or friend of human-kind,
> Poet or Patriot, rose but to restore
> The Faith and Moral, Nature gave before;

> (III.283–6)

Pope echoes his earlier *Essay* here. *An Essay on Criticism* advises critics on the relationship between nature and the rules, or conventions, governing writing:

> Those RULES of old *discover'd*, not *devis'd*,
> Are *Nature* still, but *Nature Methodiz'd*;
> *Nature*, like *Liberty*, is but restrain'd,
> By those same Laws which first *herself* ordain'd.

> (ll. 88–91)

Nature remains nature even when governed by human method. Nature is like liberty in that it is only governed by laws of its own making; or (to read the reflexive pronoun 'herself' not as part of a reflexive verb, 'herself ordain'd', but as an emphatic pronoun, leaving the 'Laws' to do the ordaining) the laws that ordain nature and liberty, God's laws of creation and natural justice, are the only laws that continue to restrain them. Pope's poetry describes and enacts the emergence of artifice out of nature, so that poetic artifice seems inherent in nature: Virgil discovers that Nature and Homer are 'the *same*' (l.135). In *An Essay on Man* the poetic restoration of values and redescription of the selfish world as the social world, of the world of chance as the world of order, is practised and described. The close of the epistle finally identifies self-love and social, but gives the divine injunction no chronological place in the rise of society nor in the progress of the epistle: 'Thus God and Nature link'd the gen'ral frame, / And bade Self-love and Social be the same' (III.317–18). The conclusion of the epistle is also its first assumption: that selfish principles of pleasure and pain which make meaning possible always have their specific meanings in communities.

Berkeley, Pope and Hume all investigate the moments at which nature becomes cultivated human society, the moment at which a specifically human world comes into existence and becomes meaningful. In Berkeley providence is evident in the meaningfulness of the world, its linguistic structure. In Pope nature often takes the place of God, only for nature to be redescribed as providence, chance as necessity, chaos as order. In Hume no such reintegration of the divine takes place, but the artificial is carefully distinguished from the arbitrary. The difference that John Sitter points out between Pope stating that 'whatever is, is right' and Hume stating that 'Whatever *is* may *not be*' is not irreconcilable.[21] Hume merely notes that one does not need God to sanction the evolution of social life from natural physiological, geographical and climatic conditions: these conditions determine the meaning of human existence, and govern its development. They could have been otherwise and could have produced a very different human world (just as Pope's proud reasoner could have been a fly), but they produced this world and no other. Hume diminishes the contingency of a meaningful human world even as he denies the necessity of a providential scheme to producing that world. These I think are the main lines of connection between Berkeley's linguistic providentialism, Pope's *Essay* and Hume's early work, and some ways in which the arguments that Pope and Berkeley share enter into later thought.

Notes

Introduction: Pope and Berkeley

1. The study of iconic relations in language and literature is ongoing in, for example, *The Motivated Sign: Iconicity in Language and Literature 2*, ed. Olga Fischer and Max Nänny (Amsterdam and Philadelphia: John Benjamins, 2001).
2. 'An Essay on Translated Verse', l. 345, in *Augustan Critical Writing*, ed. David Womersley (Harmondsworth: Penguin, 1997), p. 118.
3. *Ovid's Metamorphosis Englished*, trans. George Sandys (London: W. Stansby, 1626), pp. 54–5. This is one of the first books Pope read, and one that he 'liked extremely'. See Joseph Spence, *Observations, Anecdotes, and Characters of Books and Men*, ed. James M. Osborn, 2 vols (Oxford: Clarendon Press, 1966), I, 14, No. 30.
4. Rousseau's emphasis on the difficulty of 'inventing' language serves the important rhetorical purpose of forcing his readers to consider just how long and complex a process human evolution is. See *A Discourse on Inequality*, trans. Maurice Cranston (Harmondsworth: Penguin, 1984), pp. 92–7, p. 93.
5. Gregory A.F. Hollingshead, *George Berkeley and English Literature of the Eighteenth Century 1710–1770 With Special Reference to Swift, Pope, Blackwell, and Smart*, PhD, University of London, 1974, p. 39. Hollingshead offers an overview of the friendship, pp. 35–45.
6. For attributions of *Guardian* papers to Pope and Berkeley, see *The Guardian*, ed. John Calhoun Stephens (Lexington, Kentucky: The University Press of Kentucky, 1982), pp. 26–8, and David Berman, *George Berkeley: Idealism and the Man* (Oxford: Clarendon Press, 1994), p. 77.
7. Benjamin Rand, ed., *Berkeley and Percival: The Correspondence of George Berkeley afterwards Bishop of Cloyne and Sir John Percival afterwards Earl of Egmont* (Cambridge: Cambridge University Press, 1914), p. 110, 7 March 1712/3.
8. Hollingshead, pp. 10, 22, 34.
9. See *Guardian* No. 172, Monday 28 September 1713, and *New Theory of Vision*, *Works* I (1948), 229.
10. *Letters of Mr Alexander Pope and Several of His Friends* (London: J. Wright *et al.*, 1737), p. 203.
11. Charles Mordaunt, the third Earl of Peterborough, a famous general, later became a close ally of Pope in his altercations with Lady Mary Wortley Montagu. See *Correspondence* III, 352.
12. *Correspondence*, I, 221–2, Berkeley to Pope, 1 May 1714.
13. See Maynard Mack, *Alexander Pope: A Life* (New Haven and London: Yale University Press, in association with W.W. Norton, 1985), pp. 274–6.
14. Spence, *Observations*, I, 153, No. 344. The translation is not thought to have survived.
15. Spence, *Observations*, I, 135–6, No. 305.
16. See Andrew Keogh, 'Bishop Berkeley's Gift of Books in 1733', *Yale University Library Gazette* 8 (1933), 1–26, esp. pp. 12, 26.

17. British Library, Add, MS 39311: 27–8. Alexander Campbell Fraser, *Life and Letters of George Berkeley, D.D* (Oxford: Clarendon Press, 1871), prints this letter, pp. 235–6. A.A. Luce quotes part of the allusion to Pope, but does not note its context in the letter, *The Life of George Berkeley Bishop of Cloyne* (London: Thomas Nelson, 1949), p. 59.
18. *Correspondence* III, 358, Pope to Caryll, 20 March 1732/3.
19. See R.I. Aaron, 'A Catalogue of Berkeley's Library', *Mind*, n.s. 41:164 (October 1932), 465–75.
20. *A Catalogue of the Valuable Library of the late Right Rev. Dr. Berkeley, Lord Bishop of Cloyne. Together with the libraries of his Son and Grandson, the late Rev. GEORGE BERKELEY, D.D. PREBENDARY of CANTERBURY, and the late GEORGE MONK BERKELEY, Esq. To be sold by Leigh and Sotheby, Monday June 6, 1796, and the Five following days*, p. 5, No. 141. The annotated copy of this catalogue is in the British Library, S.C.S.28. These volumes were brought by Stanley for a shilling. The other two Pope items are a 1752 *Works* and a 1760 *Homer*. Berkeley died in 1753.
21. Hollingshead, *George Berkeley and English Literature*, pp. 44–5.
22. *George Berkeley and English Literature*, pp. 363, 370. See also Gregory Hollingshead, 'Pope, Berkeley, and the True Key to the *Dunciad* in Four Books', *English Studies in Canada* 10 (1984), 141–55.

1   Reading about language

1. John Leonard, *Naming in Paradise: Milton and the Language of Adam and Eve* (Oxford: Clarendon Press, 1990), pp. 1–22, presents this as Milton's likely relationship to Adamic and Cratylic theories of language.
2. Stephen K. Land, *From Signs to Propositions: The Concept of Form in Eighteenth-Century Semantic Theory* (London: Longman, 1974), p. 22. Other writers who refer to Locke when providing a philosophical context for the interpretation of Pope include David B. Morris, *Alexander Pope: The Genius of Sense* (Cambridge, MA and London: Harvard University Press, 1984), pp. 154–5 and Blanford Parker, *The Triumph of Augustan Poetics: English Literary Culture from Butler to Johnson* (Cambridge: Cambridge University Press, 1998), pp. 107, 111, 132–3.
3. Murray Cohen, *Sensible Words: Linguistic Practice in England 1640–1785* (Baltimore and London: Johns Hopkins University Press, 1977), p. 60.
4. Berkeley, unlike Pope, had a formal education, attending Kilkenny College and Trinity College, Dublin. Marilyn Francus remarks on the prominence of the comparative study of languages in the Kilkenny system in the years just prior to Berkeley's attendance, *The Converting Imagination: Linguistic Theory and Swift's Satiric Prose* (Carbondale and Edwardsville: Southern Illinois University Press, 1994), pp. 8, 12. R.B. McDowell and D.A. Webb, with a foreword by F.S.L. Lyons, *Trinity College Dublin 1592–1952: An Academic History* (Cambridge: Cambridge University Press, 1982) note, p. 31, that 'There is scarcely any evidence extant from which we can deduce the nature of the teaching given in Trinity College in the late seventeenth century', although they suggest a new emphasis on linguistics and mathematics. They record, p. 32, an undergraduate's complaint in 1703, when Berkeley was also

at the College, that 'philosophical teaching consists of a farrago of conflicting hypotheses from Aristotle, Descartes, Colbert, Epicurus, Gassendi, Malebranche and Locke'.

5. See, for example, Christopher Fox, *Locke and the Scriblerians: Identity and Consciousness in Early Eighteenth-Century Britain* (Berkeley and London: University of California Press, 1988). Kenneth MacLean, *John Locke and English Literature of the Eighteenth Century* (New Haven: Yale University Press; London: Humphrey Milford, Oxford University Press, 1936), states in his preface, v, that Pope, as Sterne, was influenced by no two books more than the Bible and the *Essay*, yet mostly quotes from Scriblerian parodies of Locke's work, e.g. p. 105. Leopold Damrosch, Jr, *The Imaginitive World of Alexander Pope* (London and Berkeley, LA: University of California Press, 1987), p. 139, suggests that one may 'deduce the foundations of literary practice' from the third book of Locke's *Essay*.

6. Roy Porter, *Enlightenment: Britain and the Creation of the Modern World* (London: Allen Lane at the Penguin Press, 2000), pp. 67–8. I would like to thank my excellent colleague Alex Davis for pointing me to this passage.

7. For example, Lawrence Lipking, 'Quick Poetic Eyes: Another Look at Literary Pictorialism', in *Articulate Images: The Sister Arts from Hogarth to Tennyson*, ed. Richard Wendorf (Minneapolis: University of Minnesota Press, 1983), pp. 3–25, suggests that Locke's account of words referring to mental images and his description of wit as the combination of images are highly influential, pp. 6, 18–19.

8. Joseph Spence, *Observations, Anecdotes, and Characters of Books and Men, Collected from Conversation*, ed. James M. Osborn, 2 vols (Oxford: Clarendon Press, 1966), I, 19, No. 42. Pope's copy of Locke's *Essay*, the fourth edition of 1700, was given to him by Bolingbroke, see Maynard Mack, *Collected in Himself: Essays Critical, Biographical, and Bibliographical on Pope and Some of His Contemporaries* (Newark: University of Delaware Press; London and Toronto: Associated University Presses, 1982), p. 423.

9. John Locke, *An Essay Concerning Human Understanding*, ed. Peter H. Nidditch (Oxford: Clarendon Press, 1975), III.i.2, p. 402. Further references will be given in brackets in the text.

10. See Hans Aarsleff, *From Locke to Saussure: Essays in the Study of Language and Intellectual History* (London: Athlone Press, 1982), p. 25. Land, *From Signs to Propositions*, p. 13, reminds readers of the unverifiable nature of the relationship between a word and an idea that must hold if the word is to be used meaningfully.

11. John Locke, *Two Treatises of Government*, ed. Peter Laslett (Cambridge: Cambridge University Press, 1960, 2nd edn 1967, repr. 1988), pp. 287–8, II.27.

12. 'The Epistemology of Metaphor', *Critical Inquiry* 5 (1978–79), 13–30, p. 13. De Man also claims that Locke offers an analysis of tropes, not of the understanding, p. 16. Other critics in this strand include John J. Richetti, *Philosophical Writing: Locke, Berkeley, Hume* (Cambridge, MA and London: Harvard University Press, 1983), pp. 11–16, 116; Geoff Bennington, 'The Perfect Cheat: Locke and Empiricism's Rhetoric', in *The Figural and the Literal: Problems of Language in the History of Science and Philosophy, 1630–1800*, ed. Andrew E. Benjamin, Geoffrey N. Cantor and John R.R. Christie (Manchester: Manchester University Press, 1987), pp. 103–23, p. 107; Jules David Law, *The Rhetoric of Empiricism:*

Language and Perception from Locke to I.A. Richards (Ithaca and London: Cornell University Press, 1993), p. 13; William Walker, *Locke, Literary Criticism and Philosophy* (Cambridge: Cambridge University Press, 1994), p. 208. They all suggest that philosophy's attempt to describe the understanding is destabilised by language, rhetoric and tropes.

13. See Law, *The Rhetoric of Empiricism*, pp. 44–6. Law's major interest is in the interdependence of visual and linguistic modes in the *Essay*.

14. See, for example, the classic essay by Jacques Derrida, 'White Mythology: Metaphor in the Text of Philosophy', in *Margins of Philosophy*, trans. Alan Bass (London: Harevester, 1982), pp. 207–71.

15. I am indebted on these points to Jonathan Bennett, *Locke, Berkeley, Hume: Central Themes* (Oxford: Oxford University Press, 1971), esp. pp. 3–6.

16. Saul A. Kripke, *Naming and Necessity* (Oxford: Basil Blackwell, rev. and enlarged edn 1980); first pub. in *Semantics of Natural Language*, ed. G. Harman and G. Davidson (Dordrecht and Boston: D. Reidel, 1972), p. 135.

17. Bennett is very severe on Locke's notion that words refer to mental states (what he takes Locke to mean when he says 'idea') that should correspond exactly between users, saying that this could only ever account for point one of a percentile of language use, *Locke, Berkeley, Hume*, p. 43.

18. *Philosophical Investigations*, trans. G.E.M. Anscombe (Oxford: Basil Blackwell, 1953, 3rd edn 1967), 26 *et seq.*

19. *How to do Things with Words: The William James Lectures Delivered at Harvard University in 1955*, ed. J.O. Urmson and Marina Sbisà, 2nd edn (Oxford: Oxford University Press, 1975), p. 37.

20. George Berkeley, *A Treatise Concerning the Principles of Human Knowledge*, ed. Jonathan Dancy (Oxford: Oxford University Press, 1998), Introduction, 20, p. 99.

21. See *Hermeneutics Versus Science? Three German Views*, ed. and trans. John M. Conolly and Thomas Keutner (Notre Dame, Indiana: University of Notre Dame Press, 1988), Introduction, p. 2.

22. See *The Prose Works of Alexander Pope*, ed. Norman Ault and Rosemary Cowler, 2 vols (Oxford: Basil Blackwell, 1936–86), I, 142 and 141, 'On the Origin of Letters'. In Chapter 2, I suggest that Pope may here be echoing Berkeley's *New Theory of Vision*. Pope's essay appeared in *The Guardian*, for which Berkeley also wrote, Monday, 28 September 1713.

23. For a discussion of this aspect of Pope's technique in relation to Samuel Johnson and Platonic idealism, rather than Platonic linguistic theory, see Richard Terry, ' "The *Sound* Must seem an *Eccho* to the *Sense*": An Eighteenth-Century Controversy Revisited', *Modern Language Review* 94: 4 (1999), 940–54.

24. A fuller version of my thoughts on *Cratylus* can be found in 'Plato's *Cratylus*, Dionysius of Halicarnassus, and the Correctness of Names in Pope's *Homer*', *Review of English Studies*, n.s. 53:212 (2002), 484–99.

25. The topic is still discussed in linguistic science. See *Iconicity in Language*, ed. Raffaele Simone (Amsterdam and Philadelphia: John Benjamins, 1994), *Amsterdam Studies in the Theory and History of Linguistic Science*, ed. E.F. Konrad Koerner, Series IV, *Current Issues in Linguistic Theory*, vol. 110, esp. Rudolf Engler, 'Iconicity and/or Arbitrariness', pp. 39–45.

26. *The Collected Dialogues of Plato*, ed. Edith Hamilton and Huntington Cairns (New York: Bolingen Foundation, 1961), *Cratylus*, trans. B. Jowett, 428d.

Further references are given in brackets in the text. David Berman, *George Berkeley: Idealism and the Man* (Oxford: Clarendon Press, 1994), p. 128, notes the epigraph but does not discuss its context in Plato's dialogue. I discuss this epigraph further in Chapter 4.

27. This point is made by Timothy M.S. Baxter, *The Cratylus: Plato's Critique of Naming* (Leiden, New York, Köln: E.J. Brill, 1992), pp. 14, 18.
28. See Bernard Williams, 'Cratylus' Theory of Names and its Refutation', in *Companions to Ancient Thought 3: Language*, ed. Stephen Everson (Cambridge: Cambridge University Press, 1994), pp. 28–36, p. 32.
29. Josef Derbolav, *Platons Sprachphilosophie im Kratylos und in den Späteren Schriften* (Darmstadt: Wissenschaftliche Buchgesellschaft, 1972), pp. 51–2, 63–4, emphasises Socrates' contention that words may be better or worse, and that their fulfilling their function depends on the sanction of a speech community, not on any inherent correctness. Gadamer offers an alternative interpretation whereby Socrates' moderation between the two positions is an attempt to make dialectic triumph over language by insisting that the only function of language is to make being available to knowledge. See Hans-Georg Gadamer, *Truth and Method*, trans. and ed. Garrett Barden and John Cumming (London: Sheed and Ward, 1975), pp. 368–77.
30. Williams, 'Cratylus' Theory of Names', p. 34, states that what he calls the ϕ relation (direct sonic mimesis of referents by words) is not the criterion for the name relation, but does not deny that it might exist.
31. Baxter, *The Cratylus*, pp. 136–7, notes that naming often forms a part of cosmogony: the formation of words and of reality itself have been considered coeval.
32. Thomas Stanley, *The History of Philosophy: Containing the Lives, Opinions, Actions and Discourses of the Philosophers of Every Sect* (London: W. Battersby *et al.*, 1701, 3rd edn), p. 183. Maynard Mack notes that Pope owned a copy of this third edition, *Collected in Himself*, p. 442. G.F.C. Plowden, *Pope on Classic Ground* (Athens, Ohio: Ohio University Press, 1983), suggests that Stanley's accounts of Anaxagoras, Empedocles and Aristotle may have influenced Pope, pp. 39, 101. Stanley's account of Zeno's etymology is also highly relevant:

> the first pronounced Voices, imitating the things themselves, from which the Names were afterwards imposed, by which reason they [the Greek Stoics] derive Etymologies, conceiving that there is not any word, for which there cannot be given a certain Reason. They therefore studiously enquired whence words are deduced; much pains was taken, first by *Zeno*, then by *Cleanthes*, afterward, by *Chrysippus*, to give a reason of commentitious Fables, and to explain the causes of Words, why they are called so and so.
> This beginning is to be sought, until we arrive so far, as that the thing agree in some Similitude with the sound of the word, as when we say *tinkling* of Brass, the *neighing* of Horses, the *bleating* of Sheep, the *gingling* of Chains: These words by their Sound, express the things which are signified by them. (p. 305)

33. Baxter, *The Cratylus*, pp. 96ff.
34. Geneviève Clerico, 'Lectures du Cratyle, 1960–1990', *Historiographica Linguistica* 19 (1992), 333–59, pp. 340–1.

35. See Simon Alderson, 'Alexander Pope and the Nature of Language', *RES*, n.s. 47:185 (1996), 23–34, p. 31.
36. *Correspondence*, II, 43, c.1 May 1720.
37. See David Berman and E.J. Furlong, 'George Berkeley and the *Ladies Library*', *Berkeley Newsletter* 4 (December 1980), 4–13, and Greg Hollingshead, 'Sources for the *Ladies' Library*', *Berkeley Newsletter* 11 (1989–90), 1–9, pp. 1–2, who identifies the source: 'Messieurs du Port Royale. *Moral Essays*. [Trans. Pierre Nicole.] 3 vols (London 1677–80): vol. 2, Pt 2, "The True Idea's of Things" (entire), is B's source for Pars 285–334 of "Religion" in vol. 3. 7,000 words.'
38. For a reference to the *Provincial Letters* see *Correspondence* I, 129, and to the *Pensees* III, 173; at IV, 416 Pope says that his *Essay on Man* is conformable to Pascal's opinions. Pope told Spence that in his 'first setting out' he 'never read any art of logic or rhetoric', *Observations* I, 19, No. 42. Clearly, however, Pope had read Cicero and Quintilian by the time he wrote *An Essay on Criticism*, so his supposed ignorance of rhetoric is questionable. E. Audra, *L'influence française dans l'oeuvre de Pope* (Paris: Libraire Ancienne Honoré Champion, 1931), p. 32, cites a letter from John Norris to Elizabeth Thomas, which tells her that she could learn French by browsing through a grammar and then reading French texts next to an English translation. He urges her to read Malebranche and the Port Royal *Logic*. Pope knew Elizabeth Thomas through his friend Henry Cromwell. C.J. McCracken and I.C. Tipton, *Berkeley's Principles and Dialogues: Background Source Materials* (Cambridge: Cambridge University Press, 2000), *Cambridge Philosophical Texts in Context*, ed. John Cottingham and Daniel Garber, pp. 60–9, see sufficient connection between Arnauld and Berkeley to excerpt the *Logic*. Geneviève Brykman, *Berkeley et le Voile des Mots* (Paris: J. Vrin, 1993), admits Berkeley's reading in Arnauld is a matter of speculation, yet frequently compares his thought to the *Logic*: 'La lecture des Messieurs de Port-Royal par l'étudiant de Trinity College reste à établir avec certitude, mais il est difficile ici d'ignorer la puissance toute particulière de dénonciation du voile des mots que *La Logique ou l'art de penser* avait mise en œuvre concernant les termes *être, existence, durée, ordre* et *nombre*', p. 69; 'Pour l'emploi du verbe <<to premise>>, un souvenir très direct du chapitre de *La logique ou l'art de penser*, consacré aux précautions pédagogiques exigées pour dénommer les choses, peut avoir soutenu l'initiative de Berkeley, au moment de proposer qu'on appelât les <<choses>> des <<idées>>', p. 159. For a full account of the relations between Port Royal and Britain, see Ruth Clark, *Strangers and Sojourners at Port Royal* (Cambridge: Cambridge University Press, 1932), which gives details of British interest in the Port Royal writers, including an acknowledgement of Locke's translation of some of Nicole's *Moral Essays* that can be found in *John Locke as Translator: Three of the Essais of Pierre Nicole in French and English*, ed. Jean S. Yolton (Oxford: Voltaire Foundation, 2000), *Studies in Voltaire and the Eighteenth Century*, 2000: 07. For a general account of the Port Royal Logic and its importance to English readers, see Wilbur Samuel Howell, *Logic and Rhetoric in England, 1500–1700* (New York: Russell & Russell, 1961), pp. 350–63.
39. Henry St John, Viscount Bolingbroke, *Works*, ed. David Mallet, 5 vols (Hildesheim: Georg Olms, 1968/London: David Mallet, 1754), *Anglistica & Americana* 13, ed. Bernhard Fabian, Edgar Mertner, Karl Schneider and Marvin Spevack, IV, 167, 169.

40. See Pierre Bayle, *An Historical and Critical Dictionary*, 4 vols (London: C. Harper *et al.*, 1710), I, 379ff., III, 1737ff., and III, 2371ff. Bayle has it, I, 389nY, that Arnauld invented Jansenism and Cartesianism. A copy of the 'Histoire Generale du Jansenisme, *avec portraits*, 2 tom. *Amst.* 1700' was sold from the library of Berkeley, his son and grandson. See *A Catalogue of the Valuable Library of the late Right Rev. Dr. Berkeley, Lord Bishop of Cloyne . . . To be sold by Leigh and Sotheby*, Monday June 6, 1796, p. 26, No. 825.

41. Danièle Radamar, 'La Logique de Port-Royal et Montaigne', *Romance Quarterly* 39: 4 (November 1992), 425–38, argues that Montaigne, although infrequently mentioned, is a permanent presence in the text of the *Logic*. Radamer's approach to Montaigne is similar to mine:

> L'intuition que Montaigne a de la nature du langage s'oppose, non seulement à la *Logique* de Port Royal, aux thèses réalistes ou nominalistes dont le propre est d'interpreter le schéma: 'le mot désigne,' mais aussi à toute une tradition qui voit dans la pensée une activité conceptuelle 'derrière' les signes, bref aux diverses théories qui admettent la possibilité d'une appréhension scientifique de la compétence linguistique. (pp. 434–5)

42. Antoine Arnauld and Pierre Nicole, *Logic or the Art of Thinking*, ed. and trans. Jill Vance Buroker (Cambridge: Cambridge University Press, 1996), Introduction, xxiii.

43. Murray Cohen, *Sensible Words*, pp. 35, 60.

44. [Antoine Arnauld and Pierre Nicole], *Logic; or, The Art of Thinking*, trans. John Ozell (London: William Taylor, 1717), I.i, pp. 38–9. Further references will be given in brackets in the text.

45. It is at points like this that the similarities between the Port Royal writers and Chomsky's work on generational grammar become apparent. See 'Linguistic Contributions to the Study of Mind: Past', in *Language and Mind*, enlarged edn (San Diego: Harcourt Brace Jovanovich, 1972), pp. 1–23, pp. 14–19 and *Cartesian Linguistics: A Chapter in the History of Rationalist Thought* (New York and London: Harper and Row, 1966), *Studies in Language*, ed. Noam Chomsky and Morris Halle, pp. 31–52.

46. [Pierre Nicole], *Moral Essays*, trans. A Person of Quality, 2 vols (London: J. Magnes and R. Bentley, 1677–84), I, 24.

47. Pope's edition of Cotton's translation of Montaigne was closely annotated. See Mack, *Collected in Himself*, pp. 426–31. One of the only recent treatments of Pope's relationship to Montaigne is in Fred Parker, *Scepticism and Literature: An Essay on Pope, Hume, Sterne, and Johnson* (Oxford: Oxford University Press, 2003), ' "Sworn to no Master": Pope's Scepticism in the *Epistle to Bolingbroke* and *An Essay on Man*', pp. 86–137. Parker details all of Pope's references to Montaigne, notes that Pope had read Matthew Prior's dialogue between Locke and Montaigne in manuscript and emphasises the tension in both Pope and Montaigne between art and artlessness. Audra, *L'Influence Française*, details connections between the *Essais* and *An Essay on Man*, pp. 466–80.

48. *Essays of Michael Seigneur de Montaigne*, trans. Charles Cotton, 3 vols (London: M. Gilliflower *et al.*, 1693), III, 260–62, 'Of the Art of Conferring'. Further references will be given in brackets in the text.

49. Gerard Paul Sharpling, 'Towards a Rhetoric of Experience: The Role of *Enargeia* in the Essays of Montaigne', *Rhetorica* 20:2 (Spring 2002), 173–92, discusses the linguistic background to Montaigne's vivid self-presentation in the *Essays*.
50. See *Alciphron*, I.14, in *Works*, III, 56–7.
51. See Mack, *Collected in Himself*, p. 414; *Three Dialogues Between Hylas and Philonous*, ed. Jonathan Dancy (Oxford: Oxford University Press, 1998), p. 98.
52. Thomas Hobbes, *Leviathan*, ed. Richard Tuck (Cambridge: Cambridge University Press, 1991), I.iii, pp. 22–3. Further references will be given in brackets in the text.
53. George MacDonald Ross, 'Hobbes's Two Theories of Meaning', in *The Figural and the Literal*, pp. 31–57, p. 51, notes a distinction in Hobbes's theory between the definitions of signs and the criteria for their use.
54. M.A. Stewart notes briefly that Hobbes might be seen as a precursor for Berkeley's emotive or functional theory of language, and suggests that J.L. Austin offers a modern parallel. See 'Berkeley's Introduction Draft', *Berkeley Newsletter* 11 (1989–90), 10–19, p. 16.
55. *Principles*, I.65, p. 126.
56. *Principles*, Introduction 20, p. 99. Further references will be given in brackets in the text. Berkeley's development of a linguistic philosophy in which words need not refer to ideas has been noted by Anthony Flew, 'Was Berkeley a Precursor of Wittgenstein?', in *Hume and the Enlightenment: Essays Presented to Ernest Campbell Mossner* (Edinburgh: Edinburgh University Press; Austin, Texas: The University of Texas Humanities Research Centre, 1974), pp. 153–62, p. 159.
57. *An Essay on Man* was in part modelled on Lucretius. See *Correspondence*, III, 433, Pope and Bolingbroke to Swift, 15 September 1734. Miriam Leranbaum, *Alexander Pope's 'Opus Magnum' 1729–1744* (Oxford: Clarendon Press, 1977), p. 46, states that 'Lucretius and his English translators provided Pope with specific precedents for his manner of address and his range of tone.' I presume that Pope was sufficiently interested in Lucretius to investigate Epicurus.
58. *T. Lucretius Carus the Epicurean Philosopher, His Six Books De Natura Rerum*, trans. Thomas Creech (Oxford: L. Lichfield for Anthony Stephens, 1682), pp. 170–3, and *De Rerum Natura*, trans. W.H.D. Rouse (London: Heinemann, first pub. 1924, third rev. edn 1937, repr. 1966), V.1046–51. Spence reports Pope saying that Creech 'has done more justice to Manilius than he has to Lucretius', *Observations*, I, 205, No. 479.
59. Stanley is translating Sextus Empiricus, see *Outlines of Scepticism*, trans. by Julia Annas and Jonathan Barnes (Cambridge: Cambridge University Press, 1994), pp. 92–3, II.99–101. I am presuming Berkeley would also have known Sextus Empiricus. See also Stanley's distinction between demonstrative and communicative signs in his entry on Zeno, the stoic, p. 313, which echoes the distinction here.
60. See McCracken and Tipton, *Berkeley's Principles and Dialogues: Background Source Materials*, p. 67, for Arnauld on the possibility of forming general abstract ideas of a triangle whilst looking at a particular triangle.
61. See *New Theory* 80ff., *Works* I, 204ff. and *Philosophical Commentaries*, A, 417, 443, *Works*, I, 52, 55.

62. See J.A. Faris, *The Paradoxes of Zeno* (Aldershot and Brookfield, Vermont: Avebury, 1996). Faris, approaching the paradoxes from a mathematical point of view, regards the question of infinite divisibility as a question concerning units, not things, p. 55.

63. A copy of the dictionary was sold from Berkeley's library. See A.A. Luce, *Berkeley and Malebranche: A Study in the Origins of Berkeley's Thought* (London: Oxford University Press, 1934), p. 53. Luce suggests that the article on Zeno influenced Berkeley. Pope mentions Bayle at several points in his poems and letters. He recommends Bayle's article on Penelope to Broome, *Correspondence* II, 302, 29 June 1725. Pope's 'Impromptu' to Lady Winchilsea was published in the tenth volume of a 1741 edition of the dictionary. Harry M. Bracken, 'Bayle, Berkeley, and Hume', *Eighteenth-Century Studies* 11:2 (Winter 1977–78), 227–45, p. 230 says that 'Bayle's fantastically elaborated versions of the four paradoxes, his applications of them to seventeenth-century atomists, scholastics, and Cartesians, were the locus classicus of the divisibility question throughout the eighteenth century.'

64. Pierre Bayle, *An Historical and Critical Dictionary*, II, 1679.

65. Blakey Vermeule, *The Party of Humanity: Writing Moral Psychology in Eighteenth-Century Britain* (Baltimore, MA: The Johns Hopkins University Press, 2000), pp. 95–9. Vermeule mentions Berkeley, p. 96, as another linguistic theorist who believes proper names anchor signifying systems in the world. She does not say anything about Berkeley's critique of abstraction.

66. Gregory Albert F. Hollingshead, *George Berkeley and English Literature of the Eighteenth Century 1710–1770 With Special Reference to Swift, Pope, Blackwell, and Smart*, PhD, University of London, 1974, pp. 298–343, suggests reading *Dunciad* IV next to *Alciphron*. Some of this work is published as 'Pope, Berkeley, and the True Key to the *Dunciad* in Four Books', *English Studies in Canada* 10 (1984), 141–55. I am particularly indebted to Hollingshead's work in this section of my argument.

67. Vermeule, *The Party of Humanity*, p. 115.

68. Hollingshead notes that Steele uses this phrase before Berkeley, *George Berkeley and English Literature*, p. 269.

69. *Works*, IV, 32, paragraphs 4–5. The original Latin text is as follows:

> [gravitas] est igitur qualitas occulta. Sed vix, & ne vix quidem, concipere licet quid sit qualitas occulta, aut qua ratione qualitas ulla agere aut operari quidquampossit. Melius itaque foret, si, missa qualitate occulta, homines attenderent solummodo ad effectus sensibiles, vocibusque abstractis, (quantumvis illae ad disserendum utiles sint) in meditatione omissis, mens in particularibus & concretis, hoc est in ipsis rebus, defigeretur. *Vis* similiter corporibus tribuitur; usurpatur autem vocabulum illud, tanquam significaret qualitatem cognitam, distinctamque tam a motu, figura, omnique alia re sensibili, quam ab omni animalis affectione, id vero nihil aliud esse quam qualitatem occultam rem acrius rimanti constabit. Nisus animalis & motus corporeus vulgo spectantur tanquam symptomata & mensurae hujus qualitatis occultae.

70. Aristarchus is Richard Bentley, the editor of classical texts and Milton, known for his daring emendations.

71. The clerk is falteringly identified in the *TE* as Samuel Clarke, with whom Berkeley held some staged debates, but Hollingshead suggests Spinoza on the grounds of a parallel with *Alciphron* VII, see *George Berkeley and English Literature*, pp. 21, 315.
72. *The Works of Alexander Pope*, ed. William Warburton, 9 vols (London: A. Millar *et al.*, 1766), III, xv.
73. *The Works of Alexander Pope*, ed. William Warburton, V, 247–8. Hollingshead, *George Berkeley and English Literature*, p. 203, notes this version of Warburton's note in an article by Donald Greene, 'Smart, Berkeley, the Scientists and the Poets', *Journal of the History of Ideas* 14 (June 1953), 327–52, p. 328n, but says he has been unable to find it in any edition published in Warburton's life. It seems he overlooked this 1766 edition.

2   The language of vision and the sister arts

1. Winifried Nöth's distinction between exophoric and endophoric iconicity, between verbal forms miming their meaning, and verbal forms miming other verbal forms, provides a linguistic parallel to the poetic phenomenon I am trying to describe. See 'Semiotic Foundations of Iconicity in Language and Literature', in *The Motivated Sign: Iconicity in Language and Literature 2*, ed. Olga Fischer and Max Nänny (Amsterdam and Philadelphia: John Benjamins, 2001), pp. 17–28, pp. 21–4.
2. Maynard Mack, *Alexander Pope: A Life* (New Haven and London: Yale University Press; New York and London: W.W. Norton, 1985), pp. 226–30.
3. John Locke, *An Essay Concerning Human Understanding*, ed. P.H. Nidditch (Oxford: Clarendon Press, 1975), II.viii.7, p. 134.
4. Carol Gibson-Wood, *Jonathan Richardson: Art Theorist of the English Enlightenment* (New Haven and London: Yale University Press for The Paul Mellon Centre for Studies in British Art, 2000), p. 194. The note to Locke contains a misprint,

referring to II.xxviii.2–8, when II.xxix.2–8 was intended. My thanks to Professor Gibson-Wood for pointing this out. William McGowan, 'Berkeley's Doctrine of Signs', in *George Berkeley: Critical Assessments*, ed. Walter Creery, 3 vols (London and New York: Routledge, 1991), I, 111–25, I, 114, also attributes to Locke the theory that ideas are copies of things in a manner that is very pertinent to my argument:

> In Locke's epistemological dualism, as traditionally understood, ideas are only representations or copies, however inadequate, of what we should know. The defectiveness of the argument lies not in a failure to show that ideas can be pictures, images, representations, self-portraits, or the like of original corporeal qualities... but in its failure to show the possibility of the understanding using its own ideas as signs in this or any other way.

5. Morris R. Brownell, *Alexander Pope and the Arts of Georgian England* (Oxford: Clarendon Press, 1978), pp. 45, 93.
6. Ralph Cohen, *The Art of Discrimination: Thomson's The Seasons and the Language of Criticism* (London: Routledge & Kegan Paul, 1964), p. 136.
7. Stephen K. Land, *From Signs to Propositions: The Concept of Form in Eighteenth-Century Semantic Thought* (London: Longman, 1974), p. 22.
8. *The Works of Mr Abraham Cowley* (London: J.M. for Henry Herringman, 1668), 'Verses Written on Several Occasions', p. 39.
9. *Critical Essays of the Seventeenth Century*, ed. J.E. Spingarn, 3 vols (Oxford: Clarendon Press, 1908–1909), I, 44.
10. George Sherburn, *The Correspondence of Alexander Pope*, 5 vols (Oxford: Clarendon Press, 1956), II, 106n1, suggests that there were working parties on Shakespeare of which Pope and the Richardsons were part.
11. Maynard Mack, *Pope: A Life*, p. 658.
12. *Correspondence*, II, 231, Pope to Richardson, 3 October 1731. See also Morris R. Brownell, p. 29, and James Sambrook, 'Pope and the Visual Arts', in *Writers and their Background: Alexander Pope*, ed. Peter Dixon (London: G. Bell, 1972), pp. 143–71, p. 148.
13. Richardson quotes his own poem in *An Essay on the Theory of Painting* (London: W. Bowyer for John Churchill, 1715), p. 200. Further references will appear in brackets in the text. For a good account of the relationship between Richardson and Pope, see Gibson-Wood, *Jonathan Richardson*, pp. 42, 80–6, 107–8.
14. Gibson-Wood, p. 147.
15. Rensselaer W. Lee, *Ut Pictura Poesis: The Humanistic Theory of Painting* (New York: Norton, 1967), pp. 58–9, records Leonardo, Addison, de Piles and Dryden stating that painting is a universal language, and du Bos distinguishing between the natural signs of painting and the arbitrary signs of language. In addition to these one might add Hildebrand Jacob, *Of the Sister Arts: An Essay* (London: William Lewis, 1734/University College Los Angeles: William Andrews Clark Memorial Library, 1974), *The Augustan Reprint Society Publications* 165, intro. Nicklaus R. Schweitzer, p. 6, who calls painting a universal language, and Charles Lamotte, *An Essay Upon Poetry and Painting* (London: F. Fayram and T. Hatchett, 1731, 2nd edn), p. 32, who says that painting

'speaks a Language that is understood by all Men' and, p. 37, calls it a universal language.

16. *Two Discourses* (Menston: Scolar Press, 1972/London: W. Churchill, 1719), ii, 'A Discourse on the Dignity, Certainty, Pleasure and Advantage, of the Science of a Connoisseur', pp. 25, 35.

17. *The Art of Painting and the Lives of the Painters . . . Done from the French of Monsieur de Piles* (London: J. Nutt, 1706), p. 1.

18. *Iconic Forms in English Poetry of the Time of Dryden and Pope*, PhD, Cambridge University, 1993, pp. 137, 175.

19. *The Spectator*, ed. Donald F. Bond, 5 vols (Oxford: Clarendon Press, 1965), III, 558–9, Friday 27 June 1712. Addison's theory of the secondary pleasures of imagination, those of the arts, is based on a comparison of the image of the thing in poetry, painting and so on, with the thing itself, and so still requires one to have seen the real thing in the world: 'this Secondary Pleasure of the Imagination proceeds from that Action of the Mind, which compares the Ideas arising from the Original Objects, with the Ideas we receive from the Statue, Picture, Description, or Sound that represents them' (III, 559–60).

20. The centaur is a stock example of the combinatorial power of the imagination, used, amongst others, by Thomas Hobbes, *Leviathan*, ed. Richard Tuck (Cambridge: Cambridge University Press, 1991), I.ii, p. 16.

21. That a spectator might never have seen the object to which a painting refers does not mean the painting cannot refer to that object, it merely means that the claim of universality for pictorial signs cannot operate in the fashion suggested by the writers discussed so far in this chapter. The discussion in *Alciphron*, treated in Chapter 5, of words that do not refer to any clear and distinct idea in the mind and yet are meaningful presents an analogy for the pictorial sign.

22. Nelson Goodman, *Languages of Art: An Approach to a Theory of Symbols* (London: Oxford University Press, 1969), argues that many of the images people regard as representations represent things that do not exist, p. 21. He also suggests that habits and conventions of depiction, not resemblance, are the criteria for an image being a representation:

> Realistic representation, in brief, depends not upon imitation or illusion or information but upon inculcation. Almost any picture may represent almost anything; that is, given picture and object there is usually a system of representation, a plan of correlation, under which the picture represents the object. . . . Representational customs, which govern realism, also tend to generate resemblance. (pp. 38–9)

23. *Poems on Several Occasions* (London: Bernard Lintot, 1727), 'To Mr. Pope', p. 101. Pope subscribed for four copies of this volume.

24. Harte imitates ll. 360–1: 'And praise the *Easie Vigor* of a Line, / Where *Denham*'s Strength, and *Waller*'s Sweetness join.' He also, in the penultimate line quoted, alludes to Denham's *Coopers Hill*, a famous couplet of which describing the Thames ('Though deep, yet clear, though gentle, yet not dull, / Strong without rage, without ore-flowing full.' [ll. 191–2], *The Poetical Works of Sir John Denham*, ed. Theodore Howard Banks (New Haven: Yale University Press; London: Humphrey Milford, Oxford University Press, 1928,

p. 77)) is taken as a model of imitative versification by other Restoration and Augustan poets, even to the point where Swift describes Apollo saying he can not bear to hear 'The mimicry of "deep yet clear".' 'Apollo's Edict', l. 49, in Jonathan Swift, *The Complete Poems*, ed. Pat Rogers (Harmondsworth: Penguin, 1983), p. 231.

25. See Samuel Johnson, *The Lives of the Poets*, ed. Arthur Waugh, 3 vols (Oxford: Oxford University Press, 1906), 'Life of Pope', II, 314; *Selected Prose Works of G.E. Lessing*, ed. Edward Bell, trans. E.C. Beasley and Helen Zimmern (London: George Bell, 1905), *Laokoon*, pp. 90–1.

26. *Odyssey*, V.153n, XVI.413n, XVII.224n.

27. There is a long tradition of commentary on the painterly aspects of Pope's Homer. See Robert J. Allen, 'Pope and the Sister Arts', in *Pope and his Contemporaries: Essays Presented to George Sherburn*, ed. James L. Clifford and Louis A. Landa (Oxford: Clarendon Press, 1949), pp. 78–88, p. 85; Austin Warren, *Alexander Pope as Critic and Humanist* (Princeton: Princeton University Press; London: Humphrey Milford, Oxford University Press, 1929), *Princeton Studies in English* 1, pp. 109–12; Reuben Brower, *Alexander Pope: Poetry of Allusion* (Oxford: Oxford University Press, 1959), pp. 134–5; Douglas Knight, *Pope and the Heroic Tradition: A Critical Study of his Iliad* (New Haven: Yale University Press; London: Geoffrey Cumberlege, Oxford University Press, 1951), *Yale Studies in English* 117, p. 17; David Ridgely Clark, 'Landscape Effects in Pope's Homer', *The Journal of Aesthetics and Art Criticism* 22 (1963–64), 25–8, p. 25; Brownell, *Pope and the Arts of Georgian England*, pp. 39–50; Rebecca Gould Gibson, 'In Praise of Homer: Painting and Pope's Criticism', *Notes and Queries*, n.s. 27 (1980), 395–7, p. 396; and lastly, and most directly, Peter J. Connelly, 'Pope's *Iliad*: Ut Pictura Translatio', *Studies in English Literature 1500–1900*, 21:3 (1981), 439–55, p. 449, who argues that the vividness of particular additions to Homer in Pope's translation is only indirectly related to the parallel of poetry and painting: 'Their vividness, like the moral attributes he borrowed from Dryden, is only a device to help the reader to evaluate the action.'

28. 'Postscript' to the *Odyssey*, TE, X, 384–5.

29. Reuben Brower has noted in relation to *Windsor-Forest* that Pope does not produce his poetical pictures by looking at things, but by looking 'at a picture, a picture in language consecrated to such descriptive uses through literary tradition', *Alexander Pope*, p. 53.

30. Pope makes comparative annotations on two books on the geography of Rome. See Maynard Mack, *Collected in Himself: Essays Critical, Biographical, and Bibliographical on Pope and Some of His Contemporaries* (Newark: University of Delaware Press; London and Toronto: Associated University Press, 1982), p. 440.

31. I disagree with Beate Albert, who stresses the natural connection between sign and referent in Berkeley, 'Theorising Visual Language in George Berkeley and John Paul', *Studies in Eighteenth-Century Culture* 27 (1996), 307–42, p. 314.

32. For a more sceptical approach to Berkeley's introduction of the analogy with language see Jules David Law, *The Rhetoric of Empiricism: Language and Perception from Locke to I.A. Richards* (Ithaca and London: Cornell University Press, 1993), pp. 99–100, where he states that the analogies with language 'simply reproduce rather than clarify those relationships that the language model is introduced to explain'.

33. See Benjamin Rand, *Berkeley and Percival: The Correspondence of George Berkeley, afterwards Bishop of Cloyne, and Sir John Percival, afterwards Earl of Egmont* (Cambridge: Cambridge University Press, 1914), p. 110, Berkeley to Percival, 7 March 1712/3; *The Guardian*, ed. John Calhoun Stephens (Lexington, Kentucky: University Press of Kentucky, 1982), 'Introduction', pp. 26, 28, for the attribution of numbers to Pope and Berkeley; David Berman, *George Berkeley: Idealism and the Man* (Oxford: Clarendon Press, 1994), p. 77, reassesses Berkeley's contributions to the journal.

34. *The Prose Works of Alexander Pope*, ed. Norman Ault and Rosemary Cowler, 2 vols (Oxford: Basil Blackwell, 1936–86), I, 141–3. See I, lxx–lxxi for Ault's attribution of the piece to Pope.

35. Here I differ from Stephen Land, 'Berkeleyan Linguistics', in *Berkeley: Critical Assessments*, I, 86–110, who argues that Berkeley's linguistic thought involves the analysis of utterances into underlying mental events, p. 87. Land does not take the visual language analogy very seriously, as to take it seriously would be to acknowledge that signs can be analysed in terms of other signs rather than by reference to underlying mental events – mental events are signs, they do not support signs. Berkeley is opposed to the model of substance and accidence in signification as he is in his analysis of material reality.

36. *A Treatise Concerning the Principles of Human Knowledge*, ed. Jonathan Dancy (Oxford: Oxford University Press, 1998), I.8, p. 105.

37. *Correspondence*, I, 221–2, 445–7, Berkeley to Pope, 1 May 1714 and 22 October 1717.

38. See Brownell, *Pope and the Arts of Georgian England*, pp. 78–325.

39. Arthur Williams, 'Pope's Epistle to Mr. Jervas: The Relevance of its Contexts', *British Journal of Eighteenth-Century Studies* 8 (1985), 51–7, suggests Pope argues that Rome can be reconstructed by writers cultivating personal and social virtues, p. 52. He contrasts this epistle with that addressed to Addison.

40. Howard Erskine-Hill provides a comprehensive account of this poem, concentrating on its Augustanism, and relating it to the epistles to Jervas and Burlington, in 'The Medal Against Time: A Study of Pope's *Epistle to Mr Addison*', *Journal of the Warburg and Courtauld Institutes* 28 (1965), 274–98.

41. Joseph Addison, *Dialogues Upon the Usefulness of Ancient Medals*, ed. Stephen Orgel (N.P. [London?]: 1726/London and New York: Garland, 1976), *The Renaissance and the Gods* 53, p. 147.

42. Pat Rogers, 'Time and Space in *Windsor Forest*', in *The Art of Alexander Pope*, ed. Howard Erskine-Hill and Anne Smith (London: Vision, 1979), pp. 40–51, notes that early eighteenth-century poems often claim to describe the physical appearance of a landscape whilst actually describing the history of a landscape.

43. Pliny, *Natural History*, ed. and trans. H. Rackham, 10 vols (London: Heinemann, 1952), IX, 260–3.

44. *Andrea Palladio's Five Orders of Architecture*, trans. anon., rev. Colen Campbell (London: S. Harding, 1729), 'Author's Preface', p. 1.

45. For Pope's involvement in the Palladian revival and an exploration of architecture in his work, see Howard Erskine-Hill, 'Heirs of Vitruvius: Pope and the Idea of Architecture', in *The Art of Alexander Pope*, pp. 144–56, esp. pp. 150–1.

46. Colen Campbell, *The Third Volume of Vitruvius Britannicus; Or, The British Architect* (London: The Author and Joseph Smith, 1725), p. 7.

47. For Pope's familiarity with Stowe, see Mack, *Pope: A Life*, pp. 612–20.
48. See Nigel Everett, *The Tory View of Landscape* (New Haven and London: Yale University Press for the Paul Mellon Centre for Studies in British Art, 1994), pp. 11–26, for a balanced assessment of Pope's presentation of benevolent land ownership and improvement. Everett also discusses Berkeley's works on vision in relation to landscape, pp. 17–18.
49. Julian Ferraro, 'From Text to Work: The Presentation and Representation of *Epistles to Several Persons*', in *Alexander Pope: World and Word*, ed. Howard Erskine-Hill (Oxford: Oxford University Press for the British Academy, 1998), *Proceedings of the British Academy* 91, pp. 113–34, pp. 119–25, points out the various negative descriptions of Burlington, noting the fact that in a draft of the poem it was Burlington's vanity that made good the effects of the false management of Timon's villa.

3 Money and language

1. See P.G.M Dickson, *The Financial Revolution in England: A Study in the Development of Public Credit 1688–1756* (London: Macmillan, 1967), pp. 11, 17.
2. See J.G.A. Pocock, *The Machiavellian Moment: Florentine Political Thought and the Republican Tradition* (Princeton and London: Princeton University Press, 1975), pp. 458–9. Further references will be given in brackets in the text.
3. For recent dedicated accounts of the South Sea Bubble see John Carswell, *The South Sea Bubble* (London: Cresset Press, 1960; rev. ed. Stroud: Alan Sutton, 1993); and the more popular biographical work of Malcolm Balen, *A Very English Deceit: The Secret History of the South Sea Bubble and the First Great Financial Scandal* (London: Fourth Estate, 2002). Details of the investments of Pope and Gay are given by Colin Nicholson, *Writing and the Rise of Finance: Capital Satires of the Early Eighteenth Century* (Cambridge: Cambridge University Press, 1994), pp. 63–8, 75–6. Further references will be given in brackets in the text. R.L. Hayley, 'The Scriblerians and the South Sea Bubble: A Hit by Cibber', *RES*, n.s. 24 (1973), 452–8, p. 452, gives details of Arbuthnot's substantial early investment. For the opposition to Walpole, see Mack, *The Garden and the City: Retirement and Politics in the Later Poetry of Pope* (Toronto and Buffalo: University of Toronto Press; London: Oxford University Press, 1969), and Christine Gerrard, *The Patriot Opposition to Walpole: Politics, Poetry, and National Myth, 1725–1742* (Oxford: Clarendon Press, 1994).
4. J.H. Plumb, *The Growth of Political Stability in England 1675–1725* (London: Macmillan, 1967), p. 150, talks about the Tories supporting the good old cause in financial matters. See also Louis I. Bredvold, 'The Gloom of the Tory Satirists', in *Eighteenth-Century English Literature: Modern Essays in Criticism*, ed. James L. Clifford (Oxford: Oxford University Press, 1959), pp. 3–20.
5. These poems include Alexander Ramsay, *Wealth, or the Woody: A Poem on the South Sea* to which is Prefix'd a Familiar Epistle to Anthony Hammond Esq (London: T. Jauncy, 1720); Nicholas Amhurst, *An Epistle (With a Petition in it) to Sir John Blount, Bart. One of the Directors of the South-Sea Company* (London: R. Francklin, 1720); Mr Arundell, *The Directors: A Poem* (London: E. Curll, 1720, 2nd edn); anon., *An Epistle to William Morley Esq. One of the Directors of the South-Sea Company* (London: J. Roberts, 1720). Silke Stratmann, *Myths of*

Speculation: The South-Sea Bubble and Eighteenth-Century English Literature (Munich: Fink, 2000), *Munich Studies in English Literature*, ed. Ulrich Broich, pp. 45–186, discusses the various genres of Bubble literature, including some of these poems. Hers is one of the only works of literary scholarship concerned with the relationship between literature and finance to look at this large body of minor work.

6. *The Prose Works of Jonathan Swift*, ed. Herbert Davis *et al.*, 14 vols (Oxford: Basil Blackwell, 1939–68), VI (1951), 56, *The Conduct of the Allies*; IX (1948), 32, 'A Letter to Mr Pope'.

7. See, for example, Nicholson, p. 156 on the *Epistle to Bathurst*; Catherine Ingrassia, *Authorship, Commerce, and Gender in Early Eighteenth-Century England: A Culture of Paper Credit* (Cambridge: Cambridge University Press, 1998), pp. 40–8, treats Pope's classicism as a means of masking his involvement in new financial practices.

8. David B. Morris, *Alexander Pope: The Genius of Sense* (Cambridge, MA and London: Harvard University Press, 1984), p. 183.

9. Issac Kramnick, *Bolingbroke and his Circle: The Politics of Nostalgia in the Age of Walpole* (Cambridge, MA: Harvard University Press, 1968), p. 220, calls the *Epistle* a 'direct attack on the corruption of a moneyed society'. See also James Engell, 'Wealth and Words: Pope's Epistle to Bathurst', *Modern Philology* 85 (1987–88), 433–46, p. 446. Engell presents Pope in the context of Locke's writing on language, p. 433. My own views on this poem are set out more fully in 'Pope's *Epistle to Bathurst* and the Meaning of Finance', *Studies in English Literature 1500–1900*, 44:3 (August 2004), 487–504. Earl Wasserman's *Pope's Epistle to Bathurst: A Critical Reading with an Edition of the Manuscripts* (Baltimore: Johns Hopkins Press, 1960) remains the most complete account of the financial argument of the poem. See also David B. Morris, *The Genius of Sense*, 'Property, Character and Money in the *Moral Essays*', pp. 179–213, esp. pp. 183–8.

10. Constantine George Caffentzis, *Clipped Coins, Abused Words, and Civil Government: John Locke's Philosophy of Money* (New York: Autonomedia, 1989), pp. 53, 68, identifies the possibility of accumulation with the monetary stage in Locke's account of the origins of society.

11. Laura Brown, for example, thinks that Pope in *The Rape of the Lock* 'claims an absolute disjunction between commodification and classical heroism'. See her *Alexander Pope* (Oxford: Basil Blackwell, 1985), p. 21.

12. *Authorship, Commerce, and Gender*, p. 5.

13. *Writing and the Rise of Finance*, pp. xii, 78.

14. 'How Much for Just the Muse?: Alexander Pope's *Dunciad* Book IV and the Literary Market', *The Eighteenth Century: Theory and Interpretation* 36:1 (1995), 24–37, pp. 25, 27, 35.

15. *Virtue, Commerce, and History: Essays on Political Thought and History, Chiefly in the Eighteenth Century* (Cambridge: Cambridge University Press, 1985), p. 115.

16. *Money, Language, and Thought: Literary and Philosophical Economies from the Mediaeval to the Modern Era* (Berkeley, Los Angeles and London: University of California Press, 1982), pp. 3–4. See also his *The Economy of Literature* (Baltimore and London: Johns Hopkins University Press, 1978), 'Introduction', p. 3, where Shell notes 'the formal similarities between metaphorization

(which characterizes all language and literature) and economic representations and exchange'.

17. Marx rejects the analogy between money and language:

> To compare money with language is not less erroneous [than to compare it to blood]. Language does not transform ideas, so that the peculiarity of ideas is dissolved and their social character runs alongside them as a separate entity, like prices alongside commodities. Ideas do not exist separately from language. Ideas which have first to be translated out of their mother tongue into a foreign language in order to circulate, in order to become exchangeable, offer a somewhat better analogy.

> *Grundrisse: Foundations of the Critique of Political Economy (Rough Draft)*, trans. Martin Nicolaus (Harmondsworth: Penguin, 1973), pp. 162–3.

18. *Locke on Money*, ed. Patrick Hyde Kelly, 2 vols (Oxford: Oxford University Press, 1991), I, 13, 'Introduction'. Kelly gives more details of Locke's involvement in the policy of recoinage I, 23–6. Further references will be given in brackets in the text.

19. Caffentzis, *Clipped Coins*, p. 103, notes that Locke 'invokes "common use" and "tacit consent" as only a partial solution' to the problems caused by the arbitrariness of signs. I am greatly indebted to Caffentzis's two thought-provoking books on Locke and Berkeley's monetary philosophy.

20. Constantine George Caffentzis, *Exciting the Industry of Mankind: George Berkeley's Philosophy of Money* (Dordrecht, Boston, London: Kluwer, 2000) *International Archives of the History of Ideas* 170, ed. Sarah Hutton, p. 256, compares gold to a geometrical line, in as much as they both refer to their own abstract value.

21. Alex Davis pointed out to me that gold does not rust and it is surprising that Pope seems to think it does. Another poet Pope read writes about gold's resistance to rust in a manner that is pertinent to my discussion of Pope:

> I when I value gold, may think upon
> The ductilness, the application,
> The wholsomness, the ingenuitie,
> From rust, from soil, from fire ever free:
> But if I love it, 'tis because 'tis made
> By our new nature (Use) the soul of trade.

> *The Complete English Poems of John Donne*, ed. C.A. Patrides (London: Dent, 1985), p. 179, Elegie [XVIII], 'Loves Progress', ll. 11–16. Pope seems more interested in the degeneration of ideals, of the move from a golden to a leaden world, than the science of corrosion.

22. This point is made by Ellen Pollak, *The Poetics of Sexual Myth: Gender and Ideology in the Verse of Swift and Pope* (Chicago and London: University of Chicago Press, 1985), p. 124.

23. Douglas Vickers, *Studies in the Theory of Money 1690–1776* (Philadelphia: Chilton, 1959), p. 25.

24. Caffentzis, *Exciting the Industry of Mankind*, p. 233.

25. *The Guardian*, ed. John Calhoun Stephens (Lexington, Kentucky: University Press of Kentucky, 1982), p. 286, No. 77, Tuesday 9 June 1713.

26. *The Guardian*, p. 193, No. 49, Thursday 7 May 1713.
27. See Caffentzis, *Exciting the Industry of Mankind*, p. 108.
28. 'Berkeley and Ireland', in *Berkeley and Ireland: Proceedings of the Annual Conference of the Société Française d'Études Irlandaises (SOFEIR) 15–16 November 1985*, in *Études Irlandaises* 11 (1986), 7–25, p. 14.
29. *Works*, VI (1953), 71.
30. *Works*, VI (1953), 105, Q6.
31. See Joseph Johnston, *Bishop Berkeley's Querist in Historical Perspective* (Dundalk: Dundalgen Press, 1970), pp. 51, 74.
32. *Exciting the Industry of Mankind*, p. 417.
33. Thomas Prior, *Observations on Coin in General With Some Proposals for Regulating the Value of Coin in Ireland* [Dublin: A. Rhames for R. Gunne, 1729], in *A Select Collection of Scarce and Valuable Tracts on Money*, ed. J.R. McCulloch (London: Political Economy Club, 1856), pp. 291–338, p. 294. Coin leaves the country to pay absentee landlords after the value of export drops below the rent to be paid. The lesser coin is extracted first, leaving only the highest denominations, the moidores, in Ireland.
34. See Prior, p. 316: 'The Rate of Exchange being the Sum or Praemium given on paying any certain Sum in the Coin of one Country, for receiving an equal intrinsick Value in the Coin of another, the Value of that Praemium above or under *Par*, determines the Rate of Exchange.' Prior's account makes it clear how much the Irish suffer by their exchange rate with England, paying them 11 per cent over intrinsic value in every transaction.
35. See Johnston, *Berkeley's Querist in Historical Perspective*, p. 55.
36. Joyce Oldham Appleby, *Economic Thought and Ideology in Seventeenth-Century England* (Princeton: Princeton University Press, 1978), p. 224, refers to Richard Temple's responding to Locke and pointing out that 'the proposition that an ounce of silver will buy an ounce of silver is absurd since there would be no occasion for an exchange'. Appleby's wider argument is that Locke's evaluation of gold and silver coin merely on the basis of their containing a certain mass of gold and silver was outmoded even in the 1690s.
37. Caffentzis, *Exciting the Industry of Mankind*, p. 314, states that 'For Berkeley, money was a language that needed to be learnt.'
38. William Letwin, *The Origins of Scientific Economics: English Economic Thought 1660–1776* (London: Methuen, 1963), pp. 147–8. Letwin also acknowledges that Locke's thought on money is outmoded, p. 170.
39. William Blackstone gives the twenty-first-century reader some sense of the position of 'use' in eighteenth-century law. He discusses the statute of uses passed under Henry VIII as a means of limiting the church's land ownership. The statute did this by ending a distinction between use and possession that the church had been using to retain land: 'At length the statute of uses ordained, that such as had the *use* of lands, should, to all intents and purposes, be reputed and taken to be absolutely *seised* and possessed of the soil itself.' See his *Commentaries on the Laws of England: A Facsimile of the First Edition of 1765–1769*, 4 vols (Chicago and London: University of Chicago Press, 1979), II (intro. A.W. Brian Simpson), 137. Although Blackstone praises the statute for its clarification of property law, a Catholic like Pope might have felt differently about the reclamation of land from the church.

40. For an account of the political and intellectual context of Pope's *Imitations*, see Howard Erskine-Hill, *The Augustan Idea in English Literature* (London: Edward Arnold, 1983), pp. 291–349, and Jacob Fuchs, *Reading Pope's Imitations of Horace* (London: Associated University Presses, 1989), *passim*.

41. Morris, *The Genius of Sense*, p. 196, suggests that money allows people to be self-possessed in the *Moral Essays*. Pope seems to me to be working with and against an older Horatian ideal of property ownership in his *Imitations*. Frank Stack, *Pope and Horace: Studies in Imitation* (Cambridge: Cambridge University Press, 1985), pp. 123, 127, 140, notes the opportunity Epistle II.ii gives Pope to criticise the idea of property, and recognises the extent of Horace's critique.

42. See Howard Erskine-Hill, *The Social Milieu of Alexander Pope: Lives, Example and the Poetic Response* (New Haven and London: Yale University Press, 1975), pp. 309–17, for Pope's relationship to Bethel and exploration of the country house ideal in this poem. Erskine-Hill is also interested in the idea of use in the *Imitations*, see p. 310.

43. See Lisa Jardine and Alan Stewart, *Hostage to Fortune: The Troubled Life of Francis Bacon* (London: Victor Gollancz, 1998), pp. 512–19.

44. See Blackstone, *Commentaries*, II, 2.

45. Pope's involvement in the development of copyright law might be taken as evidence of the importance of literary property to his career and writing. See Mark Rose, *Authors and Owners: The Invention of Copyright* (Cambridge, MA and London: Harvard University Press, 1993), pp. 58–66 and David Foxon, ed. James McLaverty, *Pope and the Early Eighteenth-Century Book Trade* (Oxford: Clarendon Press, 1991), esp. pp. 237–51.

46. Ralegh lost Durham House and Sherborne Abbey (which was later owned by Pope's friends, the Digbys and in which both Pope's and Ralegh's seats are still preserved), having maintained them through a period of Elizabeth's disfavour, when James came to the throne and Ralegh was accused of treason. See Stephen Coote, *A Play of Passion: A Life of Sir Walter Ralegh* (London: Macmillan, 1993), pp. 299, 314–22. Ralegh is recognised in Pope's circle as someone who lost his estate unfairly. Bolingbroke compares himself to Ralegh in a letter to Swift concerning his return to England: 'here I am then, two thirds restor'd. my person safe, unless I meet hereafter with harder treatm^t than even that of Sr Walter Rauleigh; and my Estate, wth all the other property I have acquir'd, or may acquire, secur'd to me'. *The Correspondence of Jonathan Swift*, ed. Harold Williams, 5 vols (Oxford: Clarendon Press, 1963–65), III.81–2, Bolingbroke to Swift, 24 July 1725.

47. For the passage from transient to enduring property through use, see Blackstone, *Commentaries*, II, 8:

> as we before observed that occupancy gave the right to the temporary *use* of the soil, so it is agreed upon all hands that occupancy gave also the original right to the permanent property in the *substance* of the earth itself; which excludes every one else but the owner from the use of it.

4   Providence as the language of God in *Alciphron* and *An Essay on Man*

1. Joseph Spence, *Observations, Anecdotes and Characters of Books and Men*, ed. James M. Osborn, 2 vols (Oxford: Clarendon Press, 1966), I, 135–6, No. 305. See Joseph Warton, *An Essay on the Genius and Writings of Alexander Pope*, 2nd edn, 2 vols (London: R. and J. Dodsley, 1762–82), II, 182. Warton calls Berkeley a 'sublime genius and good man', II, 259.

2. William Bowman Piper, *Reconcilable Differences in Eighteenth-Century English Literature* (Newark: University of Delaware Press; London: Associated University Presses, 1999), pp. 115–17, 127–8.

3. *Works*, III, i, 'Editor's Introduction'. See also George Berkeley, *Alciphron in Focus*, ed. David Berman (London: Routledge, 1993), *Routledge Philosophers in Focus*, ed. Stanley Tweyman, pp. 1–2.

4. *Correspondence*, III, 276, March 1731/2; III, 286, Swift to Gay, 4 May 1732; III, 289, Gay to Swift, 16 May 1732.

5. *Correspondence*, III, 209, 214, Pope to Bethel, 28 July 1731, Bolingbroke to Swift, 2 August 1731; Mack's 'Note on the Text', *TE*, III.i, 3. Berkeley was in London for the period of the publication of Pope's *Essay*.

6. See Spence, I, 131, No. 299 and *The Last and Greatest Art: Some Unpublished Poetical Manuscripts of Alexander Pope*, transcribed and ed. Maynard Mack (Newark: University of Delaware Press; London and Toronto: Associated University Presses, 1984), pp. 312–13.

7. David Berman, *George Berkeley: Idealism and the Man* (Oxford: Clarendon Press, 1994), pp. 146–8, presents what he calls Berkeley's emotive theory of religious terms in relation to the theological argument of *Alciphron*.

8. Berman, *Idealism and the Man*, p. 108, notes the quotation from *Cratylus* 428D, but does not remark on the context of the quotation in Socrates' argument.

9. Henry St John, Viscount Bolingbroke, *Works*, ed. David Mallet, 5 vols (Hildesheim: Georg Olms, 1968/London: David Mallet, 1754), *Anglistica & Americana* 13, ed. Bernhard Fabian, Edgar Mertner, Karl Schneider and Marvin Spevack, V, 2. Further references will be given in brackets in the text.

10. Brean Hammond, *Pope and Bolingbroke: A Study of Friendship and Influence* (Columbia: University of Missouri Press, 1984), p. 73.

11. *The Correspondence of Jonathan Swift*, ed. Harold Williams, 5 vols (Oxford: Clarendon Press, 1963–65), IV, 45, 18 July 1732.

12. Berman, *Alciphron in Focus*, pp. 171–5 prints some of Bolingbroke's argument against Berkeley from the *Works*, I, 176–81.

13. *Some Remarks on the Minute Philosopher in a Letter from a Country Clergyman to his Friend in London* (London: J. Roberts, 1732), pp. 52, 65. For the attribution of this pamphlet to Hervey, see *Alciphron in Focus*, p. 4.

14. David Hume, *An Abstract of A Treatise of Human Nature*, ed. J.M. Keynes and P. Saffra (Cambridge: Cambridge University Press, 1938), p. 23. I discuss the relationship between Berkeley and Hume in more detail in the following chapter.

15. Cleanthes in Hume's *Dialogues Concerning Natural Religion*, in *The Natural History of Religion and Dialogues Concerning Natural Religion*, ed. A. Wayne Colver and John Vladimir Price (Oxford: Clarendon Press, 1976), expresses

the opinion that theological language is at least as precise as scientific language, Dialogue I, p. 155. Philo, on the other hand, presents a critique of argument by analogy: 'What peculiar Privilege has this little Agitation of the Brain which we call Thought, that we must thus make it the Model of the whole Universe?', Dialogue I, p. 168.

16. Berkeley accuses Shaftesbury of poetry at *Alciphron*, V.22, p. 199 where he presents a passage from the *Characteristics* as blank verse, a tactic Pope also employs in *Dunciad* IV.488n. Pope's anxiety about poetry being secondary to philosophy is resolved, I suggest, at the close of the fourth epistle.

17. Gregory Holingshed, 'Pope, Berkeley, and the True Key to the *Dunciad* in Four Books', *English Studies in Canada* 10 (1984), 141–55, p. 148.

18. It is interesting to note Bolingbroke's definition of first philosophy:

> If you ask me now, what I understand then by a first philosophy? My answer will be such as I suppose you already prepared to receive. I understand by a first philosophy, that which deserves the first place on account of the dignity, and importance of it's [*sic*] objects, 'natural theology or theism, and natural religion or ethics.'

'Introduction' to the *Letters or Essays, Works*, III, 325.

19. A.D. Nuttall, *Pope's Essay on Man* (London: George Allen & Unwin, 1984), p. 54, states that the tension between limited human reason and complete divine reason 'is perhaps the single most important philosophical tension in the poem', but that at the level of general argument 'it becomes, indeed, mere contradiction'. I am trying to show that the tension is an analogy not a contradiction.

20. See Harry Solomon, *The Rape of the Text: Reading and Misreading Pope's Essay on Man* (Tuscaloosa and London: The University of Alabama Press, 1993), p. 92, for Pope's hypothetical reasoning.

21. See, for example, Montaigne's description of the conservative sceptic, 'unfurnish'd of Human, and therefore more apt to receive into him the Divine Knowledge', *Essays of Michel Seigneur de Montaigne*, trans. Charles Cotton (London: T. Basset, M. Gilliflower and W. Hensman, 1693), II, 283, 'Apology for Raimond de Sebonde', and Pascal, *Thoughts on Religion and Other Subjects*, trans. Basil Kennet (London: A. and J. Churchill, 1704), p. 185, 'Man knows himself to be Miserable; he is therefore exceedingly Miserable, because he knows that he is so: but he likewise appears to be eminently Great, from this very Act of knowing himself to be miserable.' For Pope's knowledge of Montaigne in this translation see Chapter 1 and Fred Parker, *Scepticism and Literature: An Essay on Pope, Hume, Sterne, and Johnson* (Oxford: Oxford University Press, 2003), ' "Sworn to no Master": Pope's Scepticism in the *Epistle to Bolingbroke* and *An Essay on Man*', pp. 86–137. For Pope's reference to Pascal in the *Essay*, see Mack, *Collected in Himself*, pp. 331–2.

22. T. Lucretius Carus *The Epicurean Philosopher His Six Books De natura Rerum*, trans. Thomas Creech (Oxford: L. Lichfield, 1682), pp. 126–7. For Pope's knowledge of this translation, see Spence, *Observations*, I, 205, No. 479.

23. Benedict de Spinoza, *On the Improvement of the Understanding, The Ethics, Correspondence*, trans. R.H.M. Elwes (New York: Dover, 1955), distinguishes between nature considered as active, that is as God, and nature considered

as passive, that is as an expression of the attributes of God, *Ethics*, p. 68, Proposition XXIX. He also states that reason perceives of everything as necessary (as resulting from the nature of God), and only imagination conceives of any event, past, present or future as contingent, p. 116, Proposition XLIV. It is not only the relatively crude accusation of pantheism which may have made critics associate the *Essay* with Spinoza's writings, but also this assertion that right reason perceives the world as the necessary result of God's being, and only false imagination which suggests the contingency of any aspect of the creation. Pope defends himself from Louis Racine's accusations of Spinozism in a letter of 1 September 1742: 'my Opinions are intirely different from those of Spinoza; or even of Leibnitz; but on the contrary conformable to those of Mons: Pascal & Mons: Fenelon: the latter of whom I would most readily imitate, in submitting all my Opinions to the Decision of the Church.' *Correspondence*, IV, 416.

24. In *An Epistle from Mr Pope, to Dr Arbuthnot*, the dull poet who cannot bear to keep his works back nine years is woken by 'soft Zephyrs', l. 42 and a 'purling Stream', l. 150, like a painted lady, is thought a worthy theme for Hervey. Such vocabulary is suggestive of regrettable as well as admirable poetic artifice.

25. Douglas H. White, *Pope and the Context of Controversy: The Manipulation of Ideas in An Essay on Man* (Chicago and London: University of Chicago Press, 1970), p. 5.

26. Anthony Ashley Cooper, Third Earl of Shaftesbury, *Characteristics of Men, Manners, Opinions, Times*, ed. Lawrence E. Klein (Cambridge: Cambridge University Press, 1999), *Cambridge Texts in the History of Philosophy*, ed. Karl Ameriks and Desmond M. Clarke, 'Soliloquy, or Advice to an Author', pp. 149–50. Further references will be given in brackets in the text.

27. Frances Hutcheson, *An Inquiry into the Original of Our Ideas of Beauty and Virtue* (London: J. Darby, 1725), II, Introduction, p. 101. See also p. 106 where Hutcheson suggests people have a superior sense that approves of moral actions in themselves and others.

28. John Balguy, *Divine Rectitude: Or, a Brief Inquiry Concerning the Moral Perfections of the Deity* (London: John Pemberton, 1730), p. 14. Balguy refers approvingly to Hutcheson's *Inquiry*, p. 17.

29. Immanuel Kant presents a more advanced version of this belief when arguing against the eudaimonist that happiness is not the reward in prospect with which people are induced to act morally, but rather that a sense of moral law must precede an action for it to be moral if the moral is to survive as a category. See *Ethical Philosophy*, trans. James W. Ellington, intro. Warner A. Wick (Indianapolis and Cambridge: Hackett, 1994, 2nd edn), 'The Metaphysical Principles of Virtue', pp. 33–4.

30. Shaftesbury acknowledges that one must learn taste through internal dialogue, that one must educate one's taste in aesthetics and morals to come to admire the most fitting objects, *Characteristics*, 'Soliloquy', pp. 151–2, raising the question of just how instinctive the faculty is if it must be educated.

31. *Works*, I (1948), 93, notebook B, No. 769.

32. Pope here seems close to William Dudgeon, *The State of the Moral World Considered* (Edinburgh: R. Fleming, 1732), pp. 21–2: 'The *Desires* are the *Springs* exciting to *Action*, our *Happiness* which is involved in that of the *Publick*, is the *End*, and *Reason discovers* or *points* out the *best Means* to that *End*.'

33. *A Letter to Dion, Occasion'd by his Book Call'd Alciphron, Or the Minute Philosopher* (London: J. Roberts, 1732), p. 47.
34. *The Ladies Library, Written by a Lady*, 3 vols (London: J.T., 1714), III, 188, 197. David Berman and E.J. Furlong, 'George Berkeley and the *Ladies' Library'* [sic], *Berkeley Newsletter* 4 (December 1980), 4–13 and Greg Hollingshead, 'Sources for the *Ladies' Library'* [sic], *Berkeley Newsletter* 11 (1989–90), 1–9, have done most of the important work of identifying the sources for passages of this work. Hollingshead lists volume three, paragraphs 190–206, which contain the two quotations I have used, amongst the passages still to be identified, p. 9. The text is actually taken from a source identified by George A. Aitken 'Steele's *Ladies' Library'* [sic], *The Athenaeum: Journal of English and Foreign Literature, Science, the Fine Arts, Music and the Drama*, 2958 (Saturday 5 July 1884), 16–17, 16, and recognised by Berman, Furlong and Hollingshead: John Scott, *The Glories of Christian Life Part I* (London: J. Leake for Walter Kettelby and sold by Richard Wilkin, 1712, 9th edn), pp. 130–1. *Eighteenth-Century Collections Online* made it possible for me to identify this passage and makes the problem of attribution little more than mechanical.
35. *The Guardian*, ed. John Calhoun Stephens (Lexington, Kentucky: The University Press of Kentucky, 1982), p. 420, No. 126, Wednesday 5 August 1713.
36. *Principles*, ed. Jonathan Dancey, p. 112, section 27. Berkeley revised this passage for the 1734 edition, adding the final sentence quoted.
37. See on this subject M.W. Beal, 'Berkeley's Linguistic Criterion', in *Berkeley: Critical Assessments*, III, 375–87.
38. Douglas H. White mentions Gay in a footnote when he discusses the 'the interplay of self-love with self-love', p. 179, n.9. Anthony Quinton, *Utilitarian Ethics* (London and Basingstoke: Macmillan, 1973), *New Studies in Ethics*, ed. W.D. Hudson, pp. 23–4, discusses Gay as a theological utilitarian. Floyd Medford, 'The *Essay on Man* and the *Essay on the Origin of Evil'*, *Notes and Queries* 194 (1949), 337–8, p. 337, notes that Law's translation was actually published in November 1730 despite being dated 1731.
39. *Works*, VIII, 33, Berkeley to King, 18 April 1710. See David Berman, *Idealism and the Man*, pp. 14–20.
40. John Gay, 'The Fundamental Principle and Immediate Criterion of Virtue', in William King, *An Essay on the Origin of Evil*, trans. Edmund Law (London: W. Thurlborn, 1731), pp. xiii–xiv.
41. See *The Works of Sir William Temple*, 2 vols (London: A. Churchill *et al.*, 1720), I, 174, 'Upon the Gardens of Epicurus'.
42. Walter Harte, *An Essay on Reason* (London: J. Wright for Lawton Gilliver, 1735), l. 222. See Pope's *Correspondence*, III, 408–9, Pope to Mallet, May or June 1734 for his remarks on Harte's essay.

Epilogue: Pope, Berkeley and Hume

1. See James F. Zartman, 'Hume and "The Meaning of a Word" ', *Philosophy and Phenomenological Research* 36 (1975), 255–60.
2. Peter Jones, 'Strains in Hume and Wittgenstein', in *Hume: A Re-evaluation*, ed. Donald W. Livingston and James T. King (New York: Fordham University Press, 1976), pp. 191–209, p. 206.

3. John E. Sitter, 'Theodicy at Midcentury: Young, Akenside, and Hume', *Eighteenth-Century Studies* 12:1 (Autumn 1978), 90–106, *passim* and p. 104.

4. *The Letters of David Hume*, ed. J.Y.T. Greig, 2 vols (Oxford: Clarendon Press, 1932) I, 200 to Joseph Spence 15 October 1754; I, 210 to William Mure of Caldwell October 1754, 'Dear Mure, I have sent to Sharpe a copy of my History, of which I hope you will tell me your Opinion with Freedom. "Finding, like a Friend, / Something to blame, & something to commend." ' I, 282 to Andrew Millar 20 June 1758, Hume notes that Pope spells honour without a 'u'. *New Letters of David Hume*, ed. Raymond Kilbansky and Ernest C. Mossner (Oxford: Clarendon Press, 1954), pp. 184–5, to John Crawford, 29 August 1768, Hume writes from Oakley Park, Bathurst's estate in Cirencester, and notes that Pope celebrated the place, and was intimate with Bathurst.

5. David Hume, *An Abstract of A Treatise of Human Nature*, ed. J.M. Keynes and P. Saffra (Cambridge: Cambridge University Press, 1938), 'Introduction', x.

6. See 'A Finding List of Books Surviving from Pope's Library with a Few That May Not Have Survived', Appendix A in Maynard Mack, *Collected in Himself: Essays Critical, Biographical, and Bibliographical on Pope and Some of His Contemporaries* (Newark: University of Delaware Press; London and Toronto: Associated University Presses, 1982), pp. 394–460, p. 420. This book is now in the possession of Bill Zachs. I owe him a great debt for allowing me to see the book, which, as Mack notes, contains marginal corrections of some of the errata.

7. Harry, M Solomon, *The Rape of the Text: Reading and Misreading Pope's Essay on Man* (Tuscaloosa and London: The University of Alabama Press, 1993), p. 132. Solomon suggests Pope directly influences Hume, p. 145, but provides little in the way of comparative reading.

8. Christopher Fox, *Locke and the Scriblerians: Identity and Consciousness in Early Eighteenth-Century Britain* (Berkeley and London: University of California Press, 1988), pp. 125–6.

9. David Hume, *A Letter from a Gentleman to His Friend in Edinburgh* (1745), ed. Ernest C. Mossner and John V. Price (Edinburgh: Edinburgh University Press, 1967), pp. 26–7.

10. See M.A. Stewart, 'William Wishart, an Early Critic of *Alciphron*', *Berkeley Newsletter* 6 (1982–83), 5–9, and 'Berkeley and the Rankenian Club', *Hermathena* 139 (Winter 1985), 25–45.

11. David Hume, *The Natural History of Religion and Dialogues Concerning Natural Religion*, ed. A. Wayne Colver and John Vladimir Price (Oxford: Clarendon Press, 1976), Dialogue 7, p. 208, alluding to *Alciphron*, p. 142, IV.2. Cleanthes finds Philo's perversion of the argument by analogy to support the idea that the world is spun out of the belly of a great spider as unconvincing as Alciphron finds metaphysical (or *a priori*) arguments for the existence of God.

12. See Michael Morrisroe, Jr, 'Did Hume Read Berkeley?: A Conclusive Answer', *Philological Quarterly* 52 (1973), 310–15.

13. *Berkeley's Principles and Dialogues: Background Source Materials*, ed. C.J. McCracken and I.C. Tipton (Cambridge: Cambridge University Press, 2000), *Cambridge Philosophical Texts in Context*, ed. John Cottingham and Daniel Garber, p. 261, quoting from 'Metacritique of the Purism of Reason', in R.G. Smith, ed. and trans., *J.G. Hamann, 1730–1788: A Study in Christian Existence, with*

Selections from his Writings (New York: Harper, 1960), p. 216. McCracken and Tipton give a good account of Hume's reading in Berkeley, pp. 208–9.

14. M.A. Box, 'How Much of Berkeley did Hume Read?', *Notes and Queries* 234 (1989), 65–6. See also Hume's *Letters*, II, 29 and Berkeley's *Works*, V, 66. Hume is talking about Rousseau's sensitivity.

15. Harry M. Bracken, for example, in 'Bayle, Berkeley, and Hume', *Eighteenth-Century Studies* 11:2 (Winter 1977–78), 227–45, p. 228, suggests that 'Bayle independently influences Berkeley and Hume', and that 'Berkeley had little or no direct impact on Hume.'

16. David Hume, *A Treatise of Human Nature*, ed. L.A. Selby-Bigge, rev. P.H. Nidditch (Oxford: Clarendon Press, 1978, 2nd edn), I.iv.7, p. 273. Further references will be given in brackets in the text. See also Solomon, *The Rape of the Text*, pp. 67, 132.

17. Solomon, *The Rape of the Text*, pp. 97, 118, suggests that Pope presents attitudes rather than arguments.

18. David B. Morris, 'Pope and the Arts of Pleasure', in *The Enduring Legacy: Alexander Pope Tercentenary Essays*, ed. G.S. Rousseau and Pat Rogers (Cambridge: Cambridge University Press, 1988), pp. 95–117, p. 100, notes the connection between Hume and Pope on pleasure and pain, citing *Treatise*, III.iii.1, p. 574.

19. Anthony Ashley Cooper, Third Earl of Shaftesbury, *Characteristics of Men, Manners, Opinions, Times*, ed. Lawrence E. Klein (Cambridge: Cambridge University Press, 1999), *Cambridge Texts in the History of Philosophy*, ed. Karl Ameriks and Desmond M. Clarke, 'Sensus Communis', p. 51.

20. One problem with both Hobbes' and Locke's schemes is that, given the preferability of a social existence on simple grounds of personal ease and pleasure, there is no conceivable point at which the self-interested person would not choose society, as Shaftesbury suggests. See Hobbes, *Leviathan*, ed. Richard Tuck (Cambridge: Cambridge University Press, 1991), Chapters 13 and 17; Locke, *Two Treatises of Government*, ed. Peter Laslett (Cambridge: Cambridge University Press, 1960, repr. 1988), p. 277, where Locke states that men keep faith and promises as they are men, not as they are men in society, and p. 334, where he says that men made agreements to form civil societies. If social contract is the fundamental agreement of human life, it seems that natural and social man are the same. Pope's image seems to describe more accurately the relationship between natural and civilised states, which is not strictly an historical development. I do not agree with Nuttall, who sees in Pope 'a very British, Lockean state of nature', *Pope's Essay on Man* (London: George Allen & Unwin, 1984), p. 112. Rousseau also recognises that the state of nature as described by many philosophers already includes much that is cultivated. His analysis of the origin of languages comes close to concluding that language could not have originated at all, *A Discourse on Inequality*, trans. Maurice Cranston (Harmondsworth: Penguin, 1984), pp. 72, 92–8. Howard Erskine-Hill states that 'Pope's moment of original contract is presented less as a public legal transaction than as a recognition of appropriate merit, and the context of the Epistle as a whole, with its emphasis upon evolution through imitation of nature, induces us to interpret the contract as a stage in a process rather than a start on a totally new foundation', 'Pope on the Origin of Society', in *The Enduring Legacy*, pp. 79–93, p. 89. My reading intends to describe this process. Miriam Leranbaum

takes it as a flaw in Pope's account of the restoration of original social principles, II.283ff., that it is 'difficult to determine just when and how Pope (normally so expert in his command of adverbs) thinks the change from a state of nature to a civil state has come about', *Alexander Pope's 'Opus Magnum' 1729–42* (Oxford: Clarendon Press, 1977), p. 80. I attempt to identify a quality in this flaw.

21. See Sitter, 'Theodicy at Midcentury', p. 104. Sitter cites the *Enquiries Concerning Human Understanding and Concerning the Principles of Morals*, ed. L.A. Selby-Bigge and P.H. Nidditch (Oxford: Oxford University Press, 1975), p. 164, first enquiry, XII.iii.134.

Bibliography

Primary sources

Manuscripts

British Library Additional MS 39311.
A Catalogue of the Valuable Library of the late Right Rev. Dr. Berkeley, Lord Bishop of Cloyne. Together with the libraries of his Son and Grandson, the late Rev. GEORGE BERKELEY, D.D. PREBENDARY of CANTERBURY, and the late GEORGE MONK BERKELEY, Esq. To be sold by Leigh and Sotheby, Monday June 6, 1796, and the Five following days, Sotheby's Catalogue, annotated sale copy, British Library S.C.S28.

Printed books

Addison, Joseph, *Dialogues Upon the Usefulness of Ancient Medals*, ed. Stephen Orgel (N.P. [London?]: 1726/London and New York: Garland, 1976), *The Renaissance and the Gods* 53.

Amhurst, Nicholas, *An Epistle (With a Petition in it) to Sir John Blount, Bart. One of the Directors of the South-Sea Company* (London: R. Francklin, 1720).

Anon., *An Epistle to William Morley Esq. One of the Directors of the South-Sea Company* (London: J. Roberts, 1720).

[Arnauld, Antoine and Pierre Nicole] *Logic; or, The Art of Thinking*, trans. John Ozell (London: William Taylor, 1717).

——, *Logic or the Art of Thinking*, ed. and trans. Jill Vance Buroker (Cambridge: Cambridge University Press, 1996), *Cambridge Texts in the History of Philosophy*, ed. Karl Ameriks and Desmond M. Clarke.

Arundell, Mr, *The Directors: A Poem* (London: E. Curll, 1720, 2nd edn).

Balguy, John, *Divine Rectitude; Or a Brief Inquiry Concerning the Moral Perfections of the Deity* (London: John Pemberton, 1730).

Bayle, Pierre, *An Historical and Critical Dictionary*, 4 vols (London: C. Harper *et al.*, 1710).

Berkeley, George, *Alciphron in Focus*, ed. David Berman (London: Routledge, 1993), *Routledge Philosophers in Focus*, ed. Stanley Tweyman.

——, *Berkeley and Percival: The Correspondence of George Berkeley afterwards Bishop of Cloyne and Sir John Percival afterwards Earl of Egmont*, ed. Benjamin Rand (Cambridge: Cambridge University Press, 1914).

——, *Bishop Berkeley's Querist in Historical Perspective*, ed. Joseph Johnston (Dundalk: Dundalgen Press, 1970).

——, *Three Dialogues Between Hylas and Philonous*, ed. Jonathan Dancy (Oxford: Oxford University Press, 1998).

——, *A Treatise Concerning the Principles of Human Knowledge*, ed. Jonathan Dancy (Oxford: Oxford University Press, 1998).

——, *The Works of George Berkeley Bishop of Cloyne*, ed. A.A. Luce and T.E. Jessop, 9 vols (London: Thomas Nelson, 1948–57).

Blackstone, William, *Commentaries on the Laws of England: A Facsimile of the First Edition of 1765–1769*, 4 vols (Chicago and London: University of Chicago Press, 1979).

Bolingbroke, Henry St John, Viscount, *Works*, ed. David Mallet, 5 vols (Hildesheim: Georg Olms, 1968/London: David Mallet, 1754), *Anglistica & Americana* 13, ed. Bernhard Fabian, Edgar Mertner, Karl Schneider and Marvin Spevack.

Campbell, Colen, *The Third Volume of Vitruvius Britannicus; Or, The British Architect* (London: The Author and Joseph Smith, 1725).

The Works of Mr Abraham Cowley (London: J.M. for Henry Herringman, 1668).

The Poetical Works of Sir John Denham, ed. Theodore Howard Banks (New Haven: Yale University Press; London: Humphrey Milford, Oxford University Press, 1928).

The Complete English Poems of John Donne, ed. C.A. Patrides (London: Dent, 1985).

Dudgeon, William, *The State of the Moral World Considered* (Edinburgh: R. Fleming, 1732).

Gay, John, 'The Fundamental Principle and Immediate Criterion of Virtue', in William King, *An Essay on the Origin of Evil*, trans. Edmund Law (London: W. Thurlborn, 1731).

The Guardian, ed. John Calhoun Stephens (Lexington, Kentucky: University Press of Kentucky, 1982).

Harte, Walter, *An Essay on Reason* (London: J. Wright for Lawton Gilliver, 1735).

——, *Poems on Several Occasions* (London: Bernard Lintot, 1727).

Hervey, John, *Some Remarks on the Minute Philosopher in a Letter from a Country Clergyman to His Friend in London* (London: J. Roberts, 1732).

Hobbes, Thomas, *Leviathan*, ed. Richard Tuck (Cambridge: Cambridge University Press, 1991), *Cambridge Texts in the History of Political Thought*, ed. Raymond Guess and Quentin Skinner.

Hume, David, *An Abstract of A Treatise of Human Nature*, ed. J.M. Keynes and P. Saffra (Cambridge: Cambridge University Press, 1938).

——, *Enquiries Concerning Human Understanding and Concerning the Principles of Morals*, ed. L.A. Selby-Bigge and P.H. Nidditch (Oxford: Oxford University Press, 1975).

——, *A Letter from a Gentleman to His Friend in Edinburgh* (1745), ed. Ernest C. Mossner and John V. Price (Edinburgh: Edinburgh University Press, 1967).

——, *The Letters of David Hume*, ed. J.Y.T. Greig, 2 vols (Oxford: Clarendon Press, 1932).

——, *The Natural History of Religion and Dialogues Concerning Natural Religion*, ed. A. Wayne Colver and John Vladimir Price (Oxford: Clarendon Press, 1976).

——, *New Letters of David Hume*, ed. Raymond Kilbansky and Ernest C. Mossner (Oxford: Clarendon Press, 1954).

——, *A Treatise of Human Nature*, ed. L.A. Selby-Bigge, rev. P.H. Nidditch (Oxford: Clarendon Press, 1978, 2nd edn).

Hutcheson, Frances, *An Inquiry into the Original of Our Ideas of Beauty and Virtue* (London: J. Darby, 1725).

Jacob, Hildebrand, *Of the Sister Arts: An Essay*, intro. Nicklaus R. Schweitzer (London: William Lewis, 1734/University College Los Angeles: William Andrews Clark Memorial Library, 1974), *The Augustan Reprint Society Publications* 165.

Johnson, Samuel, *The Lives of the Poets*, ed. Arthur Waugh, 3 vols (Oxford: Oxford University Press, 1906).

Kant, Immanuel, *Ethical Philosophy*, trans. James W. Ellington, intro. Warner A. Wick (Indianapolis and Cambridge: Hackett, 1994, 2nd edn).

The Ladies Library, Written by a Lady, 3 vols (London: J.T., 1714).

Lamotte, Charles, *An Essay Upon Poetry and Painting* (London: F. Fayram and T. Hatchett, 1731, 2nd edn).

Selected Prose Works of G.E. Lessing, ed. Edward Bell, trans. E.C. Beasley and Helen Zimmern (London: George Bell, 1905).

Locke, John, *An Essay Concerning Human Understanding*, ed. Peter H. Nidditch (Oxford: Clarendon Press, 1975).

——, *John Locke as Translator: Three of the Essais of Pierre Nicole in French and English*, ed. Jean S. Yolton (Oxford: Voltaire Foundation, 2000), *Studies in Voltaire and the Eighteenth Century* (2000).

——, *Locke on Money*, ed. Patrick Hyde Kelly, 2 vols (Oxford: Oxford University Press, 1991).

——, *Two Treatises of Government*, ed. Peter Laslett (Cambridge: Cambridge University Press, 1960, 2nd edn 1967, repr. 1988), *Cambridge Texts in the History of Political Thought*, ed. Raymond Guess and Quentin Skinner.

Lucretius, *De Rerum Natura*, trans. W.H.D. Rouse (London: Heinemann, first pub. 1924, 3rd rev. edn 1937, repr. 1966).

——, *T. Lucretius Carus the Epicurean Philosopher, His Six Books De Natura Rerum*, trans. Thomas Creech (Oxford: L. Lichfield for Anthony Stephens, 1682).

Mandeville, Bernard, *A Letter to Dion, Occasion'd by His Book Call'd Alciphron, Or the Minute Philosopher* (London: J. Roberts, 1732).

McCracken, C.J., and I.C. Tipton, eds, *Berkeley's Principles and Dialogues: Background Source Materials* (Cambridge: Cambridge University Press, 2000), *Cambridge Philosophical Texts in Context*, ed. John Cottingham and Daniel Garber.

Essays of Michael Seigneur de Montaigne, trans. Charles Cotton, 3 vols (London: M. Gilliflower *et al.*, 1693).

[Nicole, Pierre] *Moral Essays*, trans. A Person of Quality, 2 vols (London: J. Magnes and R. Bentley, 1677–84).

Ovid's Metamorphosis Englished, trans. George Sandys (London: W. Stansby, 1626).

Andrea Palladio's Five Orders of Architecture, trans. anon., rev. Colen Campbell (London: S. Harding, 1729).

Pascal, Blaise, *Thoughts on Religion and Other Subjects*, trans. Basil Kennet (London: A. and J. Churchill, 1704).

The Art of Painting and the Lives of the Painters . . . Done from the French of Monsieur de Piles (London: J. Nutt, 1706).

The Collected Dialogues of Plato, ed. Edith Hamilton and Huntington Cairns (New York: Bolingen Foundation, 1961).

Pliny, *Natural History*, ed. and trans. H. Rackham, 10 vols (London: Heinemann, 1952).

The Correspondence of Alexander Pope, ed. George Sherburn, 5 vols (Oxford: Clarendon Press, 1956).

——, *The Last and Greatest Art: Some Unpublished Poetical Manuscripts of Alexander Pope*, transcribed and ed. Maynard Mack (Newark: University of Delaware Press; London and Toronto: Associated University Presses, 1984).

——, *Letters of Mr Alexander Pope and Several of His Friends* (London: J. Wright *et al.*, 1737).

——, *Pope's Epistle to Bathurst: A Critical Reading with an Edition of the Manuscripts*, ed. Earl Wasserman (Baltimore: Johns Hopkins Press, 1960).

——, *The Prose Works of Alexander Pope*, ed. Norman Ault and Rosemary Cowler, 2 vols (Oxford: Basil Blackwell, 1936–86).

——, *The Twickenham Edition of the Poems of Alexander Pope*, ed. John Butt, 11 vols (London: Methuen, 1939–69).

——, *The Works of Alexander Pope*, ed. William Warburton, 9 vols (London: A. Millar *et al.*, 1766).

Prior, Thomas, *Observations on Coin in General With Some Proposals for Regulating the Value of Coin in Ireland* [Dublin: A. Rhames for R. Gunne, 1729], in *A Select Collection of Scarce and Valuable Tracts on Money*, ed. J.R. McCulloch (London: Political Economy Club, 1856), pp. 291–338.

Ramsay, Alexander, *Wealth, or the Woody: A Poem on the South Sea to which is Prefix'd a Familiar Epistle to Anthony Hammond Esq* (London: T. Jauncy, 1720).

Richardson, Jonathan, *An Essay on the Theory of Painting* (London: W. Bowyer for John Churchill, 1715).

——, *Two Discourses* (Menston: Scolar Press, 1972/London: W. Churchill, 1719).

Rousseau, Jean-Jacques, *A Discourse on Inequality*, trans. Maurice Cranston (Harmondsworth: Penguin, 1984).

Scott, John, *The Glories of Christian Life Part I* (London: J. Leake for Walter Kettelby and sold by Richard Wilkin, 1712, 9th edn).

Sextus Empiricus, *Outlines of Scepticism*, trans. Julia Annas and Jonathan Barnes (Cambridge: Cambridge University Press, 1994).

Shaftesbury, Anthony Ashley Cooper, the Third Earl of, *Characteristics of Men, Manners, Opinions, Times*, ed. Lawrence E. Klein (Cambridge: Cambridge University Press, 1999), *Cambridge Texts in the History of Philosophy*, ed. Karl Ameriks and Desmond M. Clarke.

The Spectator, ed. Donald F. Bond, 5 vols (Oxford: Clarendon Press, 1965).

Spence, Joseph, *Observations, Anecdotes, and Characters of Books and Men*, ed. James M. Osborn, 2 vols (Oxford: Clarendon Press, 1966).

Spingarn, J.E., ed., *Critical Essays of the Seventeenth Century*, 3 vols (Oxford: Clarendon Press, 1908–09).

Spinoza, Benedict de, *On the Improvement of the Understanding, The Ethics, Correspondence*, trans. R.H.M. Elwes (New York: Dover, 1955).

Stanley, Thomas, *The History of Philosophy: Containing the Lives, Opinions, Actions and Discourses of the Philosophers of Every Sect* (London: W. Battersby *et al.*, 1701, 3rd edn).

Swift, Jonathan, *The Complete Poems*, ed. Pat Rogers (Harmondsworth: Penguin, 1983).

——, *The Correspondence of Jonathan Swift*, ed. Harold Williams, 5 vols (Oxford: Clarendon Press, 1963–65).

——, *The Prose Works of Jonathan Swift*, ed. Herbert Davis, 14 vols (Oxford: Basil Blackwell, 1939–68).

The Works of Sir William Temple, 2 vols (London: A. Churchill *et al.*, 1720).

Warton, Joseph, *An Essay on the Genius and Writings of Alexander Pope*, 2 vols (London: R. and J. Dodsley, 1762–82, 2nd edn).

Womersley, David, ed., *Augustan Critical Writing* (Harmondsworth: Penguin, 1997).

Secondary sources

Aaron, R.I., 'A Catalogue of Berkeley's Library', *Mind*, n.s. 41:164 (October 1932), 465–75.

Aarsleff, Hans, *From Locke to Saussure: Essays in the Study of Language and Intellectual History* (London: Athlone Press, 1982).

Aitken, George A., 'Steele's *Ladies' Library*', *The Athenaeum: Journal of English and Foreign Literature, Science, the Fine Arts, Music and the Drama*, 2958 (Saturday 5 July 1884), 16–17.

Albert, Beate, 'Theorising Visual Language in George Berkeley and John Paul', *Studies in Eighteenth-Century Culture* 27 (1996), 307–42.

Alderson, Simon, 'Alexander Pope and the Nature of Language', *Review of English Studies*, n.s. 47/185 (1996), 23–34.

——, *Iconic Forms in English Poetry of the Time of Dryden and Pope*, PhD, Cambridge University, 1993.

Allen, Robert J., 'Pope and the Sister Arts', in *Pope and His Contemporaries: Essays Presented to George Sherburn*, ed. James L. Clifford and Louis A. Landa (Oxford: Clarendon Press, 1949), pp. 78–88.

Appleby, Joyce Oldham, *Economic Thought and Ideology in Seventeenth-Century England* (Princeton: Princeton University Press, 1978).

Audra, E., *L'influence française dans l'oeuvre de Pope* (Paris: Libraire Ancienne Honoré Champion, 1931).

Austin, J.L., *How to do Things with Words: The William James Lectures Delivered at Harvard University in 1955*, ed. J.O. Urmson and Marina Sbisà (Oxford: Oxford University Press, 1975, 2nd edn).

Bailey, Anne Hall, 'How Much for Just the Muse?: Alexander Pope's *Dunciad* Book IV and the Literary Market', *The Eighteenth Century: Theory and Interpretation* 36:1 (1995), 24–37.

Balen, Malcolm, *A Very English Deceit: The Secret History of the South Sea Bubble and the First Great Financial Scandal* (London: Fourth Estate, 2002).

Baxter, Timothy M.S., *The Cratylus: Plato's Critique of Naming* (Leiden, New York, Köln: E.J. Brill, 1992).

Benjamin, Andrew E., Geoffrey N. Cantor and John R.R. Christie, eds, *The Figural and the Literal: Problems of Language in the History of Science and Philosophy, 1630–1800* (Manchester: Manchester University Press, 1987).

Bennett, Jonathan, *Locke, Berkeley, Hume: Central Themes* (Oxford: Oxford University Press, 1971).

Berman, David, *George Berkeley: Idealism and the Man* (Oxford: Clarendon Press, 1994).

Berman, David, and E.J. Furlong, 'George Berkeley and the *Ladies' Library*', *Berkeley Newsletter* 4 (December 1980), 4–13.

Box, M.A., 'How Much of Berkeley did Hume Read?', *Notes and Queries* 234 (1989), 65–66.

Bracken, Harry M., 'Bayle, Berkeley, and Hume', *Eighteenth-Century Studies* 11:2 (Winter 1977–78), 227–45.

Bredvold, Louis I., 'The Gloom of the Tory Satirists', in *Eighteenth-Century English Literature: Modern Essays in Criticism*, ed. James L. Clifford (Oxford: Oxford University Press, 1959), pp. 3–20.

Brower, Reuben, *Alexander Pope: Poetry of Allusion* (Oxford: Oxford University Press, 1959).

Brown, Laura, *Alexander Pope* (Oxford: Basil Blackwell, 1985), *Rereading Literature*, ed. Terry Eagleton.

Brownell, Morris R., *Alexander Pope and the Arts of Georgian England* (Oxford: Clarendon Press, 1978).

Brykman, Geneviève, *Berkeley et le Voile des Mots* (Paris: J. Vrin, 1993).

Caffentzis, Constantine George, *Clipped Coins, Abused Words, and Civil Government: John Locke's Philosophy of Money* (New York: Autonomedia, 1989).

——, *Exciting the Industry of Mankind: George Berkeley's Philosophy of Money* (Dordrecht, Boston, London: Kluwer, 2000), *International Archives of the History of Ideas* 170, ed. Sarah Hutton.

Carswell, John, *The South Sea Bubble* (first pub. London: Cresset Press, 1960; rev. edn Stroud: Alan Sutton, 1993).

Chomsky, Noam, *Cartesian Linguistics: A Chapter in the History of Rationalist Thought* (New York and London: Harper & Row, 1966), *Studies in Language*, ed. Noam Chomsky and Morris Halle.

——, 'Linguistic Contributions to the Study of Mind: Past', *Language and Mind* (San Diego: Harcourt Brace Jovanovich, 1972, enlarged edn), pp. 1–23.

Clark, David Ridgely, 'Landscape Effects in Pope's Homer', *The Journal of Aesthetics and Art Criticism* 22 (1963–64), 25–28.

Clark, Ruth, *Strangers and Sojourners at Port Royal* (Cambridge: Cambridge University Press, 1932).

Clerico, Geneviève, 'Lectures du Cratyle, 1960–1990', *Historiographica Linguistica* 19 (1992), 333–59.

Cohen, Murray, *Sensible Words: Linguistic Practice in England 1640–1785* (Baltimore and London: Johns Hopkins University Press, 1977).

Cohen, Ralph, *The Art of Discrimination: Thomson's The Seasons and the Language of Criticism* (London: Routledge & Kegan Paul, 1964).

Connelly, Peter J., 'Pope's *Iliad*: *Ut Pictura Translatio*', *Studies in English Literature 1500–1900* 21:3 (1981), 439–55.

Conolly, John M., and Thomas Keutner, ed. and trans. *Hermeneutics Versus Science? Three German Views* (Notre Dame, Indiana: University of Notre Dame Press, 1988).

Coote, Stephen, *A Play of Passion: A Life of Sir Walter Ralegh* (London: Macmillan, 1993).

Creery, Walter, ed., *George Berkeley: Critical Assessments*, 3 vols (London and New York: Routledge, 1991).

Damrosch, Jr, Leopold, *The Imaginative World of Alexander Pope* (London and Berkeley, LA: University of California Press, 1987).

DeMan, Paul, 'The Epistemology of Metaphor', *Critical Inquiry* 5 (1978–79), 13–30.

Derbolav, Josef, *Platons Sprachphilosophie im Kratylos und in den Späteren Schriften* (Darmstadt: Wissenschaftliche Buchgesellschaft, 1972).

Derrida, Jacques, 'White Mythology: Metaphor in the Text of Philosophy', *Margins of Philosophy*, trans. Alan Bass (London: Harevester, 1982), pp. 207–71.

Dickson, P.G.M., *The Financial Revolution in England: A Study in the Development of Public Credit 1688–1756* (London: Macmillan, 1967).

Dixon, Peter, ed., *Writers and Their Background: Alexander Pope* (London: G. Bell, 1972).

Engell, James, 'Wealth and Words: Pope's Epistle to Bathurst', *Modern Philology* 85 (1987–88), 433–46.

Erskine-Hill, Howard, *The Augustan Idea in English Literature* (London: Edward Arnold, 1983).

——, 'The Medal Against Time: A Study of Pope's *Epistle to Mr Addison*', *Journal of the Warburg and Courtauld Institutes* 28 (1965), 274–98.

——, *The Social Milieu of Alexander Pope: Lives, Example and the Poetic Response* (New Haven and London: Yale University Press, 1975).

Erskine-Hill, Howard, and Anne Smith, eds, *The Art of Alexander Pope* (London: Vision, 1979).

Everett, Nigel, *The Tory View of Landscape* (New Haven and London: Yale University Press for the Paul Mellon Centre for Studies in British Art, 1994).

Faris, J.A., *The Paradoxes of Zeno* (Aldershot and Brookfield, Vermont: Avebury, 1996).

Ferraro, Julian, 'From Text to Work: The Presentation and Representation of *Epistles to Several Persons*', in *Alexander Pope: World and Word*, ed. Howard Erskine-Hill (Oxford: Oxford University Press for the British Academy, 1998), *Proceedings of the British Academy* 91, pp. 113–34.

Fischer, Olga, and Max Nänny, eds, *The Motivated Sign: Iconicity in Language and Literature 2* (Amsterdam and Philadelphia: John Benjamins, 2000).

Flew, Anthony, 'Was Berkeley a Precursor of Wittgenstein?', *Hume and the Enlightenment: Essays Presented to Ernest Campbell Mossner* (Edinburgh: Edinburgh University Press; Austin, Texas: University of Texas Humanities Research Centre, 1974), pp. 153–62.

Fox, Christopher, *Locke and the Scriblerians: Identity and Consciousness in Early Eighteenth-Century Britain* (Berkeley and London: University of California Press, 1988).

Foxon, David, *Pope and the Early Eighteenth-Century Book Trade*, ed. James McLaverty (Oxford: Clarendon Press, 1991).

Francus, Marilyn, *The Converting Imagination: Linguistic Theory and Swift's Satiric Prose* (Carbondale and Edwardsville: Southern Illinois University Press, 1994).

Fraser, Alexander Campbell, *Life and Letters of George Berkeley, DD* (Oxford: Clarendon Press, 1871).

Fuchs, Jacob, *Reading Pope's Imitations of Horace* (London: Associated University Presses, 1989).

Gadamer, Hans-Georg, *Truth and Method*, trans. and ed. Garrett Barden and John Cumming (London: Sheed and Ward, 1975).

Gerrard, Christine, *The Patriot Opposition to Walpole: Politics, Poetry, and National Myth, 1725–1742* (Oxford: Clarendon Press, 1994).

Gibson, Rebecca Gould, 'In Praise of Homer: Painting and Pope's Criticism', *Notes and Queries*, n.s. 27 (1980), 395–7.

Gibson-Wood, Carol, *Jonathan Richardson: Art Theorist of the English Enlightenment* (New Haven and London: Yale University Press for The Paul Mellon Centre for Studies in British Art, 2000).

Goodman, Nelson, *Languages of Art: An Approach to a Theory of Symbols* (London: Oxford University Press, 1969).

Greene, Donald, 'Smart, Berkeley, the Scientists and the Poets', *Journal of the History of Ideas* 14 (June 1953), 327–52.

Hammond, Brean, *Pope and Bolingbroke: A Study of Friendship and Influence* (Columbia: University of Missouri Press, 1984).

Hayley, R.L., 'The Scriblerians and the South Sea Bubble: A Hit by Cibber', *Review of English Studies*, n.s. 24 (1973), 452–8.

Hollingshead, Gregory A.F., *George Berkeley and English Literature of the Eighteenth Century 1710–1770 With Special Reference to Swift, Pope, Blackwell, and Smart*, PhD, University of London, 1974.

———, 'Pope, Berkeley, and the True Key to the *Dunciad* in Four Books', *English Studies in Canada* 10 (1984), 141–55.

———, 'Sources for the *Ladies' Library*', *Berkeley Newsletter* 11 (1989–90), 1–9.

Howell, Wilbur Samuel, *Logic and Rhetoric in England, 1500–1700* (New York: Russell & Russell, 1961).

Ingrassia, Catherine, *Authorship, Commerce, and Gender in Early Eighteenth-Century England: A Culture of Paper Credit* (Cambridge: Cambridge University Press, 1998).

Jardine, Lisa, and Alan Stewart, *Hostage to Fortune: The Troubled Life of Francis Bacon* (London: Victor Gollancz, 1998).

Jones, Peter, 'Strains in Hume and Wittgenstein', in *Hume: A Re-evaluation*, ed. Donald W. Livingston and James T. King (New York: Fordham University Press, 1976), pp. 191–209.

Jones, Tom, 'Plato's *Cratylus*, Dionysius of Halicarnassus, and the Correctness of Names in Pope's *Homer*', *Review of English Studies*, n.s. 53:212 (2002), 484–99.

———, 'Pope's *Epistle to Bathurst* and the Meaning of Finance', *Studies in English Literature 1500–1900* 44:3 (August 2004), 487–504.

Kelly, Patrick Hyde, 'Berkeley and Ireland', *Berkeley and Ireland: Proceedings of the Annual Conference of the Société Française d'Études Irlandaises (SOFEIR) 15–16 November 1985*, in *Études Irlandaises* 11 (1986), 7–25.

Keogh, Andrew, 'Bishop Berkeley's Gift of Books in 1733', *Yale University Library Gazette* 8 (1933), 1–26.

Knight, Douglas, *Pope and the Heroic Tradition: A Critical Study of His Iliad* (New Haven: Yale University Press; London: Geoffrey Cumberlege, Oxford University Press, 1951), *Yale Studies in English* 117.

Kramnick, Issac, *Bolingbroke and His Circle: The Politics of Nostalgia in the Age of Walpole* (Cambridge, MA: Harvard University Press, 1968).

Kripke, Saul A., *Naming and Necessity* (Oxford: Basil Blackwell, 1980, rev. and enlarged edn; first pub. in *Semantics of Natural Language*, ed. G. Harman and G. Davidson (Dordrecht and Boston: D. Reidel, 1972)).

Land, Stephen K., *From Signs to Propositions: The Concept of Form in Eighteenth-Century Semantic Theory* (London: Longman, 1974).

Law, Jules David, *The Rhetoric of Empiricism: Language and Perception from Locke to I.A. Richards* (Ithaca and London: Cornell University Press, 1993).

Lee, Rensselaer W., *Ut Pictura Poesis: The Humanistic Theory of Painting* (New York: Norton, 1967).

Leranbaum, Miriam, *Alexander Pope's 'Opus Magnum' 1729–1744* (Oxford: Clarendon Press, 1977).

Letwin, William, *The Origins of Scientific Economics: English Economic Thought 1660–1776* (London: Methuen, 1963).

Lipking, Lawrence, 'Quick Poetic Eyes: Another Look at Literary Pictorialism', in *Articulate Images: The Sister Arts from Hogarth to Tennyson*, ed. Richard Wendorf (Minneapolis: University of Minnesota Press, 1983), pp. 3–25.

Luce, A.A., *Berkeley and Malebranche: A Study in the Origins of Berkeley's Thought* (London: Oxford University Press, 1934).

——, *The Life of George Berkeley Bishop of Cloyne* (London: Thomas Nelson, 1949).

Mack, Maynard, *Alexander Pope: A Life* (New Haven and London: Yale University Press, in association with W.W. Norton, 1985).

——, *Collected in Himself: Essays Critical, Biographical, and Bibliographical on Pope and Some of His Contemporaries* (Newark: University of Delaware Press; London and Toronto: Associated University Presses, 1982).

——, *The Garden and the City: Retirement and Politics in the Later Poetry of Pope* (Toronto and Buffalo: University of Toronto Press; London: Oxford University Press, 1969).

MacLean, Kenneth, *John Locke and English Literature of the Eighteenth Century* (New Haven: Yale University Press; London: Humphrey Milford, Oxford University Press, 1936).

Marx, Karl, *Grundrisse: Foundations of the Critique of Political Economy* (Rough Draft), trans. Martin Nicolaus (Harmondsworth: Penguin, 1973).

McDowell, R.B., and D.A. Webb, with a foreword by F.S.L. Lyons, *Trinity College Dublin 1592–1952: An Academic History* (Cambridge: Cambridge University Press, 1982).

Medford, Floyd, 'The *Essay on Man* and the *Essay on the Origin of Evil*', *Notes and Queries* 194 (1949), 337–8.

Morris, David B., *Alexander Pope: The Genius of Sense* (Cambridge, MA and London: Harvard University Press, 1984).

Morrisroe, Jr, Michael, 'Did Hume Read Berkeley?: A Conclusive Answer', *Philological Quarterly* 52 (1973), 310–15.

Nicholson, Colin, *Writing and the Rise of Finance: Capital Satires of the Early Eighteenth Century* (Cambridge: Cambridge University Press, 1994), *Cambridge Studies in Eighteenth-Century Literature and Thought*, ed. Howard Erskine-Hill and John J. Richetti.

Nuttall, A.D., *Pope's Essay on Man* (London: George Allen & Unwin, 1984).

Parker, Blanford, *The Triumph of Augustan Poetics: English Literary Culture from Butler to Johnson* (Cambridge: Cambridge University Press, 1998), *Cambridge Studies in Eighteenth-Century Literature and Thought*, ed. Howard Erskine-Hill and John J. Richetti.

Parker, Fred, *Scepticism and Literature: An Essay on Pope, Hume, Sterne, and Johnson* (Oxford: Oxford University Press, 2003).

Piper, William Bowman, *Reconcilable Differences in Eighteenth-Century English Literature* (Newark: University of Delaware Press; London: Associated University Presses, 1999).

Plowden, G.F.C., *Pope on Classic Ground* (Athens, Ohio: Ohio University Press, 1983).

Plumb, J.H., *The Growth of Political Stability in England 1675–1725* (London: Macmillan, 1967).

Pocock, J.G.A., *The Machiavellian Moment: Florentine Political Thought and the Republican Tradition* (Princeton and London: Princeton University Press, 1975).

——, *Virtue, Commerce, and History: Essays on Political Thought and History, Chiefly in the Eighteenth Century* (Cambridge: Cambridge University Press, 1985).

Pollak, Ellen, *The Poetics of Sexual Myth: Gender and Ideology in the Verse of Swift and Pope* (Chicago and London: University of Chicago Press, 1985).

Porter, Roy, *Enlightenment: Britain and the Creation of the Modern World* (London: Allen Lane at the Penguin Press, 2000).

Quinton, Anthony, *Utilitarian Ethics* (London and Basingstoke: Macmillan, 1973), *New Studies in Ethics*, ed. W.D. Hudson.

Radamar, Danièle, 'La Logique de Port-Royal et Montaigne', *Romance Quarterly* 39:4 (November 1992), 425–38.

Richetti, John J., *Philosophical Writing: Locke, Berkeley, Hume* (Cambridge, MA and London: Harvard University Press, 1983).

Rose, Mark, *Authors and Owners: The Invention of Copyright* (Cambridge, MA and London: Harvard University Press, 1993).

Rousseau, G.S., and Pat Rogers, eds, *The Enduring Legacy: Alexander Pope Tercentenary Essays* (Cambridge: Cambridge University Press, 1988).

Sharpling, Gerard Paul, 'Towards a Rhetoric of Experience: The Role of *Enargeia* in the Essays of Montaigne', *Rhetorica* 20:2 (Spring 2002), 173–92.

Shell, Marc, *The Economy of Literature* (Baltimore and London: Johns Hopkins University Press, 1978).

——, *Money, Language, and Thought: Literary and Philosophical Economies from the Mediaeval to the Modern Era* (Berkeley, Los Angeles and London: University of California Press, 1982).

Simone, Raffaele, ed., *Iconicity in Language* (Amsterdam and Philadelphia: John Benjamins, 1994), *Amsterdam Studies in the Theory and History of Linguistic Science*, ed. E.F. Konrad Koerner, Series IV, *Current Issues in Linguistic Theory*, vol. 110.

Sitter, John E., 'Theodicy at Midcentury: Young, Akenside, and Hume', *Eighteenth-Century Studies* 12:1 (Autumn 1978), 90–106.

Solomon, Harry, *The Rape of the Text: Reading and Misreading Pope's Essay on Man* (Tuscaloosa and London: University of Alabama Press, 1993).

Stack, Frank, *Pope and Horace: Studies in Imitation* (Cambridge: Cambridge University Press, 1985).

Stewart, M.A., 'Berkeley's Introduction Draft', *Berkeley Newsletter* 11 (1989–90), 10–19.

——, 'Berkeley and the Rankenian Club', *Hermathena* 139 (Winter 1985), 25–45.

——, 'William Wishart, an Early Critic of *Alciphron*', *Berkeley Newsletter* 6 (1982–83), 5–9.

Stratmann, Silke, *Myths of Speculation: The South-Sea Bubble and Eighteenth-Century English Literature* (Munich: Fink, 2000), *Munich Studies in English Literature*, ed. Ulrich Broich.

Terry, Richard, ' "The *Sound* must seem an *Eccho* to the *Sense*": An Eighteenth-Century Controversy Revisited', *Modern Language Review* 94:4 (1999), 940–54.

Vermeule, Blakey, *The Party of Humanity: Writing Moral Psychology in Eighteenth-Century Britain* (Baltimore, MA: Johns Hopkins University Press, 2000).

Vickers, Douglas, *Studies in the Theory of Money 1690–1776* (Philadelphia: Chilton, 1959).

Walker, William, *Locke, Literary Criticism and Philosophy* (Cambridge: Cambridge University Press, 1994), *Cambridge Studies in Eighteenth-Century Literature and Thought*, ed. Howard Erskine-Hill and John J. Richetti.

Warren, Austin, *Alexander Pope as Critic and Humanist* (Princeton: Princeton University Press; London: Humphrey Milford, Oxford University Press, 1929), *Princeton Studies in English* 1.

White, Douglas H., *Pope and the Context of Controversy: The Manipulation of Ideas in An Essay on Man* (Chicago and London: University of Chicago Press, 1970).

Williams, Arthur, 'Pope's Epistle to Mr. Jervas: The Relevance of Its Contexts', *British Journal of Eighteenth-Century Studies* 8 (1985), 51–7.

Williams, Bernard, 'Cratylus' Theory of Names and Its Refutation', in *Companions to Ancient Thought 3: Language*, ed. Stephen Everson (Cambridge: Cambridge University Press, 1994), pp. 28–36.

Wittgenstein, Ludwig, *Philsophical Investigations*, trans. G.E.M. Anscombe (Oxford: Basil Blackwell, 1953, 3rd edn 1967).

Zartman, James F., 'Hume and "The Meaning of a Word"', *Philosophy and Phenomenological Research* 36 (1975), 255–60.

Index

Lightning Source UK Ltd.
Milton Keynes UK
UKOW05n1905190517
301607UK00015B/110/P